DEDICATED BY THE AUTHOR

TO

_____

_____

LAKE FOREST
ILLINOIS

History and Reminiscences
1861-1961

by *Edward Arpee*

Published by the Rotary Club of
Lake Forest
1963

My lines have fallen in pleasant places;
Yea, I have a goodly heritage.

Psalm 16:6

TABLE OF CONTENTS

AUTHOR'S PREFACE

THE PRESENT becomes the past before we know it. The past becomes history. It is important to write down the facts in some readable form before people pass on, and before many documents and newspapers, yellow with age and ready to fall apart, are gone forever and forgotten. The written records of a period are far more trustworthy than the memory of people years after the event. In view of these circumstances, it is important to preserve all that is available about our fair city, in answer to the simple question—what happened?

But the answers are not always simple. One is often faced with conflicting reports, and a choice has to be made. Many of the records are not readable; some are undated and often interesting but unusable. It is fortunate that there are a few persons still living who remember the pioneers of Lake Forest, what they were like, what their ideas were, and how they lived. I have told everyone everywhere what I was doing and received much information, some of which could not be used. Being a community of varying ideas, the balance or the omissions of this book are natural subjects of disagreements. Also with so many capable writers in our midst many types of treatment are possible. For the readers who disagree with the materials in this book or wish to add to them, blank sheets are provided at the end of the volume for private corrections or additions.

Books, newspapers, magazines, legal documents and certificates have been consulted. But two basic principles have guided the writing of this book. The advice of Dr. F. B. Meyer of London has been followed—to go among all kinds of people and listen, then write what they said, for them to read. The effort has been made to tell the truth without subterfuge and with no axe to grind. Lake Forest from beginning to end has been a community effort, demanding a balanced coverage.

The book is written for those who love Lake Forest and are proud of its past. It is hoped that an increased affection will result from an increase of information.

Many have helped in the writing of this book. Mrs. William Borland furnished historic materials about several Country Clubs of the Lake Forest area, and several stories; former Mayor Kent Chandler read the manuscript and made corrections and additions from the storehouse of information at his command going back even beyond the one hundred years; William B. Douglas read the manuscript and made several suggestions for improvement. Miss Ellen Holt wrote extended reminiscences of the 1880's onward, at my request, which I have used freely; likewise Johnathan Jackson, who wrote an account of his Lake Forest experiences during the 1890's from the school boy's point of view which were interesting and useful; L. Ellsworth Laflin, Jr., read the manuscript twice, and furnished several interesting sidelights; my colleague Richard W. Montgomery made several suggestions for improvements; Jean Rumsey loaned me her collection of interesting materials involving the period of her father and grandfather; Miss Nell Steele directed me to excellent materials about the pioneers in this entire area.

Among the most valuable interviews have been those with Miss Mary Birmingham, Mrs. Harriet Matthews Caldwell, Mrs. Carter Fitz-Hugh, Mrs. Henry Rhode, Mrs. H. T. Strenger, and Mrs. Cornelius M. Trowbridge. These have helped to round out descriptions of people and events.

Most of all I am indebted to the Rotary Club of Lake Forest for publishing this volume as a public service.

EDWARD ARPEE
Lake Forest, Illinois

February 21, 1961

CHRONOLOGY

1650 Father Allouez establishes a Jesuit mission in the area of Lake County.
1669 Father Jacques Marquette, S.J., succeeds Father Allouez.
1673 Marquette and Joliet explore the Mississippi.
1680 Chicaougou is first mentioned by Hennepin.
1769 Pottawatamies conquer the Illinois at Starved Rock and dominate Northern Illinois.

1818 Illinois is admitted to the union.
1833 Green Bay Military Road appears as a blazed trail.
1836 Pottawatamie Indians leave for Kansas.
1844 St. Michael's, first Catholic Church is erected in the Lake Forest area.
1848 The Illinois-Michigan Canal is finished.
1853 St. Patrick's, Catholic Church, is erected in the Lake Forest area.
1855 The first railroad in Lake County, the present Northwestern Railroad, is finished.

1856 The Lake Forest Association is organized.
1857 Lake Forest is platted.
1857 Lind University is chartered.
1858 Lake Forest Academy is opened.
1859 The First Presbyterian Church is organized.
1859 The Medical Department of Lind University begins.
1859 The first business house in Lake Forest is erected.
1860 A. Lincoln speaks in Waukegan. He is elected President in November.
1861 The City of Lake Forest is chartered on February 21.
1861 Civil War begins on April 12.

1865 The title Lind University is changed to Lake Forest University.
1869 Ferry Hall is opened.
1871 Chicago fire consumes the heart of the city.
1872 Chicago-Milwaukee & St. Paul railroad is built through the Lake Forest area.
1875 St. Mary's Catholic church, a frame building, is erected.
1876 Lake Forest College is begun.
1877 Original College building is burned.
1878 College Hall on the present College campus is finished.
1879 Original Academy building is burned.
1880 The first College commencement is held.
1880 North Hall is built for the Academy on the College campus.
1887 Rush Medical College is affiliated with Lake Forest University.
1887 Present building of the Presbyterian Church is dedicated.
1888 Alcott School is founded.
1890 A private water company is organized.
1893 Chicago World's Fair.
1893 New Academy Campus is dedicated just south of the college campus.
1894 The Gorton School is erected.
1895 Telephone service is installed.
1896 *The Lake Forester* is first published.
1896 Electricity is introduced.
1896 Onwentsia Club is organized.
1897 North Shore Electric line is built through Lake Forest.
1898 The Church of the Holy Spirit (Episcopal) is organized.
1898 Alice Home Hospital is opened.
1898 The City Hall is finished.
1900 The first automobile in Lake Forest creates a furor.
1902 Present Church of the Holy Spirit is erected.
1902 The Winter Club is organized.
1904 Barat College is moved from Chicago to Lake Forest.
1904 Great Lakes Naval Training Center is authorized.
1905 Young Men's Club is organized.
1907 First National Bank of Lake Forest is opened.
1908 The first Lake Forest Day is held on the college campus.

1908   J. Odgen Armour builds Mellody Farms.
1913   The first professional fire department is organized in Lake Forest.
1921   The City of Lake Forest buys the water company.
1921   The Lake Forest American Legion Post 264 is chartered.
1922   Shoreacres Golf Club is opened.
1923   First zoning ordinance is passed.
1924   Knollwood Golf Club is opened.
1924   The Prince of Wales (Edward VIII) visits Lake Forest.
1925   The Academy and Ferry Hall are legally separated from Lake Forest University.
1926   Crown Prince Gustavus Adolphus of Sweden visits Lake Forest.
1926   The Skokie (Electric) Line is finished in Lake Forest.
1931   Skokie Highway (Route 41) is completed through Lake Forest.
1931   Lake Forest Public Library is erected on Deer Path.
1933   The first government owned Post Office building is erected in Lake Forest.
1933   Chicago Century of Progress opens.
1935   Lake Forest High School is built.
1942   The present Lake Forest Hospital is dedicated.
1947   Lake Forest Academy moves to Mellody Farms.
1948   The Community Center idea is defeated at the polls.
1955   The Deer Path School is dedicated.
1957   The Academy, College, and Ferry Hall celebrate the 1857 Lind University charter.
1959   The First Presbyterian Church celebrates its centennial.
1960   The Zoning Ordinance of 1923 is amended.
1961   The City of Lake Forest celebrates its centennial.

History and Reminiscences

I

THE NATURAL SETTING

–1850

THE FIVE outstanding features of early Lake Forest were Lake Michigan, its bluff, the big ravines, the ponds, and the stands of oak and pine. These provided a picturesque and romantic setting for the city that would develop along the shore.

Geologists agree that Lake Michigan was essentially caused by glaciers during one or more of the glacial periods. It is called an ice-eroded basin, and derived from the earlier "Lake Chicago." Other factors, however, had been at work over a long period of geologic time. Volcanic action had caused warping and tilting, creating ridges and valleys, especially in the area of Lake Forest.

Lake Michigan, 365 miles long, has two basins, an upper and a lower. The deepest bottom of the Lake is in the northern basin, southeast of Sturgeon Bay, the depth being 870 feet, or 290 feet below sea level, unusual for an inland lake. The southern basin reaches its maximum depth opposite Racine, Wisconsin, at 582 feet. The greatest depth east of Lake Forest is in the center of the Lake, 252 feet. The lake bottom is said to be smooth and rounded and gradual, with few irregularities. The Racine reef is one of the few in the lake, a mile from shore and ten feet below the surface.

The shore line, too, is a smooth curve, free from bays and promontories. The strongest winds come from the north-east developing great velocity and forming waves as high as 20 feet; these bounce

3

back from the western shores of the lake and move back in a west to east direction. The water currents generally head toward the main outlet north and eastward. An exception, however, is noted in the beginning of a current in the Waukegan area. This current follows the shore line southward around the southern bend of the lake before it continues in the general pattern northward. At Lake Forest there is a definite undertow, in which a strong current at the bottom of the lake is away from the shore eastward. This has caused several tragedies.

The Lake Forest shore line has been termed a "cobble beach," poorly suited for bathing. In recent years human endeavor has made several suitable beaches along the lake front. Periodically, about every ten years the lake rises, then falls. It takes a heavy toll of the banks when the lake is high. During the first forty years of the City of Lake Forest it is estimated that 100 feet of the bluff were undermined and absorbed in the lake bottom. Trees and breakwaters have provided a deterrent in recent years.

One of the most severe erosions involved the village of St. Johns, just south of Fort Sheridan. It was laid out in June 1847 and was an active port in the 1850's with a good pier, which was lengthened and improved in 1854. The village contained a two-story building 40 by 50 feet, in which hubs, whiffletrees, various kinds of turning, and all kinds of scales were manufactured. In 1876 it was abandoned. Erosion was so drastic that even the westernmost house in the area of the village is now under Lake Michigan.

Rock bottom in Lake Forest, composed of limestone, is said to be 160 feet from the surface. The next strata upward consists of glacial drift, then blue clay, then yellow clay, then one to three feet of surface soil. Many boulders are found on and near the surface. The area of Green Bay Road is about 650 feet above sea level. Few citizens are aware that they are living on the edge of a continental divide. The area of the Des Plaines River carries the waters just west of Lake Forest into the Mississippi basin and on to the Gulf of Mexico, while water in the area east of Green Bay Road is eventually drained into Lake Michigan, and down the St. Lawrence into the Atlantic Ocean. Another significant feature is that Lake Forest is the junction point of the forest and the great prairie. Lake Forest is also on one of the main routes of birds which migrate between Canada and South America.

4

There are several theories concerning the formation of the ravines. If the simplest explanation is accepted, they are seen to be the result of slope of the surface from the area of Green Bay Road to the lake and the unusual amount of water originating in rainfall, artesian wells, and ponds seeking their way to the lake. The periodic intensity and duration of the rainfall has carried away the surface soil and created even deeper ravines. The meandering of these ravines indicates a very ancient geologic phenomenon.

Several minerals are found in Lake Forest. There is a small amount of iron ore which is found in every state in the union. Sulphur is found south of 59A and natural gas to the north of it.

The last Indian inhabitants of Lake County, in which Lake Forest is located, were the Forest Pottawatamie. They were of Algonquin stock and may not have occupied this area more than a hundred years. Pottawatamie means: "We are building a fire." Their nearest village was Mettawa, along Indian Creek at the present location of Half Day. Essentially hunters, these aborigines lived in portable wigwams made of flags or rushes, woven and lapped ingeniously. This material was wound around a framework of poles tied together at the top, permitting a hole at the apex so that the smoke could escape. The small fire burned during inclement weather as the Indian family gathered close around it, sitting on mats made of the same material as the wigwam. When no fire was burning, the hole at the top was covered. The beds were of buffalo robes and deer skins thrown over the rush mats. The door consisted of a simple opening covered with a mat or robe.

Early settlers continually described the tribe as very warlike. They were enemies of the Iroquois and often made successful attacks on them. Prof. J. J. Halsey of Lake Forest College, the pioneer Lake County historian, quotes an earlier writer who wrote that they were "tall, fierce, and haughty. Despising the cultivation of the soil as too mean even for their women and children, they deemed the captures of the chase the only fit food for a valorous people. If they understood something of the principles of the Christian religion which were told them, they listened to it as a sort of theory which might be well adapted to the white man's condition, but was not fitted for them, as they were not fitted for it. They enjoyed the wild, roving life of the prairie, and, in common with most other native Americans, were vain of their prowess

5

and manhood, both in war and in the chase. They did not settle down for a great length of time in a given place, but roamed across the broad prairies, from one grove or belt of timber to another, either in single families or in small bands, packing their few effects, their children, and infirm on their little Indian ponies. They always travelled in Indian file upon well-beaten trails, connecting, by the most direct routes, prominent trading posts. These native highways served as guides to our early settlers, who followed them with as much confidence as we now do the roads laid out and worked by civilized man."

When the first white men, traders, and missionaries came to the southwestern section of Lake Michigan, they found the Green Bay area the focal point of Pottawatamie activity.

The area of Lake Forest that the Indians frequented is marked by a great many of their artifacts: spearpoints and stone knives. A number of these have been found recently in the area just south of the present Lake Forest Academy. These artifacts are often discards, containing a blemish or having been broken by use, but as often they are in perfect condition. Another productive area was along the lake shore, which has been badly disturbed recently by the hauling away of sand and gravel and the periodic erosion caused by ice and wave. Some relics were found during the excavations for the home of the Walter Kirks, in 1913, at Mayflower and Illinois Roads, where two ravines meet. Another productive source is along the present Green Bay Road where property owners have reported occasional finds. A cannonball thought to be related to the French and Indian war was also found in this area. Seven perfect arrowheads were discovered and preserved at 1230 North Green Bay Road, when excavations were made for the cellar of *Ragdale,* the home of Howard Van Doren Shaw. Other families in Lake Forest have preserved collections, but no conclusive study has been made of the total collection because Indian tribes occupied the area in such rapid succession and often for such short periods that the subject has been an anthropologic headache. Besides, confusion has resulted from the similarity of relics of different periods. The common factor seems to be that all Indian relics fall in the Stone Age without noticeable progress. The Pottawatamies did not emerge in Lake County until the end of the French and Indian War, in 1763.

6

The Mound Builders, a much older race, built on Laurel Avenue in Highland Park, in Lake Bluff, in North Chicago, and in Waukegan, but none have yet been reported in Lake Forest proper. These were taller and larger men than the more recent Indian tribes in the area.

The Pottawatamies left many trail-marking trees in Lake Forest. These were found in the area of Green Bay Road, but several have been preserved east of the tracks along the ravines. One of these was a graceful oak in the front yard of the former Franklin P. Smith residence at 815 E. Deer Path, which was nurtured and cherished even after the tree had died about 1930. These trail marking trees were used by the Pottawatamies to indicate the direction and location of game. Young saplings were bent, about four feet from the ground, and pointed in the direction of the lake front. The bent part was fastened to the ground and after a while became permanently bent. In time the top of the branch grew vertically again, making the marker permanent.

Father Allouez, a Jesuit missionary, is said to have been the first white man to cast his eyes on the area of Lake County. He is reported to have died, in what became Little Fort (Waukegan), in 1652. At this time there seems to have been no knowledge of Lake Michigan in Europe. Cornelli's map, published in 1693, is the first to show a full delineation of the Great Lakes.

In 1673, Jacques Marquette, S.J., the French missionary and explorer, with his companion, the adventurer, explorer and fur trader, Louis Joliet, discovered the Mississippi. That spring they went down the back country from their starting point, Green Bay. They returned by the Illinois River and Lake Michigan. It was on this return trip that Joliet appreciated the area of present Chicago as a junction point for travel from the Great Lakes to the Mississippi basin. He even spoke of a canal connecting Lake Michigan and the Illinois River. Pere Marquette recorded Joliet's opinion that: "It would only be necessary to make a canal, by cutting through but half a league of prairie to pass from the foot of the lake of Illinois to the river St. Louis." One hundred and seventy-five years after this observation, the canal became a reality.

In 1674, Marquette came south again from Green Bay, past the area of Lake Forest until he reached the area of Chicago. He spent the winter in these parts, establishing the first white habitation in this place. In May of the following year he started north on the eastern shore of the Lake. He died near the mouth of the Manistee River. He is considered the founder of the Roman Catholic Church in Illinois.

Hennepin, the Belgian explorer, visited the southwestern shores of Lake Michigan in 1679 and must have been impressed by the bluffs along the north shore.

La Salle became acquainted with Lake Michigan, soon after he discovered the Ohio River. Before 1670 he was active in the present Chicago area, and wrote Journals describing his experiences. Unfortunately these have been lost, but a later anonymous *Histoire de M. de La Salle* survives. In this book La Salle's expedition south on Lake Michigan, down the Illinois River, and down the Mississippi, is described. The party set out in December, 1681. In February, 1682, it began the last stretch of the journey, reaching the mouth of the "Father of Waters" on April 9, 1682. There a monument and a cross were erected, and La Salle took possession of the area, in the name of King Louis XIV of France, calling the area Louisiana. Returning northward to Michilimackinac, he portaged from the Illinois River to the site of present Chicago and continued north to his base. Twice, during this trip, he must have skirted the area of Lake Forest.

On the basis of these and other explorations the French laid claim to the area of the Great Lakes and the Ohio-Mississippi basin until 1763, the end of the French and Indian war. With the fall of Quebec that year, the area passed into the hands of the English. In 1783, a London map of the United States area included Little Fort (Waukegan) on the western shores of Lake Michigan. In 1795, a map printed in Philadelphia marked the same location. Perhaps both of these maps were based on the explorations of Marquette and Joliet. Because at Little Fort the portage to the Aux Plaine was only four miles, less than anywhere else on the Lake, Waukegan had been used by the Indians first as a connecting point for the Mississippi, then eventually as a trading post.

The Pottawatamie Indians fought *against* the British under Chief Pontiac in 1763. They fought *with* the British *against* the United States in 1812; then in the Black Hawk War of 1832 they remained true to the United States.

8

Illinois was admitted to statehood in 1818 when a new and more formidable tide of emigrants poured into the new state from Kentucky, Pennsylvania, New England, and New York. A book published in 1818 containing a map of the new state of Illinois shows the population of the state concentrated in the southern tip. It does not show that the state touches Lake Michigan.

In 1824 a vigorous effort was made to amend the new state constitution to permit slavery in Illinois. The effort failed.

In the 1830's there was an increasing tide of immigration into northern Illinois resulting in an Indian treaty negotiated and signed in Chicago on September 26, 1833. By this treaty the Pottawatamies ceded to the United States all their lands in Illinois and Wisconsin, including Lake County, a total of five million acres, for almost one million dollars.

Numbering five thousand, the tribe crowded in camp on the prairie beyond the village of Chicago along the banks of the river. They divided themselves into prairie and forest Pottawatamies. This took place in the middle of September, 1833.

Commissioners from Washington called for a meeting at which the purpose of the conference was outlined—the purchase of all the Pottawatamie lands by the Federal Government and their planned migration to Kansas. The Indians stated that their great father in Washington must have seen a bad bird which told him a lie, because they did not wish to sell their lands. The Indians were then issued rations; then they became noisy. They wept and sang and milled around. The area teemed with squaws, children, dogs, mounted braves, and warriors on foot. Chiefs sat in grave consultation. Casks of whiskey were sold in abundance as the commissioners watched. There were repeated delays. The chiefs did not want to negotiate.

Suddenly on September 21, considering their situation hopeless, they changed their minds. Twenty or thirty chiefs met the commissioners at the present site of the north end of the Rush Street bridge. It was late in the afternoon. They had become convinced that there was no alternative except to cede their lands and to move to their new hunting grounds across the Great River. The treaty was signed by chiefs and commissioners alike. Four days later, September 26, the treaty was concluded. The Senate of the United States ratified the treaty in its final form on May 22, 1834.

It was not proclaimed, however, until February 21, 1835, when the Indian title was "extinguished" and most of the Indians departed for Kansas, in government wagons, in August, 1836, after they settled the claims of some 500 white settlers, several in excess of $10,000 each.

The departure of the Pottawatamies in 1836 made it possible to begin the construction of the Illinois-Michigan Canal; a ninety mile long project, which would connect Lake Michigan and the navigable part of the Illinois river, which in turn empties into the Mississippi. The Canal would give direct access to midwestern farm produce to the population centers of the great East and the deep South. Actually the Canal became all important to Northern Illinois and to Lake Forest because it attracted people from overseas, as well as from the Eastern seaboard, creating a great metropolis out of the wilderness. The earliest white inhabitants of the Lake Forest area were directly or indirectly connected with the construction of the Illinois-Michigan Canal.

When Illinois was admitted to the Union in 1818, the nation-wide interest in building roads and canals had become a nationally accepted program as an antidote to sectionalism. Increasing concern over the problem of slavery and its extension into the newer sections beyond the Northwest Territory, of which Illinois was a part, added to the interest of Congress to push internal improvements. Whigs and Democrats were in accord as were their leaders, Clay and Calhoun, so that the ensuing quarter of a century is referred to as the "Era of Good Feeling."

A veritable craze for canal digging had swept the country. The cost of carrying grain to the East or utensils and implements to the West by lumbering Conestoga wagons was almost prohibitive. And so a vast network of canals had been constructed, north and south, east and west, across the country, adding to the water routes already offered by the Ohio and Mississippi rivers. The steam-boat had replaced the slow barges and keel boats. The cost of transporting merchandise had fallen to a tenth of the former prices. New York City sprang into its role of chief metropolis of the East due in large part to the Erie Canal, which extended 363 miles from Albany to Buffalo. The Pennsylvanians had labored to connect Philadelphia and Pittsburgh by an artificial waterway, stepping canal boats up steep inclines with cables and sleds and carrying them across high levels by rail. The great Ohio Canal, connecting Lake Erie with the Ohio River, from Cleveland to Portsmouth, had begun in 1825. Many others were started but never completed because the building of railways suddenly interfered.

Though the people of Illinois were told a canal would cost four million dollars, while a railroad would require only one million, they insisted on the construction of a canal. So the Illinois-Michigan Steamboat Canal became a part of the national movement. In Illinois, the canal would be a symbol of unity and peace since it would give access between the two sections in economic conflict and in conflict over the slavery issue.

The legislature of the State of Illinois, beginning with the very first General Assembly, worked toward the construction of a canal. It appropriated $10,000, in 1821, to conduct a survey for a route connecting the Illinois River with Lake Michigan. A Canal Company was formed in 1825 and stock was issued and sold. In 1827 Daniel Pope Cook, who helped organize the State of Illinois, secured a federal grant of land on which to build the canal. The grant consisted of sections of land, alternating in five mile strips along either side of the canal for purposes of construction and repair. Altogether Congress donated 300,000 acres of land. For this success of D. P. Cook, the county at the eastern end of the proposed canal was named Cook County.

In 1829, a Canal Commission of three members laid out the towns of Chicago and Ottawa, the two extremities of the proposed ninety-six mile canal. In 1830, lots were laid out in Chicago and offered for sale. The plat of Chicago was filed on August 4, 1830, marking the birth of the city. In 1834 the State of Illinois loaned $500,000 to the Illinois-Michigan Steamboat Canal Company so that construction might begin. A Canal Commission composed of William F. Thornton, Gurdon S. Hubbard and Colonel William B. Archer was appointed. Engineer William Goodring planned a ditch 65 feet wide at the water level and 36 feet at the bottom, with at least 6 feet in depth.

With the departure of the Indians, on July 4, 1836, the dirt began to fly, as Gurdon Hubbard tossed the first spadeful. This was especially appropriate since he had introduced the first Canal bill into the General Assembly and his life and activities had spanned a long period of trade with the Indians and the formation of the new order under the domination of the pioneers. At this time Shadrach Bond was the Governor of Illinois, and the population of Chicago was 3,800 inhabitants. Canal workers were promised $40 per month in wages and prairie schooners were busy bringing several hundred settlers from northern Illinois to the spot in Chicago which had been used by Marquette, La Salle and a number of other explorers as a land bridge which led to the extremities and to the heart of the great continent. There were fireworks and great noise, excitement and celebration, speeches and a carnival spirit. The Canal had begun, a promise to make Chicago a great metropolis, at the same time ensuring the importation of manufactured supplies from the east and an outlet for the local farm products through New Orleans.

A great many immigrants poured into Chicago from the East, hoping for steady employment and the opportunity to buy good land at reasonable prices. Matthew Laflin drove a wagon of blasting powder for the Canal from Canton, Connecticut, in 1837. Upon arrival, he decided to settle in Chicago and sent for his wife and two sons. They lived in old Fort Dearborn in the winter of 1838. Many others with experience or skills in canal building came to Chicago, but the State of Illinois, which bore the brunt of the financial responsibility was not always able to pay the workers. In 1843 wages were cut to $16 per month. This was followed by riots in the towns of Romeo and Juliet. There was shooting and the escape of workers into the countryside. Some settlers were dragged from their homes and forced to work on the canal.

When Thomas Ford became Governor of Illinois, in 1842, matters were already at a low ebb. The State Bank had failed, and there were whispers about repudiating the public debt. Ford opposed this idea and with the help of Stephen A. Douglas defeated it in the state legislature. As a result, taxes were increased and the canal workers were paid. This tax increase caused a minor rebellion in northern Illinois. At a mass meeting in the town of Oregon, the fourteen counties above the old Ordinance Line threatened to secede from Illinois, either to form a new territory or to join Wisconsin, which was about to become a state. Governor Ford is given credit for holding the state together and resuming work on the canal, bringing the project to a successful completion.

In spite of delays caused by floods and an unusual amount of sickness among the labor force, the work was finished and the Canal was opened for navigation on April 16, 1848. Boats crowded with notables started simultaneously from La Salle and Chicago to be cheered by excited crowds in every town along the way. Bands played, a cannon was fired in the town of Juliet, now called Joliet.

The Chicago Daily Journal referred to this event as: "the meeting of the waters, an eventful period in the history of our city, of the state and of the West—the wedding of the Father of Rivers to our inland seas. A magnificent canal." The writer boarded the packet *New Orleans* at La Salle reaching the Chicago River in only twenty-two hours. He commented on the thriving towns, the beauty of the countryside, and the fine construction of locks and the aqueduct which carried the canal over the Fox River. The canal construction cost $6,557,681. The prairie farmers could now ship their grain not only south through St. Louis, but through the Great Lakes to the populous East.

For twenty years the Canal carried a heavy load of traffic. In 1866 over $300,000 of toll were collected. The long, low canal barges were pulled by mules or horses, driven by a man who watched the towpath for gopher holes which might trip the animals. Grain was carried in the hold below deck and lumber above. D. R. Holt of Chicago made the first shipment of freight—a load of lumber. He was soon to take part in the building of Lake Forest. Prosperity came to the whole canal territory. The prices of imported articles fell; the value of exports increased.

The townsfolk along the way would gather at the bridges or landing when they heard a trumpet announcing the boat's arrival. Small boys prepared to "hitch" rides. As the barge approached, the captain's wife and children stood in view. Often the family wash flapped on the line hung on deck. At some points, near Ottawa, for example, where the canal banks were higher than the street, a man could sit on his porch and watch the boats go by overhead.

So the people of Illinois at last realized their dream—an unbroken waterway connecting them with the East and the South. During sixty years of operation the canal received $6,610,067 in tolls and spent $4,995,316 for operation and maintenance. It was not a financial success, but it played an important part in developing northern Illinois. As Governor Ford wrote: "It transformed the raw region of northern Illinois into a settled and prosperous community. Its influence on the economic development of the adjacent region surpassed the local influence of any other American canal except the Erie." In addition, it held the state of Illinois together.

The canal had taken twelve years to build. It was of primary importance for another twelve years. Then alas for the canal, the Railroads claimed Chicago, making it the railroad capital of the United States by 1850. At that time trains were operating from Chicago to Elgin on what has become the Galena division of the Northwestern Railway. The Rock Island trains were operating from Chicago to Rock Island in 1854. The Illinois Central began service to Centralia by 1856.

In 1882 the canal moved over a million tons of freight, but collected only $86,000 in tolls. The triumph of the railroad was complete. The canal, however, did continue to operate until 1907 when it was abandoned.

II

THE PIONEERS

1832–1857

"We the surface broad surveying,
We primeval forests felling,
We the virgin soil upheaving,
We the route for travel clearing,
O resistless, restless race!
Pioneers! O Pioneers!"
                                    —*Walt Whitman*

THE MAGNET which drew overseas immigrants to the Chicago area and thence to the open spaces west of Lake Forest was the Illinois-Michigan Canal. Even before the Canal was finished, settlers began to come. Some of these had worked on the Erie Canal. Many more had worked on the canal in Chicago and received farmlands as part payment for their labors, since the Canal Company was unable to pay them in cash. These early families were attracted by the beauty of the forest and the small streams backed by the Des Plaines River. Besides, the area was accessible because of the famous Green Bay Road, or Military Road, which connected the settlements of Chicago, Milwaukee and Green Bay, and passed through what was to become a part of Lake Forest.

When the region of Northern Illinois had been brought to the attention of the country at large during the Black Hawk War in 1832, General Winfield Scott visited the area and recommended the building of a thoroughfare which became known as Green Bay Road. Although the road was rerouted many times, the general direction remained.

The survey began in October 1832 with a congressional appropriation of $2,000, and construction began by detachments of soldiers in 1833. At first it was "a narrow track through the forest." Andreas, the Chicago historian, says that the road was "somewhat improved by cutting out trees to the width of 2 rods and laying puncheon and log bridges over the impassable streams." Generally it followed the route of the Indian trail and crossed 24 streams between Chicago and Green Bay. No grading was done for several years, and as late as 1836 it was only a "blazed trail" through the forest between the three settlements of Chicago, Milwaukee and Green Bay. In addition to being a military road, it also provided transportation, especially in the winter-time, when sailing vessels could not be used. As time went on, its military purpose was diminished and its use for local travel and for mail routes became dominant. The first real support came in 1838 when Congress appropriated $15,000 for improvements on the Road. The following year, Bishop Jackson Kemper (Episcopal), a pioneer missionary in the mid-west, left Chicago, arriving in Kenosha 24 hours later, though the scheduled time was about ten hours.

In 1865 Green Bay Road was relocated and brought within the limits of Lake Forest. The question is, where was the original Green Bay Road in the vicinity of Lake Forest? Lieutenant Center's plat is no doubt buried somewhere in the archives of the state of Illinois and without it we hazard a guess that the road was on or near the present Waukegan Road. To support this theory we present the following facts and inferences: First, the road ran parallel to Lake Michigan, and at Waukegan it was three miles west of the Lake. Since this was so, it is reasonable to assume that the road was also three miles west of the Lake in the Lake Forest area. Secondly, the road is repeatedly described as passing through "open prairie in Illinois." This, too, points to the same area, much more suitable for a road of this description since this area alone is treeless, and grading and tree cutting would be reduced to a minimum. Besides, the "impassable streams" and "getting mired" is more likely here than on the ridge which is the present location of the road. Thirdly, the 1830 pioneers are said to have come out on Green Bay Road from Chicago. It is reasonable to suppose that they carved out farmsteads on or near the thoroughfare to maintain communication with Chicago, Waukegan and Milwaukee. Finally, the two Post Offices, the earliest within the boundaries of present Lake Forest, were in the Waukegan Road district.

There was an alternate Green Bay Road through Wheeling, Half Day and Libertyville. A mile north of Libertyville it "veered to the northeast, recrossed the Des Plaines and joined the main Green Bay Road three miles beyond that point."

Stage coaches began operations in the spring of 1836. By 1850 the *Waukegan Gazette* reported "five to six coaches pass daily through Waukegan, full, inside and out."

By 1836, the land along Green Bay Road, in the general area of the present Waukegan Road, was easily accessible from Chicago, and so people came in the best tradition of the pioneer to carve out homesteads, unhampered by possible contention with Indians, most of whom had departed two years earlier. The first families arrived as squatters, with the hope of later buying the land at low prices. Many of these left their families on the farms as they worked on the Canal in Chicago.

On March 1, 1839, Lake County was detached from McHenry County by an act of the Illinois State Legislature. Independence Grove, now Libertyville, became the first County Seat. Two years later, Waukegan became and has remained the county seat of Lake County. This county derived its name from the fifty fair sized lakes within its boundaries. The County consists of 460 square miles with 24 miles of Lake Michigan shoreline.

In 1844 there was a large enough population in the area of west Lake Forest to organize a Catholic church—St. Michael's, one of the earliest Catholic churches in the state. It was a log church erected on the west side of Waukegan Road in the southeast quarter of section 7 in west Deerfield Township. The land was donated by Michael Yore, and the logs were hewn by men of the parish. The church was forty feet long and thirty wide, and was a meeting place for four adjacent townships. Father O'Mara was the first priest. When the population moved northward, the log church was sold to Michael Vaughn, in 1855, who moved it south a half a mile on the same road and made it his family home.

Soon after this first log church, another was erected at Meehan's settlement. This was named after Michael Meehan, who had arrived in this area in 1835 from Ireland. He is said to have brought the first cattle, pigs and cats to the area of Lake Forest. Like many others of this period he went to California during the gold rush, to seek his fortune. This second log church is said to have stood at the northwest corner of the present St. Patrick's Cemetery. In the forties it was a mission of Little Fort (Waukegan), and its first priest was a French missionary, Father John Guegnin. In quick succession came Fathers McGorish, Kean, Hampston, Coyle, and Magee.

Father Coyle undertook the building of a more permanent structure—St. Patrick's. On March 24, 1853, two and a half acres of land were conveyed by Peter and Margaret Bichel to the Very Reverend James Van de Velde, Bishop of Chicago, for $86.00. This property is described as occupying the S.E. quarter of the S.E. quarter of section 31 in Shields Township, on the east side of Waukegan Road, near the intersection of Mellody Road. The clay for the bricks was secured on Patrick Melody's farm. James Durkin moulded the bricks and the parishioners furnished the wood necessary to fire the kiln. A great misfortune was averted one night when the watchman fell asleep, and had it not been for the timely arrival of Patrick Carolan with a load of wood, the whole kiln of bricks would have been lost, for the fire had almost gone out.

When the bricklayers arrived from Chicago, they stayed at the Melody home until their task was finished. The corner stone was laid on October 22, 1853. The church and parish house together cost $14,000. Father Magee was the first resident pastor. The log church now became the community school with as many as 137 pupils crowding into its cramped quarters. They sat in the loft, on the stairs, or on benches. This school continued until 1905. St. Patrick's was variously called the "Brick Church," or "Corduroy Church." After Father Magee, it was served also by Fathers M. Edwards, Michael Ford, James Coyle, William Herbert, William Phew, Patrick O'Dwyer, and J. W. Kennedy. The last-named bought the present property on which St. Mary's church was erected in 1875. St. Patrick's served the parish until one night in

18

July 1895 it was struck by lightning and burned to the ground. A new church building was erected to replace the original brick building. It, too, suffered a fire on August 20, 1908, and the site was abandoned. The present building of St. Patrick's was built on the corner of Everett and Waukegan Roads in 1910.

Titles to all properties in Lake County and the State were somewhat uncertain and subject to change, except for those held by deeds from the Federal Government. Between 1835 and 1855 there were squatters who occupied the lands, hoping to purchase them eventually at the minimum price, and settlers who paid cash for their property. After 1835 Senator Thomas Hart Benton's land theory of "graduation" was in vogue. It called for the reduction of the price of unsold lands until the price reached 25¢ per acre. Then the unsold lands would become the property of the State. In 1841 "Preemption" was the principle everybody favored. This theory would give settlers the right to buy the lands on which they had settled, at the minimum price. When Congress passed the Homestead Act in 1862, all settlers and squatters received greater surety in their titles and ownership. This act permitted the ownership of 160 acres of public land after five years residence and use, for a nominal fee.

Otis and Sarah Hinkley were the first to settle in the original area of the first Lake Forest plat. They built their cabin on the present south-west corner of Deer Path and Green Bay Road in 1835, but they moved to Waukegan before Lake Forest was incorporated. One of the first settlers who came and stayed in the Lake Forest area was Matthew Steele. Born in Scotland, he came to Shields Township in 1839, after several years of labor on the Illinois-Michigan Canal. He was on the West coast during the gold rush period where he made a fortune. Returning to Shields Township in the 1850's, he purchased a large farm on Waukegan Road and married Helen Atteridge. His three sons married into the Swanton and Connell families of the area. His extensive farm became a part of the J. Ogden Armour acres and of the R. O. Boehms' property.

Michael Yore arrived from Ireland by way of the Erie Canal and the Great Lakes, in 1838. His ship was supposed to land in Milwaukee but a storm blew them off course to Little Fort. At first he thought of purchasing property along the shore of Lake Michigan, where the Stanley Field property now stands, but decided against it, thinking the bluff might be washed away. He settled, instead, in the area of the Everett School which was then called Corduroy.

Michael sent for his wife and children who made three attempts to set sail from Ireland, but were forced back each time. They finally arrived after a trip of three weeks across the ocean, having lost all their belongings except a small red trunk. This trunk remained a prized possession of the family until recently.

The first town meeting was held in the Yore house, also Sunday services. Neighboring farmers came to Mass and stayed for Sunday dinner. In the 1840's Mrs. Yore is said to have walked to Waukegan to sell eggs. Michael Yore secured sufficient property so that he provided a farm for each of his five sons.

John Birmingham came from Dublin, Ireland, through Hartford, Connecticut, in 1852. At one time he had squatter's rights south of Woodland Road and east of Sheridan. He cut trees and sold them to the railroad company for railroad ties and for fuel. In 1859 he bought a farm including the present Owen Jones property from the Lake Forest Association and built a homestead. The hill on Deer Path just west of Green Bay Road was for long called Birmingham Hill.

Some of the earliest names on the pioneer role in the Waukegan Road area were: Atkinson, Barker, Bolger, Burns, Carolan, Carroll, Cole, Conway, Dawson, Doyle, Duffy, Dulanty, Dwelley, Dwyer, Fagan, Gibbons, Hickox, Hinckley, Kennedy, Lancaster, Ludlow, Masterson, McGuire, Meehan, Melody, Murphy, Nullery, O'Boyle, O'Connor, Redmond, Swain, and Yore. The descendants of many of these original settlers still live in Lake Forest.

The first Post Office in the present area of Lake Forest was established on May 28, 1846, at the northwest intersection of Kennedy and Waukegan Roads. Andrew Steele was the first Postmaster. This was also called the Emmet Post Office. This office was discontinued in 1859, then reestablished in 1870, then discontinued again in 1875. The first telegraph line between Chicago and Milwaukee was laid in 1847, following the old Green Bay Road, the present Waukegan Road. This is the origin of the name Telegraph Road which has been retained north of Route 176.

The Pioneers, 1832–1857

In 1852 Elijah M. Haines of Waukegan, a school-teacher, published his *Historical and Statistical Sketches of Lake County*, the first history of any Illinois County to be published in book form. In the meantime, new names began to appear near the lake shore area, from the present Green Bay Road eastward and north and south of present Deer Path. These were the families which owned clearings in the area included in the first plat of Lake Forest in 1857. The area west of the present Green Bay Road was not joined to Lake Forest until May 12, 1926.

Those living within the first plat include Thomas Atteridge, Thomas R. Clark, Patrick Conlon, Jacob Felter, Edward Lee, Francis McCandry, Michael Mooney, Peter Mooney, Joseph Sammons, and William Swanton. Thomas Atteridge is said to have come to this area in 1837. He built a log cabin on the N.W. corner of Sec. 19, and dug a well. A few years later, he married Mary Cole Swanton, widow of Robert Swanton who had arrived the same year as Atteridge. Thomas Atteridge later moved south to the Cole farm where he raised six children and six step-children. One of these, William Atteridge was the first white child born in Lake Forest proper.

The first reported Protestant services were held in the log house of William Atteridge which stood near the present corner of Deer Path and Green Bay Road. Three families gathered for religious services in 1850, and the Rev. Mr. Tate, a Methodist minister, preached several Sundays. A Rev. Mr. Howe conducted services to another group at the present intersection of Waukegan and Deer Path at about the same time. In 1856 a Sunday School was held at Shields' Corners, four miles north of Deer Path and Green Bay Road. When the railroad was finished, Sunday School and regular services began in a log house on Green Bay Road just south of Lake Bluff. These services were supplied by Methodists from Evanston and gradually were assimilated by the Lake Bluff Camp Meeting Association.

In the eighteen fifties, stage coaches ran on Green Bay Road from Chicago to Milwaukee until the completion of the Chicago Milwaukee Railroad which ultimately became a part of the Northwestern system. These stage coaches were regular Concord coaches, with a baggage rack behind and four horses. At one time Parmalee was the promoter of this line. Ed. Gunn, McGovern and James McVay, all later Lake Forest residents, were among drivers of these coaches.

The assessed valuation of real and personal property in all of Shields Township, in 1850, was $44,300.

The early settlers in the Lake Forest area were pioneers in the real sense, suffering all the hardships involved in making clearings, locating drinking water, cutting wood for fuel, cutting paths or roads, making their own clothes often, and supplying their families with home-made candles, and generally eking out a mere existence. They contended with wild animals and were sometimes startled by stray Indians who peeked through windows at families gathered around the dinner table in the kitchen. These families made a real contribution in preparing the area and making it especially suitable as the site for a village to the east, soon to be chartered as the City of Lake Forest.

ANOTHER GROUP of pioneers originating in New England, New York, and Pennsylvania, settled in the Chicago area, then moved to Lake Forest after the formation of the Lake Forest Association. All who came from the Eastern seaboard could have made the trip to the Illinois country by covered wagon as early as 1836 and more certainly by 1840, over the National Road which was authorized by Congress in 1806, reaching the Ohio River by 1830, the Indiana border by 1840 and Illinois the same year. They came in various ways. John Tillson and his wife Christiana went from Massachusetts to Baltimore by sail boat, then crossed the mountains by wagon to Pittsburgh and then took a flat-boat to Shawneetown. A Vermont family of Elkanah Brush journeyed by covered wagon along Lake Erie and down the old Vincennes Trail to St. Louis, up the Mississippi and the Illinois rivers to a spot known as Yankee Settlement and later named Bluffdale.

These young pioneers often left home to seek elbow room, independence or new opportunities. The depression of 1837 had caused many to turn to the West with the hope of better luck in the new country. One Lake Forest grandmother, Elizabeth Downs, left an account of her trip to Illinois, made in 1837, ending in Chicago.

The trip began in Hanover, Connecticut. Fellow townsmen by the name of Rockwell had gone ahead, formed the Rockwell Land

Company and wrote back to their Eastern friends of the fine land and opportunities in Illinois. Times were hard in Connecticut. There seemed to be no openings for a young man, and certainly every bit of land had long been in the possession of families from early colonial times.

Barzilli Bishop persuaded his 18 year old bride-to-be, Lydia Elizabeth Allen, to set their wedding date for the earliest possible moment and be ready to start with others from their town for the land so alluringly described by the Rockwell brothers. According to strict New England custom it was announced on two successive Sundays in Church the intention of the young people to marry. Then came the Sunday in April when the wedding should take place, the day before the departure to the West. Mr. Bishop was taken suddenly ill. The distraught bride was not allowed by her father, Deacon Ebenezer Allen, to go to see him. Monday morning, the 17th of April, Bishop was sufficiently recovered to drive over to the home of his bride. They were married at ten o'clock and caught the stage for Norwich. There they joined the party bound for Illinois, boarded a steamer and went down the Thames River on their way to New York. When Deacon Allen bade farewell to his daughter, he said: "I will come to visit you when I can make the trip in 36 hours." "That means you will never come," she said. "Yes, my daughter, I expect to live to see the day when I can come by railroad in that length of time." Had he not died soon afterwards, it would have been possible for him to see her again.

There was no mention of the Bishops' sea voyage to New York. Two days were spent in New York City, then the "steam cars" were taken on the next lap of the journey. Arriving in Philadelphia, the couple changed cars and went to the end of the line at Hollidaysburg. Now travel by water was resumed, for here the party took a boat on the Pennsylvania Canal. When they reached the Allegheny Mountains it was Saturday, six days since the departure from Connecticut. A discussion ensued among the passengers: should they continue over the mountains or rest where they were over Sunday? The party was divided. It was not surprising that Elizabeth and Barzilli Bishop were among those who decided to wait. Their stopping-off-place was not too desolate, for there was a church which they attended.

Crossing the mountains was achieved by means of a stationary engine on the summit. The cars would be drawn up one mountain side and let down the other. When the Bishops were safely over and on their way, Monday morning April 24th, they learned that when the cars went over the mountains the day before, the safety car had got loose going down and had nearly smashed. The members of that party were thereby delayed and reached Pittsburgh only one hour earlier than the second party, after travelling since Saturday night. Some nodded wisely, not surprised that Sabbath-breaking resulted in misfortune. When the Bishops reached Pittsburgh, the first important objective of the trip, they were amazed to see everyone with dirty hands and faces, caused by the use of soft coal.

After spending 24 hours in Pittsburgh they took a river boat to Cincinnati, arriving on April 29, almost two weeks after leaving Norwich, Connecticut. They took another ship after spending three days in Cincinnati. This vessel, termed "a fine steamboat," carried freight and passengers down the Ohio River with the danger of snags the only threat to progress. In order to avoid them the captain would "tie up to a tree" at night, waiting until daylight to proceed. The Bishops must have been impressed by the beautiful series of hills which lined the banks of the Ohio all the way to the even more impressive confluence of the Ohio and the Mississippi at Cairo, Illinois. The "fine steamer" plodded up the "Father of Waters" to St. Louis, the Queen city of the West, arriving on May 8 after three weeks of tedious travel. They did not linger in the city, but took a small steamboat up the Illinois River as far as it was navigable at that time.

They landed at a settlement called Peru on a dark rainy night. Standing ankle deep in mud, they watched the boat chug out of sight on its way back to St. Louis. They made their way to the two buildings which comprised Peru, one of which was a log tavern already crowded to capacity. The other building was the Post Office, a frame building with no plastering. It did not take much to make our travellers happy.

Tuesday morning dawned bright and clear. The previous miseries were forgotten, and everyone wanted to start out for Rockwell immediately. They were told the goal of their travels was only two miles distant. A blast from a horn announced the arrival of the stage. Everyone clamored to get on, and soon every available space inside and out was quickly taken. The rest of the company started out on foot, stopping every few paces to scrape the clay from their shoes so that they could walk more easily. The young Bishops must have been among the latter group, as the record says: "After walking a mile and a half, they came to a river, Little Vermilion. On the way they passed a few shanties occupied by men digging the Illinois-Michigan Canal. At a shanty close by the river, they inquired of a woman how they could cross the stream. 'You see the little boat there? Get into it, row over, and tie it up on the other side,' she said. They asked how far it was to Rockwell. She replied: 'Two miles.' After crossing the river they walked up a long, steep bluff; then through the prairie grass which was a beautiful green and full of flowers." The young girl-bride, tired as she was, must have felt her spirits lifted by the sight. Years later, she told her Lake Forest grandchildren: "Never saw anything more beautiful."

Looking ahead they saw a little village and soon detected a man sawing boards. When they reached him they inquired how far it was to Rockwell. He replied with a pleasant smile: "You are in Rockwell." Soon the young couple purchased land from the Rockwell brothers, put up a house and made a good start with their farm. At the time of their arrival Elizabeth Bishop and the keeper of the boarding house were the only women in Rockwell.

One night Elizabeth had a bad dream in which all had died and she alone was left. A dark-haired man appeared and consoled her saying that he would take care of her. A few days later the Bishops drove to the nearby village and there in the store Elizabeth saw the clerk and said to her husband: "That is the man I saw in my dream." This was the store, constructed for the Rockwell Land Company, for which the man was sawing boards the day the Bishops arrived. Mr. Charles L. Palmer of Norwich, Connecticut, was the carpenter to whom they had spoken. He remained a friend of the family and died in Chicago in 1892.

Elizabeth bore a son the following year after their arrival in Rockwell. Though the child seemed strong and healthy, he died suddenly at the age of three months. Two months later her husband died of typhus fever, leaving her with the payments for the farm still incomplete, the crops unharvested and a scamp of a land owner to deal with. Her father sent word for her to come home to Connecticut, but she married the man in her dream, Myron Day Downs.

The Downs moved to La Salle in the fall of 1839, and three years later, in 1842, they drove to Chicago in a buggy, their household goods following them by team, over Frink and Walker's stage road. The journey took two days for the hundred miles. In Chicago the family prospered selling lumber from the Downs' Lumber Yard which stood on the land which is now the corner of Michigan Avenue and Wacker Drive. Soon after the Civil War, one of her daughters moved to Lake Forest. Thus this town became the home of six of Elizabeth Downs' grandchildren.

In ADDITION TO the Illinois-Michigan canal, another factor which led to the founding of Lake Forest was the Iron Horse. It all started when the State of Illinois granted a charter to the Illinois Parallel Railroad Company with the right to construct a railway from Chicago, contiguous to the shore of Lake Michigan, via Waukegan, to the Wisconsin State line. The charter to this first railroad in Lake County was issued February 17, 1851. Work began immediately, and the name was soon changed to the Chicago and Milwaukee Railway, which extended to the Wisconsin line, where it disembarked its passengers, who then boarded the Milwaukee and Chicago Railway and continued their journey to Milwaukee, Wisconsin. These two railroads were subsequently united into the Chicago and North Western system in 1854.

The tracks were built through this section of the present North Shore, partly because there was so much timber in the area, especially pine. The ties were secured, on the spot, in the section between the boundaries of Chicago and Waukegan. Local labor was employed. James Swanton and John Birmingham cut many of the ties which were originally laid in this area. It was supposed that there was enough timber in this district to furnish ties and fuel for the engines for the next fifty years. The tracks cost the company $10,000 per mile.

The road was completed to Waukegan, and the first train left Chicago on January 11, 1855. The passengers included officials of the Company and the Chicago City Council. The train left at 9:30 a.m. and travelled the thirty-five miles in three hours, reaching Waukegan at 12:30 p.m. Upon arrival Colonel Swift's Artillery, from Chicago, shot a brass field piece. It was thought that this trip had achieved a new world's speed record—nearly twelve miles per hour. This can be appreciated if the 1855 model of a train can be visualized, together with the primitive wooden rails covered with iron sheathing. The arrival was also greeted with the ringing of the church bells and the playing of the local band. The Mayor of Waukegan made a speech of welcome.

A large banquet was prepared for the first passengers, officials and celebrities. Among those present were William Bross of the *Democratic Press,* who was to become the President of the Board of Trustees of Lake Forest University (1865–1890), and Dr. C. Volney Dyer, the "Prince of Wits" and director of the Underground Railroad, a staunch friend of Lake Forest in the years to come. Samuel F. Miller who had previously built the first Chicago bridge, over the north branch of the Chicago River, as well as the tracks from Chicago to Waukegan, made a speech on "Our Railroad." Three years later he was elected the first Principal of Lake Forest Academy, and six years later he was to become the first Postmaster of the newly chartered City of Lake Forest, and its first Superintendent of Schools.

The railroad track, now dividing the future Lake Forest, emphasized certain features. Next to the lake was the highest bluff along the north shore, varying from 50 to 90 feet above Lake Michigan, and commanding a view of the shore line and the lake unsurpassed in beauty and serenity. Ravines penetrated from the area of the railroad eastward, achieving an increasing depth and beauty as they descended into the waters of the great lake.

Three large ravines traversed the area from west to east. Many more small ones followed the same pattern. The northernmost and most precipitous one, called Clark's Ravine in the early days of Lake Forest, contained a spring. The families living north and south of this ravine have done much to maintain its original beauty. In 1961, Mrs. Donald R. McLennan lives just north of the intersection of the ravine and the lake while the Stanley Keith home is to the south. The largest ravine, which ends near Ferry Hall, combines two branches, one beginning at Deer Path and the railroad tracks, the other beginning at Illinois Road, a quarter of a mile south. These two branches go around the College south campus uniting east of the Campus circle. The third largest ravine was near the south end of town, and came to be called The Mc-Cormick Ravine.

Until the 1880's these ravines were deep in water and were a favorite resort of youthful fishermen and gatherers of wild flowers. When the wind was from the northeast, the backwash from the lake increased, making the ravine waters deeper. Some recall that trout were caught in these ravines. J. V. Farwell, Jr., remembered counting one hundred lady-slippers in his father's ravine in the 1870's.

The area of the railroad contained many ponds which were the source of continually running water in the ravines. Many of these ponds consisted of standing rainwater and gradually disappeared as soon as real estate became valuable and scarce, and sewers were installed and roads built. Other ponds were fed by springs.

Ponds large enough to deserve a name included the Atteridge Pond, the Brewster Pond, the Farwell Pond, the Holt Pond, the Kelley Pond, and the Quinlan Pond. The Holt Pond was between Deer Path, Green Bay Road and Oakwood, and was always a gathering place of skaters in the early days of Lake Forest. In the summer time it might have been used for swimming except that it contained snakes. This pond was filled with dirt from the excavations for Market Square around 1915 and is now part of the area of West Park. The Farwell Pond, just south of present Deer Path and east of Mayflower, provided early Lake Forest youngsters additional skating space, College, Academy, and Ferry Hall students using this pond freely through the generosity of Senator C. B. Farwell.

The crowning glory of the area, east of the tracks, were the beautiful stands of trees. Jack Pines four feet or more in diameter towered over hickories, elms, maples and even over giant Swamp Oaks.

Ravines, abundant waters, ponds and forest attracted the wild life recorded by early residents, namely, "herds of deer, moose, raccoons, weasels, woodchucks, wolves, bear, fox, squirrels, partridges, prairie chickens, wild pigeons, quail, ducks, geese, swans, meadowlarks, bobolinks, blue jays, red-headed woodpeckers, owls and snakes." Was this the state of nature described by Rousseau, or was it Longfellow's forest primeval?

III

THE LAKE FOREST ASSOCIATION

1856–1861

CHICAGO, which had been incorporated as a city in 1837, was in a turmoil during the 1850's. The eyes of the nation were focussed upon this sprawling pioneer city which had nearly tripled its population between 1850 and 1855, from 28,000 to over 80,000 inhabitants. The newly finished Illinois-Michigan Canal had in large part caused this bulge in the population, but now that it was the projected railroad hub of the North American continent, even greater commercial activity and an accelerated growth of population were indicated.

There was need for cultural and educational continuity, progress, stability and growth to maintain an enduring city. Chicago had established a public school system of a dozen grade schools and two high schools. But the promise of a phenomenal expansion of the city suggested the need not only for more units of secondary education but for copying the models of eastern and European colleges and universities and establishing independent institutions capable of producing trained professional men.

Colleges begun in the older parts of the state gave impetus to a movement in Chicago. Illinois College had been started by Presbyterians in Jacksonville as early as 1829, graduating the first college class in the state. In 1841 Knox College, another Presbyterian institution, opened its doors and became established in

29

Galesburg as a pioneer college. Monmouth was begun by the United Presbyterians in 1856. These beginnings in the state influenced the Chicago Presbyterians directly, because they were a part of the Synod of Peoria at the time, and the feeling became general that higher education should also be promoted in the newly developed section of the state which now promised to become the center of Illinois population.

An added impetus came from the religious revivals which were sweeping the country. The leadership in these Chicago educational projects was therefore furnished by the various religious groups of the city, since they had the vision and the will to begin. The first group to become effectively organized was that of the Methodists. It made elaborate plans, founding a school that began in 1851 with a faculty of four and a student body of two. This was chartered in 1855 and grew to become Northwestern University, in Evanston. The Baptists founded the University of Chicago in 1857.

Inspired by all these beginnings, and following many and long discussions, the congregations of the First and Second Presbyterian churches of Chicago were at last ready for definite action. Their respective pastors, the Rev. Harvey Curtis and the Rev. Robert W. Patterson, organized several committee trips in all directions from Chicago, in order to locate a home for their dream university. These together with the Rev. Ira M. Weed, agent for the Home Missionary Society, residing in Waukegan, agreed that the institution should be located somewhere between Evanston and Waukegan. During another exploratory trip these three ministers decided on the location in the area which was later named Lake Forest.

On a trip soon after this, another committee also arrived by means of the newly finished railroad. They were let off at a point later called Farwell Crossing, since there was no station of any kind in the entire area. They made their way from the train to the lake shore, all the while searching for a suitable name for the new educational community. This committee, besides the three ministers named above, included the Rev. J. J. Slocum of Cincinnati, who had had experience in starting several educational institutions, and a layman, D. R. Holt. The Rev. Slocum, who was a visitor in Chicago at the time, looked about and asked the members of the committee what lay before them. They replied: "A lake." He then asked what stood behind them. They said: "A forest." He then rejoined: "Why not call it Lake Forest?" To this they all replied: "Amen." And so it has remained.

Rev. J. J. Slocum continued to be instrumental in "getting the ball rolling," as he informed the congregations that he knew a Mr. Gibson in Cincinnati who would give $100,000 for this project, if it were called Gibson University. When it became known that Mr. Gibson had gained his wealth by distilling whiskey, people were reluctant to pursue the matter, and he, taking the hint, withdrew the offer. This incident was not without profit however, since another benefactor, Sylvester Lind, a Chicago Presbyterian layman, soon made the same offer of $100,000, on condition that a like sum be raised by the Presbyterian community of Chicago.

The first step presented the problem of purchasing the land in the area. Mr. Thomas R. Clark was one of the first to offer land: forty acres, at reasonable prices. Other properties were held in small areas by earlier settlers and a few railroad construction workers. A subscription book was made, and the Rev. J. J. Slocum became the collecting agent for purchasing the properties which might be for sale. In a short while $59,000 was collected from ninety-four subscribers, and a meeting of all subscribers was called to organize a permanent body. The largest donations came from T. R. Clark, D. R. Holt, D. J. Lake, and Peter Page. Each of these gave $750. C. B. Farwell and Amzi Benedict each gave $375.00.

The Second Presbyterian Church of Chicago had been built in 1851. It was called the Spotted Church, because its gray stones were covered with black spots. These bituminous limestones had been quarried near the intersection of Chicago and Western Avenues. This church stood on the corner of Wabash Avenue and Washington Street, and became the headquarters for meetings and all details of organization. On February 26, 1856, a meeting was held with a clear purpose: "To establish an institution of learning of a high order in which Christian teaching would hold a central place." Hiram F. Mather presided, Horatio G. Shumway was secretary. Thomas Butler Carter, the city's most popular merchant, wealthiest citizen, and founder of the Chicago Bible Society, stood up and made a motion that a Lake Forest Association be formed to purchase land and sponsor the contemplated educational institutions. The motion carried. T. R. Clark, David Lake, and H. F. Mather were elected Trustees, and empowered to purchase land to consummate the purposes of the Association.

On February 29, 1856, the first meeting of the Trustees was held in the office of Mather and Taft. All members were present. H. F. Mather was elected chairman, Peter Page, Treasurer, and David J. Lake, Secretary. "The Treasurer was required to give bonds in the sum of $60,000 for the faithful performance of his duties. The Secretary was authorized to procure the necessary books for the Association." On March 3, 1856, the Trustees met again and "authorized Mr. Page to proceed to purchase the lands in such way as he might deem proper."

The subscribers were presented with the articles of the Association, to be known as the *Lake Forest Association,* which were accepted. The capital stock was to be not less than $50,000, nor more than $60,000, the shares being $500.00 each, and the articles of the Association were not binding until $50,000 had been subscribed in good faith. The purchase of twelve hundred acres was contemplated, the quantity not to exceed the purchasing power of the capital stock. Fifty acres were to be set apart by the Trustees for three institutions of learning: thirty acres for College grounds, ten for an Academy, and ten for a Female Seminary. In case there were only twelve hundred acres purchased, the residue of lands remaining after the appropriation of this fifty acres was to be divided equally among the Association and the institutions of learning; but if more should be purchased, the institutions were to have one half of the lands, not exceeding eight hundred acres (including streets) besides the fifty, and the residue should belong to the Association.

Article 9 stated that these educational institutions shall "at all times be subject to the ratification and approval of the Synod of Peoria or its legal successor." The board was told that within five years from July 1, 1856, buildings must be erected and other improvements of the lands of their institution made to the estimated amount of $30,000; otherwise all their appropriated land that then remained unused, should revert to the Association.

The land was described as containing about thirteen hundred acres, twenty-five miles north of Chicago, two and a half miles along the shore of Lake Michigan, and one mile wide from the lake to the railroad track which was to be the western boundary. It was said to rise boldly from fifty to ninety feet above the lake, covered with a rich forest, intersected with beautiful ravines, and most suitable for the objects intended, and unsurpassed by a plat of equal size anywhere to be found.

The Lake Forest Association now sold shares to those who wished to purchase it. Enough money was collected so that the required lands could be bought. The first purchaser was Franklin Ripley, Jr., who bought two shares. The shares were worded:

This certifies that Franklin Ripley, Jr., is the owner of 2 shares of the capital stock in the Lake Forest Association, created in furtherance of the Articles of Association bearing date February 28, A.D. 1856. Said shares being $500 each and that he has this date paid the sum of $250 on account of his subscription to such stock. Said share is liable to further payment evidenced by three notes payable to the Trustees of said Association dated February 28, 1856, for the sum of $250 each and severally payable in 6, 12 and 18 months after date with interest at 6% per annum in pursuance of said articles and subject to all the provisions and covenants contained in said articles to which reference is made.

This certificate is transferable by assignment below to the extent of the payment made and by the surrender of this certificate to the Trustees when a new certificate will be issued by them to the person or persons named in the assignment, such person or persons first affixing his or their name and seal to the said articles as provided therein.

Signed,

	H. F. Mather	David J. Lake
Chicago, Illinois	Sylvester Lind	E. H. Aiken
April 5, 1856	Peter Page	

In a few weeks sufficient money was available so that the lands in the area could be purchased. Mr. Page owned a farm at nearby Wadsworth. He was a former Presbyterian minister of Devon, England. He had raised fine trotting horses, and had twice gone to California during the period of the gold rush. In Chicago he was the director of the Chicago Mutual Life Insurance Company and the Internal Revenue Assessor. He was a capable executive as well as a man of character and determination. He employed Samuel Dowst of Waukegan to act as purchasing agent. The latter

33

examined the purchases and Judges Henry W. Blodgett and Clark W. Upton examined the titles, in Waukegan. In the summer of 1856 purchases were made from the following property owners: Edward Lee was paid $2,000, William Swanton $1,794, Patrick Farrel $1,500, Patrick Conlin $1,000, Peter Mooney $840, and James Swanton $470.

The Charter of Lind University was received on February 13, 1857. It was titled: "An Act to Incorporate the Lind University." Issued by the State of Illinois, it was written in longhand. This charter became the foundation of what was to become first of all a university in the classic sense, having four faculties, and secondly a supporting community which the Charter named Lake Forest.

The Charter described the projected institutions as "schools of every description and grade, together with a college and seminaries or departments devoted to instruction in Theology, Law, Medicine, General or particular Sciences and Literature or the (Liberal) Arts." It specified "equal privileges of admission into all departments for students of every denomination of Christians."

The Charter named a board of Trustees, limited to twenty names. Sylvester Lind was designated the *first trustee,* "the donor of one hundred thousand dollars to found a Theological Department in honor and recognition whereof the University (shall) bear his name." The complete roll of the trustees included:

1. Amzi Benedict	11. Lewis H. Loss
2. Asabel L. Brooks	12. Hiram F. Mather
3. William H. Brown	13. Peter Page
4. Thomas B. Carter	14. Robert W. Patterson
5. Franklin W. Chamberlain	15. Charles H. Quinlan
6. Harvey Curtis	16. Benjamin W. Raymond
7. Ansel D. Eddy	17. Shubert G. Speer
8. Devillo R. Holt	18. Charles R. Starkweather
9. SYLVESTER LIND	19. Harvey M. Thompson
10. Samuel D. Lockwood	20. Ira M. Weed

Sylvester Lind's life-long ambition had been to found a Theological Seminary for the training of Presbyterian ministers. It was natural that much was said at this time about the location of the proposed Seminary. There was a diversity of opinion in the minds of the shareholders and of the Board of Trustees on the subject. Section 7 of the Charter provided that: "The Theological department of the University may by a vote of ¾ of the entire Board of Trustees of said University be located *in or near* the City of Chicago." This decision was affirmed by passing a resolution during the Association meeting of March 1857 which stated: "This Association will and does hereby approve of the location of the Theological Department of Lind University on the Lake Forest grounds or at or near Chicago."

Another problem was dealt with at this time when the Association passed a resolution stating that: "The trustees be and are hereby instructed to lay out the cemetery grounds in the north portion of the lands belonging to the Lake Forest Association in the best manner for the interest of the Association."

In the meantime, when the Association had collected in excess of $100,000 and the Lake Forest dream seemed to be progressing, Olmstead, Vaux and Company of New York City, who had just planned South Park in Chicago and Central Park in New York, was asked to design Lake Forest. This company recommended a young engineer, Jed Hotchkiss, from St. Louis, a landscape architect, who went to work immediately and designed the future city of Lake Forest.

Hotchkiss laid out the city in park style, as South Park in Chicago and Central Park in New York had been designed. He made the Lake Forest streets follow the natural curves of the ravines, as did the Deer Path which went from the second slough along the Milwaukee Railroad tracks, through the first slough, later known as the Skokie, winding its way eastward to the shores of Lake Michigan. He planned beautiful winding streets and spacious residential lots, affording privacy, and insuring sites for the construction of homes which would have natural drainage down to the streets on which they were located. The resulting maze of winding streets with irregular intersections has been a fertile source of humorous remarks and the cause of an unusual number of lost souls looking for particular addresses. Deer Path was designed eastward to present Sheridan Road; then it turned northeast to what is now Westminster, all the way through Lake Road to the edge of Lake Michigan. Nearly all of this original area was located in Shields township.

In the Hotchkiss map every alternate lot was set apart for Lind University so that the proceeds from the sale of these lots would help finance the future institution. This left a surplus of 1,000 acres which when sold for residential purposes, or for farming, would furnish the Lake Forest Association with sufficient funds for improvements.

Four years later, Hotchkiss became the famous advisor, topographer, confidant and important source of military success of the Confederate General Thomas J. "Stonewall" Jackson. In the first year of the Civil War, General Jackson and Jed Hotchkiss met a Union General in the Shenandoah valley, a man already distinguished and decorated for gallantry in the Mexican war. He had fought at Vera Cruz and Cerro Gordo. This latter General was James Shields, Senator from Illinois in the 1850's and the man after whom the township was named in which Hotchkiss had designed Lake Forest.

It must be said that the Hotchkiss map was a work of art. Even today it impresses one with the beauty of his general plan, the rhythm of curves and the irregular contours created by the ravines, even suggesting the waves of the adjoining lake, and combining into an artistic whole.

The Trustees of the Association now employed Samuel S. Greeley, the surveyor of the City of Chicago, to survey the lands purchased, and to plat the entire area designed by Hotchkiss. This was necessary before lots could be sold and recorded. The plat was recorded on July 23, 1857. It is possible that a large crew of surveyors took part in such a large project which was finished so quickly. The name Greeley does not appear on the plat. The name of Edmund Bixby is there as deputy County surveyor of Lake County. The plat was accepted by Judge George Manierre of the 7th Judicial Circuit Court of Illinois.

Judge Manierre literally rode the circuit, either on or behind a horse. He was to become a delegate to the Republican Convention which nominated Lincoln in 1860, and the chairman of the Resolutions Committee of that convention. He was the grandfather of Lake Forest Mayor Francis E. Manierre.

Additional lands were purchased almost continually, even after the plat. In September 1858 William Swanton was paid $1,794.32, Thomas Cole $1,224.33, and Pat Farrell $1,000. When it became generally known that the entire area was in the process of being purchased, several property owners required prices in excess of the original estimates. Others refused to sell properties

36

east of the railroad tracks, unless their properties west of the tracks were also purchased. The result was that twenty-three hundred acres were purchased instead of the contemplated twelve hundred acres. Most of the land was secured at $25.00 per acre, but some as high as $100 per acre.

Lot 342 was bought by Joseph Sammons in 1844 for an undisclosed sum. In 1849 William Swanton bought it for $400. Thomas Swanton purchased it for $450 in 1851. James Swanton bought it for $150 in 1854 and sold it to the Lake Forest Association in 1856 for $1,340.

The Association having purchased most of the area now announced the terms for their sale to the general public. One fourth was to be paid in cash, the balance in one, two or three years, with 6% per annum. Discounts, at the rate of 10% per annum were offered for pre-payment. On July 23, 1857, when the plat was recorded in Waukegan, the following sales were also recorded:

W. A. Baldwin	1.6 acres	for $	300
Amzi Benedict	1.8		700
T. B. Carter	2.6		700
J. P. Chapin	2.2		300
T. R. Clark	9.5		800
Charles R. Day	3.66		500
C. B. Farwell	4.66		900
W. R. Gould	2.76		300
D. R. Holt	4.75		1,300
D. J. Lake	6.9		1,150
S. J. Learned	.47		200
Sylvester Lind	4.41		1,400
Joseph Meeker	3.86		500
M. A. Neefe	3.36		600
George W. Newcomb	2.8		850
Nathaniel Norton	1.22		500
R. W. Patterson	5.78		1,200
B. W. Raymond	3.0		1,200
A. J. Sawyer	5.55		500
H. G. Shumway	5.41		900
Mark Skinner	7.11		1,300
H. M. Thompson	6.23		800
W. B. Topliff	2.15		600
Chauncey Tuttle	3.65		900
S. D. Ward	6.0		800
P. L. Yoe	3.69		1,000

In addition Edmund Bixby bought 7 acres at $51 per acre; and a man named Hight bought 14 acres at $57 per acre. Also on July 23, 1857, a deed was recorded, transferring Lot no. 99 in Lake Forest, to John V. Farwell and Charles B. Farwell by the Trustees of the Lake Forest Association for $1,320. The trustees witnessing the deed were Sylvester Lind, Peter Page, David J. Lake, Hiram F. Mather, Edward H. Aiken and Thomas R. Clark, all residents of the City of Chicago. W. F. Merriam, Notary Public, of Chicago, notarized it.

A number of deeds issued between 1857 and 1861 contained a clause providing that: "No spiritous liquor shall at any time or under any pretense be ever made an article of traffic or sale except for strictly medicinal purposes in or upon said premises or at or in any house, store, or other building to be erected thereon." This clause persisted in many deeds even after 1900.

The Trustees held several meetings at which bills against the Association were considered and paid. The Rev. J. J. Slocum presented a claim for $1,250 for his services. The trustees decided that the claim was not just and that they would not pay it. Two weeks later they offered him $400 which he accepted. S. M. Dowst presented a bill for services in purchasing land and for other services rendered the Association. It was voted to pay him $500 for said services, and Mr. Dowst agreed to receive that sum in full payment. E. H. Aiken and D. J. Lake were appointed a committee to build and superintend the Hotel construction for which purpose $5,000 had been donated. They were to dig a well on the hotel lot. When the Lake Forest Hotel construction was completed, it was put in charge of Peter Page who operated it as a hotel and was paid $2,700 for three years of service as hotel manager and general superintendent of the Lake Forest Association 1859 to 1861. E. Mather was employed to superintend the contemplated improvements in Lake Forest. He accepted. Jed Hotchkiss was paid a total of $1,500 for his design of the City of Lake Forest. D. J. Lake was paid $700 for his service as Secretary-Treasurer. Peter Page, Mark Skinner and Rev. R. W. Patterson were appointed a committee to confer with the railroad company with reference to a depot and to make arrangements for the same. This resulted in the erection of the first station which was a modest structure.

The major problem facing the Association in the spring of 1858 involved the clearing of sick and dead trees, grubbing out stumps, levelling, filling, and general cleaning operations. On May 15 a committee composed of Aiken, Page and Lake was chosen to con-tract for the cleaning of the streets and tending to the other prob-lems. If possible, they were to operate with no expenditures of additional moneys, hoping that the timber when sold would pro-vide the necessary finances. In one year Deer Path and West-minster were put in perfect order. The following year, 1859, the committee concentrated on the rest of the town plat, commencing with the most central part of Lake Forest, especially on those streets which would more readily show the results of labor.

A road "back in the country to half day" (sic) was proposed and $100 was voted for the construction of the same. This was very likely due to Half Day's being the junction point from Lake County communities to Chicago by all horse-drawn transportation. It was also well known for its great number of saloons. The village itself may have been named after the local Indian, Chief Half-Day. However, in the 1880's and 1890's the fact that the village was considered a half day's carriage ride from Chicago gave rise to the popular belief that it was named for that reason.

Peter Page was instructed to build a bridge on Winona Avenue across the "Raveine" between lots 18 and 19, the present Elm Tree Road north of Woodland Road, across the Clark's ravine, the northernmost and largest. He was also instructed to build a bridge on Mayflower Avenue between lots 180 and 191. This is the same spot by Ferry Hall where there is now a steel bridge. Also on Mayflower near lot 268 where there is another steel bridge about a half mile south. These bridges were to be completed within 30 days, as were the grading of Westminster and several other streets near the center of the village.

By 1861 it became necessary to raise or reconstruct the bridge on "Deerpath Avenue," now filled in, north of the present Durand Art Institute. Reconstruction and repairs of roads and bridges be-came a continual activity as these were poorly built by modern standards and heavy rainfalls often damaged or completely washed away parts of roads or whole bridges.

Hotchkiss had made Deer Path the most important street in Lake Forest. The earliest maps and documents variously refer to it as Deerpath or Deerpath Avenue or Deer Path. The original road had followed the natural deer path which led from the Skokie to the edge of Lake Michigan. In 1915 the route of Deer Path east of Sheridan Road was altered to make it less confusing to people; but the original natural path to the lake was thus concealed. Before the coming of the white settlers, herds of fifty deer were said to have moved back and forth between the Skokie and the lake. In the early sixties there were still occasional deer wandering toward the lake but never in large herds. A few have been reported in the Lake Forest area even during the City of Lake Forest Centennial.

IV

LAKE FOREST ACADEMY

1858–1863

WHEN the General Assembly of the Presbyterian Church met in Chicago in May 1858, a considerable portion of those convened made an excursion to Lake Forest, to see the situation of the new Academy and the proposed University. This visit introduced the project to the country at large. The Assembly saw the location of the Academy building, which was being built approximately where the Durand Art Institute now stands. Meals were eaten from the tree stumps in Triangle Park, at the present intersection of Deer Path and Washington and Walnut Roads.

This visit produced Lake Forest's earliest recorded joke. When the passengers were discharged, somewhere near Deer Path, they made their way eastward, through clearings which were not exactly suitable for a comfortable walk. One of the party stumbled and fell into a deep hole. The next person in the party looked down and remarked: "Huh! A lay man!" The layman was the distinguished theologian Dr. Henry B. Smith, and the punster was a famous preacher of the day, Dr. Roswell D. Hitchcock.

The first public building in Lake Forest had been completed in 1857, the Lake Forest Hotel, later called the Old Hotel, and sometimes the Clark Hotel. This hotel provided food and lodging for those who came from Chicago intending to examine and purchase lots. It was a white frame building and stood in the middle of

41

present Triangle Park, just east of the railroad station. It cost $6,400, raised by $100 subscriptions. E. H. Aiken superintended the erection of the building. This hotel entertained many pioneer Lake Foresters, among them D. R. Holt, the Farwell brothers, the Durand brothers, Lockwood Brown and others. It was the meeting place for many picnic parties which came out from Chicago for a day in the country. In the 1860's the City Council met here part of the time.

The Lake Forest Hotel was the first building used by the Lake Forest Academy. Just before the opening of school, a hotel employee named Long was asked, for some reason, to leave his job in the Hotel immediately. He was paid $150 for doing so. Here classes were held in 1858 until January 3, 1859, when the Academy building was formally occupied. A Chicago newspaper advertisement advised prospective students to make application for the Academy at the Lind Block, in Chicago. This appeared on March 21, 1859. The Boys' Classical School which boasted of fifty pupils and held classes in the basement of the First Presbyterian Church of Chicago was disbanded in 1860 as the enrollment of Lake Forest Academy increased by the same number of students.

The first students in 1858 were John C. Patterson, John Johnson, Ellery S. Miller, and William Atteridge. The station attendant, named Daniel A. Jones, was a part-time student. "Prof" Samuel F. Miller was the first teacher, and his first professorial chair consisted of a board across a nail keg. This was at least a variation of Mark Hopkins' proverbial log with himself on one end and a student on the other.

Prof. Miller was an Amherst graduate, a member of the class of 1848. After finishing his work of building the railroad tracks from Chicago to Waukegan, he lived in the latter city, until the Academy building was completed. He then lived in an apartment in the Academy building, where his son, Spencer, once crawled across the hall into the study hall and paid an unofficial visit, to the pride of the father and the delight of the students. Prof. Miller paid rent at $150 per annum for his apartment in the Academy building, until 1860, when his house east of the old Academy, and north of present Deer Path was completed.

At first Prof. Miller taught all subjects, but his favorite was mathematics. He was a very religious man and had an important role in the organization of the first Presbyterian Sunday School, and then the Church. He was in the prime of life, strong and dignified. He believed the millennium was at hand. He helped organize the City of Lake Forest. His Academy salary was $1,400 per annum. Among his duties he was bursar for the school, sending out bills to parents at the middle of each term, made payable to him until the close of the year when he rendered account to the executive committee. In the fall of 1862 he devoted himself to surveying projects in Lake Forest. At this time Prof. Milford C. Butler became the Principal of the Academy. In 1868 Prof. Miller returned to Amherst, Massachusetts, becoming a professor of mathematics and engineering.

During the first year of the Academy, the Lake Forest Hotel served as the school's dining room. Here student John C. Patterson established a local record by consuming 17 pancakes at one sitting. Until the turn of the century this Hotel continued to serve citizens and institutions. Families waiting for the completion of their homes resided here for a while. Parents visiting their student children found the Old Hotel convenient.

The first Academy building stood on the approximate site of the present Durand Art Institute of Lake Forest College, and at the same angle. The contractor was William Loughlin; the architects were Carter & Drake. It was surrounded by a twelve acre forest of oaks, elms, hickory, and majestic pines. The latter dotted the edge of the ravines surrounding the area. The white frame structure with green shutters underscored the idea that Lake Forest was the New England town of the West. At night, when the student candles or kerosene lamps gleamed from the windows, the sight was especially impressive.

The cost of this building, $4,000, was raised by special subscription. Besides quarters for the head of the school, the first floor contained a chapel and a study hall. Second and third stories were dormitories. In May 1859 it became evident that the contractor would be unable to complete the erection of the building, and the roof was in a defective condition, demanding immediate repairs. The agreed price was too low for the specifications. Peter Page accepted the responsibility and supervised the needed construction and repairs. Sylvester Lind and Dr. Charles H. Quinlan as a committee took the responsibility for removing certain red oaks and other trees partly or wholly decayed, and also "such smaller trees or trunks as were not desirable for shade or primeval beauty of the Academy grounds." These were replaced with saplings.

Meals were served away from the Academy—first at the Hotel, later at the home of the Rev. and Mrs. Brainerd Kent, across the street on Deer Path. This house had been built by Sylvester Lind for the Kents. Mrs. Kent cooked, while her son Fred carved. When a friend of his asked for another *small* slice of meat, it was understood that a large one was wanted and he got it. Mrs. Kent was a motherly soul who would keep a plate on the back of the wood stove for a boy returning from Chicago too late for the regular meal. The earliest graduates remembered her with affection. The boarding department was moved to the Academy building after March 1860. Mr. and Mrs. I. M. Snodgrass were the caretakers of the school building during the early years. The students were granted half holidays on condition that they would work on the streets, grubbing out stumps, or shingling the Church roof.

Most of the Academy classes were held in the one classroom with each boy occupying a separate desk. Prof. Miller sat on a platform. On the two top floors, where the boys roomed, there was no faculty supervision whatever. Discipline was enforced by the boys themselves. An early catalogue says: "It is expected that the students will govern themselves in this school as they would in a well regulated and refined home, and never forget that it is upon earnest work in the study room, and faithful teaching, that the reputation of any school should rest."

The earliest debating society was formed in April, 1863, and called the Philologian Society. The constitution of the Society stated: "We the undersigned do declare ourselves an association for natural improvement in elocution, composition and debate; in the pursuit of which we desire to exhibit a due consideration for the feelings of others, and to seek truth in all our exercises."

The first president was F. H. Kent; vice-president George Manierre; secretary-treasurer, C. R. Wilkinson. During the May first meeting it was jocularly moved that President Abraham Lincoln be elected an honorary member. The motion was lost when Mr. Gage objected. A week later, "William R. Stokes moved to consider the vote of the last meeting on the election of Abraham

Lincoln as an honorary member." This motion carried.

The first catalogue, published during the school year 1861–1862, showed S. F. Miller, A.M., as Principal and teacher of Mathematics; Rev. William C. Dickinson, A.M., teacher of Languages; C. E. Dickinson, A.B., a tutor. It said: "Applicants for admission must not be less than twelve years of age, and must pass examinations in the primary studies, including written arithmetic as far as common fractions." Forty-nine students were listed. The studies offered included Greek, Latin, Mathematics, English, Grammar and Geography. The estimated expenses listed were:

Tuition—Collegiate Department	$30.00 per year
Higher branches of the Academic course	24.00 per year
Common English branches	20.00 per year
Room rent in the Academy building	6.00 per year
Incidentals	2.25 to 2.50 per week
Washing	.50 per dozen
Wood	2.50 per cord

There was a friendly feeling between the village and the school. Thomas R. Clark, President of the yet unchartered Lake Forest; Dr. Charles H. Quinlan, the only medical man in town; and "Pappy" Lind, the number one citizen, were frequent visitors at the school.

At first there was no gymnasium, and with the amount of physical exertion required to maintain life, none was needed. As the Academy enrollment increased to fifty in three years, there was a round of required daily industry. Each boy fetched water from the well, cut wood for his own box stove, cleaned and supplied his lamps with oil, swept his room and made his bed. A full bath was a luxury, taken only in warm weather, and in the lake. The lake could be reached by the ravines which contained splendid springs where boys could always get a cold drink in hot weather. Hickory nutting was a favorite pastime, and many jagged holes were torn in clothing of boys who climbed the trees to shake the nuts to the collectors below. A favorite pastime, after supper, was to walk to the depot to see the trains come in. These were a source of interest and amusement for a good many decades, as records were kept of the names of the engines, which were those of the towns through which they passed.

The boys' rooms were decorated with birds, butterflies, bugs and skins of animals. There were live creatures too. One boy kept garter snakes in his room, another entertained on his window ledges two beautiful flying squirrels, which were sleepy in the day-time but lively at night. Near Christmas time, a number of boys took a wagon, with Ellery Miller as driver, and drove into the woods near Lake Bluff to gather pine branches and trailing vines with which to decorate the Academy.

While there were no organized sports, fishing tackle and a sixteen pound rifle were standard equipment in every boy's room. Rabbits, quail, duck and pickerel provided all the sport needed, as well as delicacies for Mrs. Kent's table. Hunting, fishing, and trapping were the most loved sports. There was an infinite variety of wild songbirds in the area, also game of every kind. Around the school area were black and fox squirrels and partridge, while west of the track were quail and prairie chicken in abundance. On the Skokie and in nearby ponds it required little shooting skill to get good bags of mallard, teal, wood duck, swans and other waterfowl. John Patterson and Vilasco Chandler got forty mallards in a little pond in the woods west of the track, and these two with George Manierre shot a hundred wild pigeons in the area of the Des Plaines River. On one occasion two Academy boys encountered three deer, but the bird-shot in their guns had no effect beyond causing the beautiful animals to bound gently out of sight.

The ravines were wild and full of flowers, notably the lady slipper which grew profusely. In the spring, when the water was high, suckers used to run up the ravines and could be caught in great quantities. One spring the Academy boys reported a large pickerel in the Skokie marsh. Skokie, an Indian word, is said to mean "open marshy land." This area afforded the most pleasant sights and sounds: the booming of the prairie chickens, the twittering of countless red-winged blackbirds, the notes of meadowlarks and bobolinks. Red-headed woodpeckers and blue jays added their harsh cries in contrast to their beautiful plumage. Throughout the night the weird hooting of the owls echoed through the forest.

Lucien G. Yoe, a student 1860–1863, wrote: "In the spring the passenger pigeons flew north in flocks that almost obscured the sun. In the autumn during their migration south, when they lit in the oak trees to feed on acorns, one could bag three and four in a single shot." These pigeons have been extinct a long time but are described as having soft rose breasts with delicate blue heads, wings in changeable green, blue and bronze with a pearl-like luster. They came to the Lake Forest area when the Michigan nut-bearing trees had been stripped. Audubon claims that a flock consumed eighteen million bushels of acorns or beechnuts per day. Flocks are described as a mile broad, 240 miles long, each bird moving a mile a minute, and containing more than two billion birds. They came out of the sky with a great roar, the sun was darkened, but their wings flashed in the light. The sound was like the roar preceding a tornado. They landed in the trees. The forest boughs swung in rhythm like the waves on the stormy lake. The sound of their voices filled the air in an unending din. Boughs broke and crackled under the enormous weight. The whole forest became a vast chicken house, complete with the smells. Droppings covered the ground. Farmers resented their visits as one hour in a cornfield the flock could make a clean sweep of it. Farmers' pigs got fat on the dead pigeons. People shot them by the score and ate so much pigeon pie it came out of their ears.

On June 25, 1859, occurred a massive picnic which the *Waukegan Gazette* reported: "A pleasant gathering met at the grounds of Lake Forest. At 9:45 a special train put out 700 individuals of both sexes and all ages, residents of Chicago, all bent on an innocent frolic. The party was accompanied by the Great Western Band and the Highland Guards in its peculiar uniform, not without the bagpipes."

At 11:00 o'clock a Waukegan train brought three hundred additional picnickers. They were met by the Great Western Band and the Highland Guards at the station. They paraded the serpentine Deer Path, nearly a mile in length, arriving at the picnic grounds in the beautiful grove on the banks of the lake. Many had come from Libertyville, Half Day, and from Shields and Deerfield Townships.

Peter Page was the master of ceremonies. He ascended the platform and made a few remarks in praise of Lake Forest. He explained what the Association had done and intended to do. He said the future was cheering, then introduced William Bross of the *Chicago Tribune* who made a brief speech. He was followed by Dr. C. Volney Dyer, the prince of wits and director of the

47

Underground Railroad, who made some humorous sallies. As a former army surgeon it was appropriate that he had everybody in "stitches." One of his witticisms is recorded by Thomas Hoyne who met him downtown in Chicago. The old cemetery was in present Lincoln Park. Beyond this, in 1840, only a scattering settlement existed. At that time Dr. Dyer moved to this area. Hoyne said to him, "Hello, Dyer, I don't see you often. Where do you live now?" "O, I am very comfortably situated, I have a new home beyond the grave," was the Dyer retort.

The Chicago crowd left at 5 o'clock. The Waukegan crowd left soon after. Several Waukegan young ladies "waited for the 10 o'clock train, fascinated no doubt by some of the Academy boys."

BASEBALL was introduced at the Academy in 1860. It had been invented at Cooperstown, New York, in 1839. At least that has been a persistent report. It was an intramural sport in the 1860's and was played on the athletic field behind the Academy building. A home-run could be achieved by driving the ball into the ravine. This was the first and only athletic field in Lake Forest for several decades. The first baseball game with an outside team was reported in 1867, when the Academy team played the Waukegan Amateurs. The Academy team won 39 to 14. Edward D. Clark was the umpire. "Shinny," the antecedent of hockey, was popular. Football and tennis were as yet unheard of.

IN 1860 there was a Young Ladies' Seminary, supported by the Lake Forest Association, a sister institution of the Academy. Its head was the Rev. Baxter Dickinson. His amiable daughters formed the faculty. Occasionally the girls came to the Academy to meetings of the Philologian Society to hear debates or elocution. There were also informal picnics including students from the Seminary and the Academy. This school, the antecedent of Ferry Hall, was located just south of the Holt residence and was discontinued when Ferry Hall was begun in 1869.

When serious rumors of war were heard in 1860, Colonel Elmer Ephraim Ellsworth of Mechanicsville, N.Y., came to the Academy during successive week ends and put the students through drills of various kinds and taught them to handle rifles. This was the cause of much excitement at the Academy and in Lake Forest. These drills were held on the baseball grounds. The government had provided a Springfield army musket for each student. One of the boys trained, Edward J. Bartlett, later gave his recollections of the drilling and the long hikes taken through the country surrounding Lake Forest, the miles of double quick marching, the bivouac and the camp, and most of all how they enjoyed their gay yet dignified young commander. They called themselves the Ellsworth Guards.

Elmer Ellsworth was already famous throughout the country as the organizer of military companies called the Zouaves. Arrayed in oriental costume: wide trousers, fez, and loose jackets, the original Zouaves were noted for their rapidity of movement and ferocity of courage as fighters in Algeria. Ellsworth, romantic by nature and a lover of the novel and dramatic, was attracted by the now famous and spectacular system, and sent to France for books fully explaining it, and set himself to acquire the language that he might read them. He drilled companies in Elgin, Rockford, Chicago and Lake Forest in Illinois, and in Madison, Wisconsin. In 1860 he drilled a company of infantry which travelled about the country and gave military demonstrations, including one at West Point, by invitation, and another for President James Buchanan on the White House lawn.

Ellsworth had studied law in Abraham Lincoln's law office in Springfield, Illinois, and was in charge of the train which carried Lincoln as President-elect to Washington. When the Civil War was imminent, President Lincoln called him to Washington, with the rank of Colonel. Ellsworth was the first officer to give his life for his country in the Civil War. He was shot by an innkeeper named James W. Jackson, in Alexandria, Virginia, after he had personally retrieved a Confederate flag from the roof of the Marshall House Hotel.

Other favorite people of the Academy boys included Sylvester Lind who loaned his hunting dog for an expedition. When the dog was found reluctant to leave his master, Mr. Lind accompanied the boys until the dog was willing to continue with them. Captain McLaughlin was another favorite. He was a carpenter and builder in Lake Forest. He never denied the use of his tools to any boy when the maple sap was running. Jock Steel entertained the boys with his clog dancing. Mayor and Mrs. T. R. Clark were very special friends of the Academy boys. "Nigger Joe," the village handy man, always whistling, always cheerful, was a popular figure, a helpful companion to the boys. Dr. Charles H. Quinlan took care of the boys in all their medical needs. Thomas Atteridge, Sr., who had built his log cabin in 1837 just west of Green Bay Road, frequently entertained Academy boys on his farm, especially during the hunting season. Everyone knew William Atteridge, his son, who was a member of the original Academy class.

Lake Forest Academy was far away from the confusion and distractions of the city, where boys and their teachers could find communion with nature and with God, as the founding fathers had intended. All town boys attended the Academy from the beginning until the turn of the century. Other students came from Chicago, a few from other states. The air, termed "salubrious" in the earliest catalogues, invigorated body and mind. Truly the early Academy students could agree with Pliny that Diana (Goddess of the chase) and Minerva (Goddess of wisdom) are natural bosom companions. By 1861, the faculty had increased to three, permitting Prof. Miller to concentrate on his great love—the teaching of mathematics. Studies included Greek and Latin, as mentioned before, but Military Science was added in 1861 which study continued for two decades. Music was optional. Until the end of the Civil War the Academy offered a three year course.

The first graduating classes were partial to Williams, Yale, Amherst and Princeton, in that order. The school library, just after the Civil War, boasted of 2,000 volumes. The first prize was the Peter Page Oratory Prize. References in the 1869 catalogue included well known Lake Forest and Chicago names, also Rev. Henry Ward Beecher, Brooklyn, N.Y.; Hon. Schuyler Colfax, Vice-President of the United States, Washington, D.C.; George L. Dunlap, General Manager of the Chicago and Northwestern Railroad Company; and Hon. Horace Greeley, Editor of *The New York Tribune*.

Early family names in the earliest school lists include Charles G. and George D. Dyer, Walter Neef, Charles L. Page, Charles E. and George H. Quinlan, Richard Stokes, and Edward L. Webster.

On April 11, 1859, the Trustees of Lind University had a seal designed for the institution. It was an open Bible with a closed one beside it, with the motto "Christo et Ecclesiae," for Christ and the Church. This is essentially the present seal of Lake Forest College.

Among the early students was George Manierre, the author of the best description of the early days of the Academy and of Lake Forest. He attempted to practice the flute in the Academy attic, against the protests of his classmates. He was absent from Lake Forest long enough to be present in the Wigwam, convention hall in Chicago, where President Abraham Lincoln was nominated. He remembered that the boys had a lot of fun "jumping from one table to another before the delegates entered the Wigwam and came to order." One of his close friends in Lake Forest was young Bill Atteridge. Both loved to hunt with muzzle-loading guns. George furnished the powder and shot; Bill furnished the Atteridge farm stocked with game. George Manierre was the son of Judge George Manierre who signed the original plat of Lake Forest.

V

EARLY HOMES

AND PRESBYTERIAN CHURCH

1859–1862

When the Lake Forest Association purchased all the lands to be included in Lake Forest, there were already a dozen or more farmhouses in the area: quaint, small, and simple. Several of these houses have survived as a whole or in part. A charming example of a house of this period is the west section of the Preston house at 1260 North Green Bay Road.

When the Academy building was finished, there were several new houses under construction. William Loughlin, the contractor of the Academy, was perhaps the first to build a home for himself, though he may not have been the first to occupy one. He is said to have moved into his own home on January 1, 1859. His house was erected on the south side of Deer Path and later moved across the street. It was occupied by Dr. Theodore Proxmire for several decades, in the new location, until it was torn down in 1960, and the land converted to a parking lot for the Presbyterian Church.

The Quinlan house, on the property just east of the present Lake Forest Library, is said to have been the first home to be occupied. Dr. C. F. Quinlan moved to Lake Forest in 1859 and built his house that same year. A description by Mrs. Quinlan stated that the house was frame, built in Grecian style with large fluted columns, and stood on a terrace. A central walk, bordered with evergreens, led from the front of the house to a large tulip bed and a marble urn. A driveway around the house formed a semi-circle in front leading to the outside entrance.

The grounds were well wooded, east and west, and contained giant oak trees while a parterre west of the terrace was ornamented by many choice flowering plants and numerous shrubs, as well as "scotch roses." In the front garden there was a large "grapery," as it was known in those days, filled with a variety of the most luscious white grapes. The house was white with green blinds. The rear grounds contained a large yielding orchard of pear, peach and apple, extending east, with a central walk bordered by currant bushes and the kitchen garden on the west. This house burned down in 1869. Dr. Quinlan built the present house the following year and sold it to S. B. Williams. This second Quinlan home was later occupied by Capt. I. P. Rumsey, and is now the home of Mrs. John Baker, Sr.

Dr. Quinlan was one of the first medical men in Chicago to produce anesthesia by the use of sulphuric ether. He was a dentist, and the only medical man in Lake Forest until Dr. Henderson, a surgeon in the Civil War, came to town. Dr. Quinlan was also one of the founders of the Lake Forest Presbyterian Church and of the City of Lake Forest.

In 1859 several other houses were built. Harvey L. House, a gardener, built just east of the present City Hall. Hugh Samuels, a carpenter who had worked in the construction of the Academy building, built on two lots immediately west of the present Christian Science Church. The Hortons bought this house some ten years later and it is now lived in by members of the same family, the Wadsworths. This house stands in its original location on Deer Path. Rev. Yates Hickey built on Deer Path south and east of the present Lake Forest Public Library. Sylvester Lind built a cottage just east of the railway station, which was occupied by James Anderson until the completion of the latter's own house in 1863.

Francis Nelson Pratt had come west on the Erie Canal. He settled in Waukegan. In 1857 he came to Lake Forest and took part in the construction of bridges, the Old Hotel, and the Academy. He served as depot-master when there were six trains a day. He also became postmaster and had a dry goods store next to his home, which he built in 1859. This house stood about where Martin's Drug Store stands. In the early days Mr. Pratt could see deer going by as he sat on his porch. This house was moved to the corner of Vine and Green Bay Road and is a part of the present home of the Wyndham Haslers.

Gilbert Rossiter built in 1859 a house costing $1,200, on Deer Path south of Triangle Park. It had a porte cochere and a little bridge over the stream. In 1920 this house was moved to a lot just east of the Gorton School. Mrs. Norman B. Judd was a sister of Gilbert Rossiter and she together with her famous husband were frequent guests in this house. The Lawrence Robbinses and the Howard Gillettes owned it at various times.

The Dickinson house stood in the middle of the block just south of present College Road and west of Sheridan. It was built in 1859 by the Rev. Baxter Dickinson for his wife and four daughters; but at the same time it served as the home of the "Dickinson Seminary for Young Ladies," beginning in 1859. Rev. Dickinson and his family, supported by the Lake Forest Association, operated this school until the establishment of Ferry Hall. At that time the Dickinson home became a boarding house. In 1877 it became a dormitory for girls of Lake Forest College, and the name was changed to "Mitchell Hall," after Maria Mitchell, a pioneer woman astronomer. In 1879 it was used by the Academy boys when their first building burned down. In 1900 Mitchell Hall was moved to the site near Hixon Hall of Lake Forest College, to become the South School. In 1917 part of Mitchell Hall was bought by the Charles B. Frenches and incorporated into their home on Mayflower Road.

The D. J. Lake house was erected north of the Academy building, on Deer Path, and was named "Forest Lawn." This is the 1961 H. E. Muzzey residence. The Lind House was the predecessor of the one now occupied by the Frank Woods family on the northeast corner of Deer Path and Washington Road. The first shed to serve as the Lake Forest railroad station was converted into the Lind kitchen.

Sylvester Lind was the man after whom Lind University was named. He was a small but very bright man with penetrating eyes. A leader in the organization of the Lake Forest Association, he became the key figure in the chartering of the City of Lake

Forest. He was well acquainted with the area of Lake Forest, when as a young bank messenger in George Smith's Bank in Milwaukee, he made weekly rounds to the Chicago branch bank with exchanges in his saddle bags. Four times he was to become Lake Forest's mayor.

Lind had been a carpenter by trade when he first arrived from Scotland. He had been in the employ of Lord Aberdeen, Prime Minister of England, for five years. Arriving in Chicago in 1837 he became a lumberman, a realtor, then an insurance executive. In the early 1850's he erected the Lind Block in Chicago which still stands in 1961, on the northwest corner of Wacker and Randolph, one of the first Chicago skyscrapers, and seven stories high. This building survived the Chicago fire of 1871, one of the few structures in the loop area to escape.

Lind was a very religious man, and his life ambition was to found and support a Presbyterian Theological Seminary in the Chicago area. However, during the world-wide depression and panic of 1857, just as Lind University received its charter, he lost so much of his fortune that he was unable to meet his promise to the Lake Forest Association, to make a donation of $100,000. Soon afterwards, Cyrus McCormick of the South Presbyterian Church of Chicago made enough money from his Henrietta reapers to import a Presbyterian Theological Seminary from New Albany, Indiana, to Chicago. This institution became the McCormick Theological Seminary.

In Lake Forest "Pappy Lind" was a favorite throughout his life. When he visited the Reid family, the children would capture his hat and cane, so he would have to stay for dinner as they knew he wanted to do. At the end of the meal he would push his plate away and say three times: "And there we are," patting his knees with his hands.

Several more houses were built in 1860. The Samuel F. Miller house was built east of the Academy and on the north side of Deer Path. It was later torn down and a brick structure succeeded it, which was for long known as the Russel D. Hill house. In 1961 it is owned by the Owen Wests.

The Holt and Thompson homes were built simultaneously next door to each other. D. R. Holt was busy with his lumber business in Chicago, but Harvey Thompson persuaded him to build, saying he would watch the construction along with that of his own. The Thompson house stands today on the southwest corner of Deer Path and Sheridan Road. Harvey Thompson was quite artistic and had elaborate flower beds. The ravine was laid out in terraces, with vistas displaying statuary. Like other places this one had iron deer, and great urns here and there on the lawn. For years afterwards the college boys would knock down the deer at Hallowe'en. There has been a succession of owners, among them the J. B. Durands. When a Mr. White owned it, he put up a fence so that the Holt children could not see the property to their north—one of the Holt horses had gotten into the White flower beds. The 1961 owners are the Paul Rowans.

The Holt house, "The Homestead," is just about as it was in 1860. It stands at the north corner of College and Sheridan Roads. At one stage it was painted brown, a popular color at the time. When the family first arrived they lived in the back part of the house while construction was being completed. At first it was supposed to be for summer use only, though built substantially of brick covered with wood, with the first floor concrete. In 1861, the Holts stayed the year around and never went back to the city to their former home on Michigan Avenue where Orchestra Hall now stands. Mrs. Holt was thrilled with the educational facilities in Lake Forest—the Academy for her boys and the Dickinson School for her girls: "They were private and there was nothing to worry about." The Holt gardens have been a great joy to Lake Forest residents for a hundred years, since the variegated colors and shapes of the flowers have been easily seen from close quarters by all passers-by. Red and yellow in the nineteen twenties, they became a more pleasing pink and blue in the nineteen fifties.

In 1860 Captain James H. Stokes built on Deer Path just east of the Academy grounds. His son attended the Academy next door. Captain Stokes was a West Point graduate. He enlisted in the Union army and as commander of the famous Board of Trade Battery became a Brigadier General of Volunteers. This property passed on to Carl Bradley, then to Henry C. Durand, and Clayton Mark. When the original house burned to the ground in 1912, the Finley Barrells built the present brick structure. This house was next purchased by C. Frederick Childs, and is now owned by Newell Childs.

Nearly all the early homes had either greenhouses or conservatories, besides gardens and orchards. Houses had cozy fireplaces to heat them, long before central heating systems were invented. One grandfather spoke of his fireplace as "the bonniest flower in the garden." Almost all the upstairs shuttered windows opened out into little balconies, where children loved to go. Attics were filled with trunks and cedar chests, another favorite spot where children played. Oil lamps lighted these early houses. The simple "facilities" placed in some unobtrusive spot in the back yard were often of the same architecture as the house itself.

Peter Page as manager of the Lake Forest Association, recorded that these early houses cost from $1,000 to $12,000.

During the summer of 1858 Mr. Lockwood Brown and Mr. T. R. Clark of the Second Presbyterian Church of Chicago were two guests at the Old Hotel who wished to hasten the beginning of Christian education. On July 4, 1858, they called for a Sunday School class to be held in an old public schoolhouse which stood on Green Bay Road. Seven pupils reported for the first session, at which Mr. Brown presided as Superintendent, while Mr. Clark became the first teacher. Preaching services were conducted during that summer in the Lake Forest Hotel by the Rev. I. M. Weed, who resided in Waukegan.

In March 1859, Sunday School was continued in the Hall of the newly finished Academy building. The superintendent was now Dr. Quinlan; Prof. Miller was the teacher, and Charles Vilasco Chandler, an Academy student, was the first Secretary-Treasurer.

Church services soon followed Sunday School. By July 19, 1859, the church members numbered fourteen, including two elders, Dr. C. H. Quinlan and Prof. Samuel F. Miller. At a special meeting of the Presbytery of Chicago, which was held at the Protestant Orphan Asylum near Wabash and 22nd Street, a petition was presented, signed by several Lake Forest Presbyterians, requesting to be organized into "The First Presbyterian Church of Lake Forest." The petition was granted. Rev. C. L. Bartlett, Rev. Yates Hickey, and D. R. Holt, all of Chicago, were appointed to organize the church on Sunday July 24, 1859. Dr. Quinlan and Prof. Miller were ordained and installed as Ruling Elders. Prof. Miller became the first clerk of the session. The first Trustees,

Erastus Bailey, Harvey L. House and C. H. Quinlan, were elected at a meeting on November 23, 1859.

Other charter members of the Presbyterian church were James Anderson, Mrs. Elizabeth Baldwin, Miss Elizabeth Desencamper, Mrs. Jessie House, Miss Mary Lynch, Mrs. Charlotte H. Miller, Mrs. Ruth E. Quinlan, Hugh Samuels, Mrs. Elizabeth Samuels, James H. Wright, and Mrs. Eunice Wright.

On the same Sunday evening, the Ruling Elders met with acting Moderator, the Rev. A. T. Norton, presiding, and completed the organization of the newly formed church.

For the next two years church services were held in the Academy chapel. At first there were no ministers to conduct the services and sermons were read by laymen. However, in the fall of 1859, when the Rev. William C. Dickinson, a minister of a Kenosha church, joined the Academy faculty as teacher of Latin and Greek, he began to conduct most of the Sunday services, sometimes assisted by the Rev. Yates Hickey and others. He served the church as part-time minister until 1862, when he felt that he could not discharge his duties as teacher during the week and preacher on the sabbath, so he was replaced in July 1862, by a stated supply, the Rev. A. H. Post, a student at Lane Theological Seminary of Cincinnati.

After the church services had been held at the Academy for a short while, it became apparent that the room was too small for the congregation as well as the forty-nine students. Moreover, it had not encouraged reverence on the part of the Academy boys to have Church in their school building.

During a meeting on August 7, 1861, plans were made to erect a church building. On motion of Yates Hickey, it was resolved: "That the Trustees of this Society be requested to go forward as fast and as far as practicable in building a chapel 32 feet by 60 feet in lot number 116½ at the point now staked for the purpose and that voluntary subscriptions in money and labor be obtained which it is possible to secure, and the same be expended on the building, with the understanding that the title to the said lot 116½ is first to be secured before the commencement of the building." The lot was bought from Dr. C. H. Quinlan, the present property, which cost virtually $300. By July 15, 1862, the building was ready for occupancy.

It was a Gothic cottage in the form of a cross, with a pointed roof and two low spires on either side of the front door. The windows were of clear glass. The building was completed with voluntary subscriptions in money and labor. A loan of $300 for three years, without interest was arranged with the Synod of Peoria. This loan was subsequently paid back. The building was simple and small. It included a ten foot platform and a stove, which was later replaced by a furnace. The building had no basement. In 1867, then in 1877, the building was enlarged to provide additional room for the rapidly growing congregation. This church was torn down and the present church edifice was used for the first time in June 1887.

D. R. Holt transferred his church membership from Chicago to Lake Forest in 1861, when the Holts became permanent Lake Forest residents. He was elected an elder and became the Superintendent of the Sunday School, preparing his lessons every Sunday afternoon for the next Sunday morning's lesson. His son Charles played the church organ.

In July 1863, the Rev. W. C. Dickinson was again pressed into service and began to preach, giving up his teaching entirely. Several members of the small college class which he had been instructing, suddenly was absorbed by the Union army. He was installed as the first pastor of the first Presbyterian Church on May 10, 1864, and served until his resignation on June 24, 1867. His salary as pastor was $400 per annum.

When the church was completed, the furnishings included red cushions and a green carpet, which to some did not harmonize, creating a sharp difference of opinion. Mrs. Gurdon S. Hubbard's offer to buy the carpet, at cost, was accepted, and a new red carpet was bought, and harmony restored. The color of the outside paint also caused variations of opinions. This, too, was resolved when it was decided that whenever any color was unsatisfactory to anyone, that person had the right to change the color, at his own expense.

The first business house in Lake Forest was a simple store on the northeast corner of Deer Path and McKinley in 1859. The first owner was James H. Wright, who sold it to Dr. C. H. Quinlan. The latter rented the building to Joel Hulbert, who lived upstairs and came down to open the store whenever a customer appeared. Many meetings of the early town trustees were held on the second floor of this building. Youthful Lake Foresters bought odds and ends here to break the monotony of school schedules. They could also buy chocolate creams. In 1862 James Anderson bought the building from Sylvester Lind and the business from F. B. Burchard and continued in this location until 1867 when he moved the building across the tracks, to the corner of Deer Path and Western. This new location became a landmark for the next thirty-five years.

As construction continued in the early days the problem of creating a town cemetery was faced by the Lake Forest Association. During the March 7, 1859, meeting, the Trustees were "instructed to lay out, adorn, beautify and fence in, in a suitable manner, the ground appropriated by a former meeting for cemetery purposes, to be called 'Ever Green Cemetery' and offer the same for sale. However, objections appeared immediately as it is undesirable to have the cemetery located within the limits of the village because it is regarded by the best physicians as objectionable on the score of health and because it will seriously impair the value of adjoining lots." As a result a Cemetery Association was formed and the Lake Forest Association Trustees conveyed the deeds for lots 1, 2, 3, and 7 (the present cemetery property) to the Cemetery Association.

In February 1860 $450 was raised by subscription to improve the cemetery. Fences were built, the grounds were cleared, the property was surveyed and platted and ten acres were added to the property. In 1863 the entire cemetery problem was absorbed by the City of Lake Forest when it received title to all the cemetery properties and a Cemetery Commission, composed of five residents, was appointed by the Mayor.

On April 2, 1860, Lake County entertained a Springfield attorney named Abraham Lincoln. The incident would have been forgotten had it not been reported in the *Tribune* on the next day and had it not become the favorite story of James Anderson of Lake Forest who was always proud to tell about it.

This happened six months before the Republican convention in the Chicago Wigwam. Mr. Lincoln had been attending court in Chicago when "at the ernest solicitation of Lake County citizens" he came to Waukegan to deliver his address. His speech "followed the precepts of his Cooper Union address which was delivered in New York last

February. It was a masterful effort, characterized by precision of state-
ment, simplicity of language, unity of thought, and withal a perfect
sincerity that carried conviction. The address terminated somewhat
prematurely due to a conflagration in town, which distracted the
audience." The fire broke out on the flats on the Little Fort River,
southeast from the hall where the rally was held. The glare could
easily be seen shining in the windows of the room. Elisha P. Ferry, the
chairman, rose and assured the audience that the fire was not near
enough to endanger any of them. Mr. Lincoln made a second beginning, but the audience grew inattentive and gradually slipped
away. Only a few remained, among them Jim Anderson. Mr. Lincoln
turned to him and said: "Guess we might as well go to the fire too!"
Had this rally been held six months later, after Abraham Lincoln had
been nominated the Republican candidate for the President of the
United States, the whole of Lake County would have been present
and stayed to the end, come fire or high water.

According to the *Tribune* story of April 3, the party which also
included John G. Nicolay, Mr. Lincoln's Secretary, Norman B.
Judd who nominated Mr. Lincoln to the presidential candidacy
and was chairman of the Republican State Committee, were "entertained, following the address, in Lake Forest, at the home of
Mr. Judd's brother-in-law," Gilbert Rossiter. At the time this house
stood south of the Triangle Park and is now the home of the Jay
G. Ridingers, on Illinois Road.

In 1860 there were probably two public schools in existence in
the Lake Forest area. The first public school east of the tracks was
a small white building on North Washington Road and just north
of Triangle Park. It was sometimes called the Quinlan School.
Roxanna Ward Beecher was the first teacher. She was a niece of
Henry Ward Beecher, the famous Congregationalist preacher of
Brooklyn, N.Y., and of his sister Harriet Beecher Stowe, the author of *Uncle Tom's Cabin*. Her father, Edward Beecher, was the
president of Illinois College in Jacksonville, the first institution
of higher education in Illinois. The Beechers were known as a
family of reformers. Another little white school was soon built,
perhaps in 1870, on the north end of the village near the intersection of Western and Noble Avenues. Nearby stood the brick
city jail. At this time one train each way each day provided the
only contacts with Chicago.

The promise of rapid growth of Lake Forest made the city

fathers realize the need of drawing up a charter to incorporate the city. On June 3 and 6, meetings were held at the home of Sylvester Lind to make plans for an election to be held at the Lake Forest Hotel: "for the purpose of incorporating said town under the general laws of the State of Illinois." M. A. Neef was chairman of these meetings, C. H. Quinlan, Secretary. Other members of the election committee were William M. Loughlin and E. Mather. A notice was issued for an election to be held on June 17, 1859, at the Lake Forest Hotel to decide whether or not to incorporate. The voters were required to have resided in Lake Forest six months or to be owners of freehold property on the 17th of June, 1859. The voters convened at 9:00 in the forenoon and voted in favor of incorporation, whereupon a request was drawn up and filed with the Secretary of State. On August 29, 1859, the store building of James H. Wright, on the corner of Deerpath Avenue and Depot Avenue was secured for a suitable place for town meetings and office for the Justice of the Peace. The room was 17 by 22 feet, with a closet, and cost $50 per annum for rent.

The first town election was conducted in the Lake Forest Hotel on July 16, 1859, for the purpose of establishing officials for an interim government until the charter should be received and approved. The supervisors of the election were Thomas R. Clark, Erastus Bailey, William M. Loughlin, Harvey L. House and Charles H. Quinlan. Thomas R. Clark was elected President of the Trustees of Lake Forest. R. G. Rossiter was elected Secretary and James H. Wright, clerk. William M. Loughlin became Notary Public. A marshal was elected to take care of the Council Room. Thirty-five "Rules and Order of Business of the Board of Trustees of Lake Forest" were drawn up.

On November 19, 1859, the city fathers issued a petition stating that "Side-walks (boards) from the railroad crossing to the Hotel Crossing (Washington Road) on the north side of Deerpath Avenue is incomplete and broken in many places, consequently dangerous to pedestrians. Therefore it is ordered by the President and Trustees that side-walk be repaired and replaced in safe condition." This sidewalk construction became a perennial activity as frost and weather caused the need for continual repair and replacement, until cement came into vogue just before 1900. Mayor William S. Johnston, Jr., spent a great deal of time supervising the building of sidewalks in the 1860's. W. B. Popliff and E. Reuding did the work of construction. The property owners paid for the adjoining board walks.

Another petition required the repair of the streets immediately in front of people's houses. Citizens hauled gravel from the lake shore and dumped it along the street in front of their properties. When the rains washed away these roads, citizens made continuous trips to the beach for more gravel, to make the necessary repairs. A. J. Sawyer, who lived just west of the Presbyterian Church on Deer Path, refused to sign the petition, and refused to make the necessary street repairs. This refusal may have precipitated the employment of a city attorney in the spring of 1860. In August of that year Francis N. Pratt was sworn in as constable. He took this oath, which has survived:

> I Francis N. Pratt do solemnly swear that I will support the Constitutions of the United States and of the State of Illinois, and that I will faithfully perform the duties of the office of Constable within and for the County of Lake in the State of Illinois according to law and to the best of my understanding, and I do solemnly swear that I have not fought a duel nor sent or accepted a challenge to fight a duel the probable issue of which might have been the death of either party, nor in any manner aided or assisted in such a duel, nor being knowingly the bearer of such challenge or acceptance since the adoption of the Constitution and that I will not be so engaged or concerned directly or indirectly in or about any such duel during my continuance in office. So help me God.
>
> Taken and subscribed before me
> this 17th day of August A.D. 1860.
>
> WILLIAM LOUGHLIN
> *Notary Public for the Town of Lake Forest*
> Lake County, Illinois

This same oath was taken by several hundred officials of the City of Lake Forest, before 1900.

In 1860 a copy of the Revised Statutes of Illinois was purchased by Lake Forest. Also a Market Clerk was appointed and hay scales were purchased, to insure honesty and fair dealing when farmers brought their loads of hay to Lake Forest. "Naturae et Scientia Amor"—the love of nature and science—was chosen as a motto of the City of Lake Forest and was placed on the city seal.

The Charter arrived. It was titled "A Bill for an act to Incorporate the City of Lake Forest," bearing the date February 21, 1861. It was signed by Governor Richard Yates and O. M. Hatch, Secretary of State. This document was written by hand and dealt with the usual subjects of taxation, police department, fire department, street and water departments. It also established a school district. It provided for a Mayor to hold office for one year. It established two wards, to be divided equally as to population, with two Aldermen to be elected from each ward. The Aldermen and Mayor were to constitute the City Council.

The Charter required that voters should be "all free, white, male and over 21." Provisions were made: "to restrain, prohibit and suppress tippling houses, dram shops, gaming houses within two miles of the University Park; within said City and within the limits of one mile beyond the boundaries of said city." A Mayor's court was established with "jurisdiction in all cases arising under the ordinances of said city" and declared the Mayor "entitled to such fees as are allowed in justice of peace for like services." The office of Mayor, although elective, has been occupied for a hundred years, by prominent citizens in turn, as a civic duty, with no pay (with one exception), and all efforts have been made to keep it free from political patronage.

On March 23, 1861, a poll was held at the Lake Forest Hotel, in order to approve or reject this document. There were four dissenting votes. The list recorded twenty-nine voters:

1. E. Bailey
2. C. L. Bartlett
3. John Black
4. Frank Calvert
5. Patrick Clark
6. George Cook
7. Baxter Dickinson
8. William C. Dickinson
9. M. J. Dunlap
10. John Giles
11. Yates Hickey
12. Harvey L. House
13. J. H. Hulburd
14. John Jackson
15. Matthew Kelly
16. S. W. Kellogg
17. Fred Lake
18. William Loughlin
19. S. F. Miller
20. Andrew Moody
21. William Norkat
22. F. N. Pratt
23. C. H. Quinlan
24. Gilbert Rossiter
25. Luther Rossiter
26. Hugh Samuels
27. Terry Shealer
28. James H. Stokes
29. Harvey M. Thompson

On April 9, 1861, three days before the firing on Fort Sumter in Charleston harbor, South Carolina, which is considered to be the beginning of the Civil War, another election was held to fill the offices of mayor and aldermen. Harvey M. Thompson was elected the first Mayor. Erastus Bailey and J. H. Hulburd were chosen aldermen from the first ward; William M. Loughlin and Luther Rossiter from the second ward.

The first city council meeting was held on April 13. S. F. Miller was named superintendent of public schools; S. W. Kellogg, city clerk; C. H. Quinlan, treasurer; E. Mather, assessor; W. M. Loughlin, marshal; and Erastus Bailey, street commissioner. The city marshal was the first police officer of Lake Forest. During this meeting the fee of the city clerk was fixed at $1.00 per session. In 1862, H. T. Helm became the Superintendent of Public Schools in place of S. F. Miller, who became the first Postmaster.

The first ordinance approved by the City Council read: "Be it ordained by the common council of the city of Lake Forest that no person elected to the office of Alderman of said city shall receive any salary for his services as Alderman." In 1861 the city of Lake Forest had one park, Forest Park, on the lake front, with 3,200 feet of lake frontage, a gift of the Lake Forest Association.

VI

CIVIL WAR AND RECONSTRUCTION

1860–1870

IN JANUARY, 1860, Chicago was the eighth largest city in the United States, with a population of 109,260, a fourfold increase in ten years. The total United States population was 31,443,000.

The Medical School of Lind University had opened in 1859 with thirty-three students, in the Lind Block in Chicago. Dr. Nathan S. Davis, a young Chicago physician, is given credit for this beginning. He was assisted by the following men in establishing this school: Edmund Andrews, William H. Byford, Titus Deville, Ralph N. Isham, Hosmer A. Johnson, and David Rutter. Dr. Davis had been a pioneer in starting the American Medical Association in 1847. Now he and his faculty became pioneers in establishing the first basic requirements for entrance to and graduation from Medical School. The curriculum included a three year course.

There were sounds of discord, however. On national issues Sylvester Lind had become involved in the Underground Railway. Increasing numbers of runaway slaves were coming, generally from St. Louis, and with the help of several Chicago leaders were escaping to Canada by means of railroads, steamships and sailing vessels on Lake Michigan. Dr. C. Volney Dyer was the Chicago director of the Underground Railroad. As an executive of the Chicago, Burlington and Quincy Railroad he secured transportation for thousands of Canada bound passengers. He harbored many in his own home. He fought extradition of runaway slaves in the courts. In 1863 President Lincoln made him Judge of the mixed court for the suppression of the African slave trade. Captain Blake of *The Illinois* was a most efficient assistant of Dr. Dyer. He is said to have transported several hundred slaves from Chicago to Collingwood in Ontario, Canada. Philo Carpenter, a Chicago druggist, who established the first Sunday School in Chicago, escorted 200 fugitive slaves to Canada in one trip. The issue of slavery now overshadowed all other problems after the Dred Scott decision of the Supreme Court in 1857 decreed that slaves were property; and it was therefore illegal to consider them free when they crossed into a free state. The whole country now seemed open to slavery.

The news that the fanatic abolitionist, John Brown, had seized the federal arsenal at Harper's Ferry, Virginia, was published abroad on October 16, 1859. Brown had hoped that all slaves in the area would join him and he would lead them to freedom. After frantic calls for help, Governor Henry A. Wise finally brought the insurrection under control when Colonel Robert E. Lee invaded Harper's Ferry, with a company of marines and captured those still alive, including the leader, John Brown. The latter was executed for murder, criminal conspiracy and treason against the State of Virginia.

Events were moving rapidly toward war. The Republican convention met on May 16, 1860, in the huge wooden Chicago Wigwam with 10,000 seats. It stood on the corner of the present Wabash Avenue and Wacker Drive. The nominating speech was made by Norman B. Judd, a Chicago attorney and an intimate friend of several Lake Forest residents and promoters, including the Rossiters and the Farwells. His speech was greeted with a prodigious response of screams, yells, shouts, and a stamping of feet that resounded in the panelled walls and shook the building. Thousands of black hats and white handkerchiefs were tossed into the air to the accompaniment of a mighty crescendo of cheering. Lincoln was nominated unanimously on May 18th as the crowds poured out into the Chicago streets to yell themselves hoarse. There was much carrying of fence rails, shooting of cannon, beating of drums, and general bedlam. Everybody wanted to shake hands with the "next President." On November 6, 1860, Abraham Lincoln was elected President of the United States.

There were many future Lake Foresters for whom the nomination and election were banner days of their lives. Ezra J. Warner had come from Walpole, New Hampshire, to the Republican convention. He was so impressed by Chicago and the spirit of the West that he decided to stay, building his home in Lake Forest after the war. Calvin Durand, aged 20, went to the Tremont House after the nomination and shook hands with the Republican nominee. He built his home in Lake Forest after serving throughout the Civil War with the Board of Trade Battery.

In contrast with the stimulation afforded by the nomination and election, the chartering of the city of Lake Forest, and the apparent progress made by the Lake Forest Association, prosperity had not claimed Lake Forest. People had begun to feel the panic of 1857 and its consequences, and the quarrels over slavery made people cautious about new ventures. Several stockholders openly criticized the Association. Peter Page, Treasurer and agent, felt compelled to print a twelve page defense of himself and the Trustees, which he distributed to all members just before the meeting of March 1, 1861.

It was known that several trustees had received pay. D. J. Lake had received $1,600, Peter Page $800, H. F. Mather $750, E. H. Aiken $300, T. R. Clark $100. Many Association members contended that the Trustees should not be paid, that improvements were unnecessary. Others objected that improvements had not been crowded forward rapidly enough. Some said that mortgages should be foreclosed and dividends paid. Other criticisms involved an improper accounting of disbursements.

Peter Page answered each criticism point by point. He said Trustees were paid only for labors outside of their duties as Trustees, never anything like a full compensation. It was merely token pay for expenses incurred. He himself had spent far more out of his own pocket to serve the Association than he received. Improvements were authorized in Article 7 of the Association by-laws; besides they were voted by the members in a special election on May 28, 1859. Foreclosing mortgages would serve no good purpose, because the embarrassment of many is only temporary. A little patience would serve both good business and good religion.

68

Every member was entitled to inspect the books of the Association, which were open to all at all times.

Peter Page concluded: "During the past two years (and for which I have received no compensation), I have collected and disbursed more than $16,000, procured abstracts of title, perfected a number of titles, disposed of a number of lots, contracted for and superintended the building of three bridges and the grading of some miles of streets, most of which have been paid for in lands, and labored with many parties to induce them to pay up their last notes; have gone to Lake Forest, from Chicago, on the business of the Association, more than 300 times, collected about $2,000, paid out of my own pocket all my personal expenses, have examined personally and procured estimates for grading and bridging."

In August 1859, Rev. Robert Patterson and Hiram F. Mather had been appointed a committee to procure the services of the Rev. William Dickinson as an additional instructor at the Academy, to assist Prof. Samuel F. Miller to organize a college class in the fall. The Church promised to raise $300 toward Rev. Dickinson's salary. Some college subjects were taught beginning in the fall of 1859.

The first Lake Forest Academy commencement occurred in June, 1861. The first graduates included Charles Vilasco Chandler, Frederick Chapman, George Manierre, John C. Patterson, William D. Price and Ralph E. Starkweather. These continued as freshmen in the college course. Some of the boys were only 14 years old. Their college studies included Cicero's *De Officis*, Livy, Xenophon's *Memorabilia*, Homer's *Iliad* and *Odyssey*, geometry, conic sections, declamation and English composition. The college course continued until the spring of 1862 when it was discontinued, as the older boys joined the armed forces. John C. Patterson and George Manierre later attended Yale University. Starkweather went to Williams College after the war and studied medicine later on. He practiced medicine in Chicago until his death in 1892.

There were financial problems which forced the discontinuance of the Medical School of Lind University, though it lived on independently, and exists now (1961) as the Northwestern University Medical School. The Theological School of Lind University was advertised to open in the fall of 1861; then the opening was deferred to 1862; then it was postponed indefinitely. This uncertainty was partly due to the fact that another Presbyterian theological school, McCormick Theological Seminary, had just been moved to Chicago from New Albany, Indiana, on May 13, 1859. This school was at first called the Northwestern Theological Seminary. Cyrus McCormick's gift of $100,000 caused the transference of the institution to Chicago.

Lake Forest with perhaps less than four hundred people, nursing a boys' and girls' preparatory school, continued during the war years as normally as possible. The first male child born in Lake Forest after the city was chartered was a war baby. Robert Davis Samuels was born in the house just west of Deer Path and Washington, in 1862.

The Academy boys were more than ever serious about military drill. Lake Forest Academy had its little share in the armed service and its losses too. C. Vilasco Chandler was wounded at Chickamauga. "A bullet went through one of his legs and made him lame for life." Chandler later became a Colonel on the staff of Governor Tanner of Illinois. Frederick Chapman was missing in action and was presumed killed. Wilbur T. Norton, the first editor of the *Forest Gem,* published in 1861, was a member of the 133rd Illinois Infantry. William Delano Price of Chillicothe, Ohio, a member of the 53rd Illinois Regiment, became a second lieutenant and lost his life in the battle of Big Hatchie on October 5, 1862. He had been an Academy student for two years. He had been sick when General Grant ordered his regiment to Corinth. During the battle "Willy" ordered his men to lie down and commence firing. He sat a little behind his men "telling them to keep low, and cheering them, when he fell. He fell, and died without a struggle." These four were Academy students.

James Swanton of Lake Forest served in reconnaissance parties during the western campaigns, going ahead of the main body of the army to clear ambushes and to locate the Confederate army.

Captain James H. Stokes, a West Point graduate and a teacher of Artillery at that institution, had built his home on Deer Path in 1860. On July 23, 1862, the Board of Trade Battery was formed in Chicago, and Stokes was elected Captain by acclamation. In September the Battery became a part of General Don Carlos Buell's army stationed at Louisville, then at Nashville. The story of this battery is the history of the war in the west, as it fought continuously in successive campaigns until the end of the war. After the battle of Nashville on December 15 and 16, 1864, when all organized confederate resistance terminated in the western theatre, the Board of Trade Battery remained in Nashville until May, 1865. One of the memorable days for the Battery was during the battle of Murfreesboro or Stone's River. Confederate General Breckinridge made a bold charge on the Union left. It seemed as though this would turn the Union flank and cause its retreat; but Captain Stokes and his comrades opened fire from a knoll on the massed columns with 58 guns. General Braxton Bragg retreated after the failure of this final assault. General Negley said: "The promptness displayed by Captain Stokes in bringing his battery into action by my orders, and the efficient manner in which it was served, affords additional evidence of his marked ability and bravery as an officer and patriot." Stokes was commissioned Brigadier General before the end of the war.

A considerable group serving in the Civil War from various states made their homes in Lake Forest sometime after the war. This group included Samuel Dent, an ex-slave, born in Tuscumbia, Alabama, according to his grave stone in the Lake Forest Cemetery. "Escaping from slavery he entered the Union army in 1862," and served to the end of the war. He came to Lake Forest in the 1870's, and until his death in 1898 was a much beloved citizen.

Calvin Durand served throughout the war in the Chicago Board of Trade Battery, taking part in the campaigns of Generals Grant and Sherman. For a few weeks he was in Chicago in the winter of 1863–1864 on a recruiting mission. Returning, he took part in the battles of Chickamauga and Chattanooga, then in the several battles culminating in the battle of Atlanta. On July 10, 1864, just north of Atlanta, he was ambushed by Wheeler's cavalry and taken to the General's headquarters for questioning. The wagon train under his command had escaped. Sergeant Durand was then shipped to Andersonville. He said: "After entering the stockade and closing the gates, the sights that met our eyes were simply appalling, and our hearts dropped within us. It seemed to me that we were really in the land of the Inferno."

When Andersonville was under threat from Sherman's army,

Durand was one of many transferred to other prisons. He was taken to Charleston, S.C., where 150 a day were being carried outside and buried in long trenches. Then he was taken to a stockade at Florence, S.C., where he preserved his sanity by cutting wood outside the stockade, purchasing beans from Negroes, and selling them to his fellow prisoners. His next confinement was in Libby Prison in Richmond, Virginia, from which he was exchanged and returned to Chicago, arriving home at 3:00 in the morning. His family had presumed him dead. He returned to his Battery in Nashville, but the war was soon over. He built a Lake Forest home in 1875 and served as Mayor from 1891 to 1895.

David Fales served throughout the war. Returning to Chicago he studied law and became a charter member of the Chicago Bar Association. He moved to Lake Forest, after the Chicago fire, and lived here until his death in 1926.

Michael Fitzgerald was a member of the First Wisconsin Heavy Artillery. He volunteered at the age of sixteen in 1863 and served till the end of the war. He came to Lake Forest in 1880 and helped to organize the Lake Forest Post of the G.A.R. in 1889, becoming one of the commanders. He died in 1927, the last survivor of the G.A.R. in Lake Forest.

Marvin Hughitt, a long time resident of Lake Forest after the war, aided the nation signally by keeping the trains moving to supply Union Generals Grant and Sherman with horse, gun, food and other supplies from Cairo, Illinois, southward, earning his title, "the Grand Old Man of the Railway World," and a promotion in 1865 at the age of twenty-eight as General Superintendent of the Illinois Central Railroad. Hughitt served the Northwestern Railway, from 1872 until his death in 1928, as General Superintendent, President, Chairman of the Board, and Chairman of the Finance Committee.

George W. Huntoon, as a member of the Eighth Illinois Cavalry Regiment, fought throughout the war in the eastern campaigns. He took part in the long Peninsular campaign and at Mechanicsville the Regiment fought a critical rear guard action until the rest of the command retreated to safety. At Gettysburg the Eighth Illinois, together with the Eighth of New York and Third Indiana Cavalry, a total of 800 men, were ordered to Cashtown, to make contact with the enemy. This they did, only to be overwhelmed by three Confederate divisions commanded by General A. P. Hill, 25,000 rifles in all. In the retreat that followed into Cemetery Hill at Gettysburg, the Eighth Illinois was assigned to General Abner Doubleday, who later thanked the regiment publicly for saving his division from annihilation. The last assignment of the Eighth Illinois Cavalry was after the war, when the Regiment went into Maryland in search of the assassin of President Lincoln, John Wilkes Booth, whom they failed to find. During the four years of the war the Regiment captured seven Confederate flags, inflicted 4,000 casualties and freed 3,000 slaves. Huntoon came to Lake Forest after the war, and for years operated a bakery.

Henry McIntosh, a former slave, escaped from a Kentucky plantation through the Underground Railway and joined the 102nd Regiment of the United States Volunteers at Detroit, in 1863. He was nineteen years old at the time. He fought in several engagements in Georgia and South Carolina, taking part in Sherman's March to the Sea. He was discharged on September 30, 1865, at Charleston, S.C. He came to Lake Forest in 1871 and worked as a coachman and gardener.

Abram Poole served in the quartermaster's department and was involved in the battles of Chickamauga, Chattanooga and Atlanta. He came to Lake Forest and built one of the first homes on the bluff, in 1884.

Captain Israel Parsons Rumsey was the first to enlist in Taylor's Battery in Chicago, which he helped organize in April 1861. He was elected Second Lieutenant, then became Assistant Adjutant General on General W. H. L. (Lew) Wallace's Staff, then Chief of Artillery of the Second Division of the 15th Army Corps. He was commissioned Captain in July, 1864.

Captain Rumsey fought under Grant, Logan, McPherson, Sherman and W. F. Smith. He took part in the battles of Fort Henry and Donelson, Shiloh, Vicksburg, Missionary Ridge, Lookout Mountain and Atlanta. General Wallace, after the capture of Fort Donelson called Captain Rumsey: "Active, intelligent and brave. Always ready to undertake orders, riding to any part of the field amid the hottest fire, his daring and coolness contributed much to the success of the day." Captain Rumsey brought his family from Chicago to Lake Forest in 1887 and lived on Deer Path on the old Quinlan property until his death in April, 1921.

His son Henry Axtell Rumsey was Mayor of Lake Forest 1919–1926.

Captain Albert Robbins Sabin raised a company of volunteers in Vermont which became a part of the 9th Vermont Infantry. As part of Colonel Dixon S. Miles' command at Harper's Ferry, he was one of 12,000 captured by Stonewall Jackson on September 15, 1862. This force had been trapped in a pocket and waited too long for reinforcements, which were so near, yet they never arrived. His regiment was paroled and sent to Kansas to fight Indians. At the end of the war they were mustered out in Chicago where Sabin began his teaching career in the public school system. He became a Principal of Lake Forest Academy, 1874–1879.

General Joseph Dana Webster, related to Daniel Webster, was a Dartmouth graduate and a civil engineer by profession. Early in the war he was attached to General U. S. Grant and became his Chief of Staff. He took part in the Forts Henry and Donelson campaigns; then at Shiloh he was credited with saving General Grant's headquarters when Confederate General Pat Cleburne made his final drive at nightfall on April 6, 1862. General Webster hurriedly collected miscellaneous artillery in time to defend it from capture. He was Chief of Staff to Grant again during the Vicksburg campaign, then became Chief of Staff to General W. T. Sherman during the last year of the war. General Sherman spoke in glowing terms of General Webster's service when he said: "He was one in whose keeping General Grant and I could always repose any trust with a sense of absolute security." General Webster came to live in Lake Forest, on Deer Path, next to the Presbyterian Church, after the war. He became the collector of internal revenue in Chicago in 1872, and about that time moved his family back to Chicago, where he died at the Palmer House in 1876.

The war brought tragedy to The White House. When President Lincoln's body was brought through Chicago from Washington to Springfield, the Ellsworth Guards of Lake Forest Academy acted as escort and guard of honor. They were taken from Lake Forest to Chicago in box-cars, the only available transportation at the time. They escorted the coffin to the City Hall where it lay in state. They took part in a parade in Chicago, then escorted the body to its resting place in Springfield. Nelson Green Edwards was the drummer boy for the Ellsworth Guards and, during the funeral services, for the President. He later became a Colonel in the United States Army.

There were hard times in Lake Forest during the war years. Many properties changed hands, as people wished to sell, but the buyers were few in number. The effects of the war, misunderstandings, bitterness of mind and spirit, and the final state of exhaustion made their impact on Lake Forest; but this city somehow held on to its original ideals, and continued to build on its original foundations. One of the staunch supporters of Lake Forest was a dynamic little Scotsman with bushy eyebrows and a deep voice, named William Bross. He joined the board of trustees of Lake Forest University in 1865 and continued in this capacity until 1889. He was a former Principal of Ridgeway Academy at Goshen, New York, and a Lieutenant Governor of Illinois. He founded the *Chicago Tribune*. With his rich background of experience, William Bross was a constant visitor to Lake Forest and contributed much to the development of her institutions.

On February 16, 1865, the State of Illinois issued a new charter to the University. The first section stated: "Be it enacted by the people of the State of Illinois, represented in the General Assembly that the name and style of Lind University created by the act mentioned in the title to this act, be, and the same is hereby changed to 'Lake Forest University' by which name it shall hereafter be known."

The reason for this change has often been said to be that Mr. Lind had been unable to fulfill his promise of giving $100,000. It must also be noted that the name "Lake Forest University" had been used in the minutes of the Association as early as June 6, 1856, and had appeared again in March 1861, indicating that this popular name would sooner or later supersede the legal title. Moreover, from the beginning, the first installment of the University to be built was called Lake Forest Academy and not Lind Academy. Since Lake Forest Academy was the only visible part of the University during the years 1858–1865, it was natural that people continued to call the parent institution Lake Forest University, even though the legal title was Lind University. The law was bound to follow the custom established earlier. Mr. Lind's chief interest in the University was the establishment of a theological school. Now that McCormick Theological Seminary had been confirmed, the name Lind University was no longer significant.

From 1860 to 1870, Lake Forest increased her population to about 800. By the end of the Civil War, there were Negroes in sufficient number so that the members of the Presbyterian Church organized a Sunday School for Colored children, which met in the first public schoolhouse in the city of Lake Forest, just northeast of Triangle Park. In 1866 the first Negro church was organized, The African Methodist Episcopal Church. A frame church building was erected at the present corner of Maplewood and Washington Road in 1870. This building was abandoned and early in the 1920's was moved north about fifty feet where it served as the Academy Infirmary for two decades.

There was little home construction during the Civil War period. In 1861 the Alonzo Sawyers built a home just west of the Presbyterian Church. After the war this house was occupied by General J. D. Webster. It is possible he was in Lake Forest on leave as his name is mentioned in the Council minutes of April 15, 1863.

James Anderson purchased lot 324 for $350 on December 19, 1860. Payments were made in labor in University and Mayflower (Ferry Hall) Parks. "He excavated and removed all dead and decayed trees and all stumps, also all logs and rubbish. He filled up all excavations to a smooth and level surface. Burning of logs and stumps was done on such locations so as not to expose to injury any standing trees." Having finished the work, he received the deed on June 1, 1861. He began to excavate for his house on the day of the battle of Shiloh, April 6, 1862. This Anderson home became a landmark. It stood next to the southwest corner of Western Avenue and Illinois Road.

In 1862, Henry T. Helm, a new superintendent of schools, built a home on the property now owned by William H. Mitchell on Rosemary Road. In 1863 a house was built for the Rev. William C. Dickinson, opposite the Stokes' on Deer Path, later known as the E. J. Learned house. Amzi Benedict built a home in 1865 at the eastern end of present Deer Path. It has been occupied by the Bowes, the A. B. Dicks, the Colonel Harvey T. McElwees, and is the 1961 home of the Kimball Salisburys. Walter Frazier, architect, restored this house in the 1940's to its original appearance. Dr. C. H. Quinlan remodelled the first schoolhouse at the corner of Walnut and Washington into a small home in 1867. For a time it became the home of Miss Annie M. Brown. In 1906 it was bought by Ezra J. Warner, Sr., and his granddaughter Jane Warner Dick was born in this house. When the Warners built a large home on this location, the original house was moved to 334 E. Westminster. In this location this house was for long known as the Sidney Burridge house. It is now occupied by Dr. A. J. Wurth.

E. S. Barnum built on Sheridan Road, incorporating in his home the first store in Lake Forest, the Wright store, the forerunner of Anderson's. For long this was known as the Edward Samuel house and is now occupied by the Charles S. Werners. This house was completed soon after the Civil War.

The J. V. Farwells built the present Robert Lehmann house, in 1869. The contractor was Leonard Double, who came from England to Lake Forest for this pioneer project: the first concrete house in America. The cement for this house was imported from England. The construction was described as "hand poured concrete." The architecture was said to be "a turreted baronial castle, quaint and picturesque." The interior was finished in black walnut and cherry. Three other buildings were built in the same way —the J. V. Farwell barn which has been converted into a home, the house of Abby Farwell Ferry, just north of Lake Park, which has been razed to make room for a ranch house, and the house which Double built for himself with the remaining cement, on the corner of Spruce and Elm Tree Road. He also built many of the earliest Lake Forest cement sidewalks. For years the Farwell barn was the sports arena for all the young Farwells and their friends. Here boxing, wrestling, and cock fights took place. All four concrete buildings were built within a few years.

Senator Charles B. Farwell built a house in 1869, across the street and south of Deer Path. He and his brother had bought their joint property in 1857 but did not build for twelve years because of their activities during the Civil War, and frequent trips to England. The C. B. Farwells stayed at the Lake Forest Hotel from time to time before their house was finished. He named their home

"Fairlawn." The architect was Frederick Law Olmsted. This property contained the famous Farwell Pond, and the house was especially remembered for an extension which was an art gallery, lighted through windows in the roof. Both Farwell homes on Deer Path had elaborate formal gardens and each had a large greenhouse. The C. B. Farwell house burned to the ground in January 1920; the estimated loss was $150,000.

In 1870 the Henry C. Durands moved into the Carl Bradley house, which had originally been built by Captain James H. Stokes in 1860. This house was described as "a large English cottage." Lands were sold several times during the 1860's at low prices, in order to make up deficits for the Lake Forest Association. There were even outright gifts of land, to families which had donated moneys when the Association was first formed. J. V. Farwell received several acres along the lake front as a present, because he had bought a share for which he had donated $500. At this time land along the lake and at the end of town, so far from the business district and transportation, was considered almost worthless. The lake front was thought to be damp and unhealthy for year around habitation. As the town grew during the later decades, the lack of adequate sewer systems in these areas made these properties somewhat less than desirable.

City Council problems, during the 1860's, revolved chiefly around the subject of money. Sale of lands, taxes, special assessments, improvements, schools, salaries, streets, alleys, sidewalks, bridge-building, repairs and elections were the principal subjects dealt with. In 1860, a sidewalk on the south side of Linden (College Road) was authorized. In 1861 a "side walk 5 feet 4 inches in width, well spiked down was ordered for the north side of Deerpath Avenue." S. F. Miller was paid $18 for surveying in the Cemetery. In 1862 the Public School Library was given a sum of money for the purchase of new books. F. N. Pratt and Gilbert Rossiter were elected inspectors, the publication of taxes in the *Waukegan Gazette* was permitted, and a poll list of 34 names was compiled. In 1863, the Forest Cemetery Association lots and premises were transferred to the City of Lake Forest for Cemetery purposes, the city accepting it. In 1864 it was decided that evening school for adults should be discontinued. This school had been conducted, for three Negro and ten white men, three times a week, and was taught by H. D. Din who received $8 per month for his services. The sessions were two hours long, from seven to nine, at night. The city clerk was authorized to procure signs and place them upon bridges, with the notice of an ordinance against fast driving. On December 31 a citizen's meeting was held "for the purpose of considering the expediency of amending the City Charter." In 1865 Miss Sweet was hired by the City Council at $45 per month as a teacher in the public schools. S. F. Miller was paid $16 for surveying for the city. In 1868 an ordinance was passed "That no person shall without permission of the City Council slaughter, dress, or pack, any cattle, calves, sheep or swine within the limits of the City of Lake Forest." This ordinance was frequently disobeyed even after 1900.

The City Council reports showed that Roxanna Beecher received $25 per month as teacher 1860–1863. The superintendent's report indicated that the number of pupils in the Public Schools increased to 48, in 1862, then dropped to 36 in 1864. In 1865 the number of pupils increased to 46, while the 1868 report showed an enrollment of 106 pupils.

During one quarter of Miss Beecher's teaching, $13.25 was spent for the installation of a lightning rod on the schoolhouse. I. M. Snodgrass undertook to supply heat for the school during the winter of 1862–1863, but had trouble obtaining sufficient fuel. $2.00 was spent for washing and cleaning the school, 90¢ for chalk pencils, 30¢ for a school register. A suitable bookcase for the school library was furnished by private subscription. Rules for the library were submitted to the City Council for approval. A school clock was recommended, the want of which had been felt by the teacher and the school.

The Townline Road, later called 59A or Kennedy Road, separating Vernon and Libertyville townships, was laid out and surveyed in March 1862. Judge George Manierre of the Circuit Court in Waukegan approved and accepted the survey on March 20.

In the fall of 1863, when the school enrollment had dropped to 36 pupils, the new superintendent, Prof. M. C. Butler, who also served as Principal of Lake Forest Academy, recommended that: "Text books in the common school of Lake Forest shall be the same as are used in the public schools of Chicago for scholars of the same grade." The following year it was reported that "Music had been used with good success, and a prize for good attendance (was) provided by the Superintendent out of his own pocket." The subjects taught included geography, practical arithmetic, writing, history of the United States, algebra, and mental arithmetic.

In 1868 Hugh Samuels, the carpenter, built a new public school—on Noble Avenue, near Western, on the west side of the track. In 1861 a public meeting was held in School House No. 3 and it would be logical to assume that at that time there were already three schools in the area. The exact number of schools in the 1860's is difficult to determine because of the lack of evidence. But there was no confusion in the mind of Luther Rossiter, the Superintendent of Schools 1865–1869. He philosophized on teachers and students: "There have been some scholars in the school of such unruly dispositions as to severely try the patience of the teachers. There is no such thing as a perfect teacher. It is often the case that women can maintain better discipline and give pupils a better intellectual drill than the majority of men."

Soon after the Civil War, "Guv" Marshall, an ex-slave, came to Lake Forest Academy to be the janitor. He was exceedingly religious, and very popular with the boys. He served the Academy for about thirty years and was a well known person about town throughout his life.

The Academy building was rebuilt and enlarged in 1865 at a cost of $20,000. This improvement nearly doubled the amount of floor space. Towers and a full basement were added, and the building was raised so that it now had four stories, the new basement becoming a dining room and kitchen.

In February 1865, Green Bay Road, also known as the "Military Road" or the "Chicago and Milwaukee Road," was relocated to come within the corporate limits of the city of Lake Forest. This change from the present area of west Lake Forest, was no doubt due to the need for higher ground, to insure better facilities and drainage for the ever increasing traffic, especially between Chicago and Milwaukee.

The first record of a cultural community evening was a "Soirée Musicale," given in the Hall of the Academy on June 28, 1866. Joseph Matteson was the soloist. Other performers were Miss E.

French, Mr. and Mrs. Ansorge, William A. Bond, and Miss Kitty Lind, the only child of Sylvester Lind. Miss Lind is remembered for driving about town in her carriage with a bow on her whip.

The first newspaper, *The Forest Gem,* an amateur effort, was published by two Lake Forest youngsters, Wells C. Lake, 15, and William J. Fabian, 13. They set up a little printing press in the back of David Lake's grounds, across the street from the Academy building, and published monthly missives. Advertisements included one for Anderson, Lind & Company—Dry Goods, Stationery, Crockery and Wooden Ware. Another for John Giles, advertising ice cream and fruits. In July 1867, they wrote: "We notice horses and hogs still running at large. These horses seem to have the full run of the city. They run up and down the streets, get in the way of trains, besides scaring children into fits. Will not someone pen them up? The city promises to pay five dollars for each animal so taken up, and fifty cents a day for keeping the same." A year later, on July 7, 1868, the boys were repaid for their efforts, as the City Council voted: "That the Mayor be directed and empowered to employ a suitable person to enforce the city ordinances and the laws relating to stock running at large and that said person be paid out of the city treasury for such work."

In the early sixties the business section of Lake Forest was on the east side of the railroad tracks. By the end of the decade it had gradually moved to the west side, on Western Avenue. In 1867 Augustus Taylor opened the first meat market. Samuel Blackler bought the business in 1874, and in 1895 built the present Blackler building—the first three story building, setting a pattern for the future business district. In 1868 Joseph O'Neill, a coppersmith, tinsmith and sheet metal worker, opened a hardware store as well, near the present Jaeger Pastry Shop. His wife operated the hardware store at first. During the first year of the hardware store, the stock was valued at $1,000. The following year the hardware store was moved a half block south, opposite the railroad station.

In 1867 there was heavy erosion of the bluffs along the lake front. Mayor Harvey Thompson had Forest Park hill repaired that year. There was a heavy traffic of wagons and teamsters to the beach, where free sand and gravel were secured and delivered for a fee to the front of any homeowner who wished to be free of mud and dust. Gradually the city fathers became aware that this traffic may have been at least partial cause of periods of heavy erosion. Suits were brought against the teamsters, and free procurement of sand and gravel was finally stopped.

On SEPTEMBER 2, 1869, Ferry Hall, the sister institution of the Academy, opened her doors. The first catalogue published that same year declared that: "Ferry Hall, the spacious and elegant edifice occupied by the institution, is a model of fine architecture, constructed of Milwaukee bricks and commanding an extensive view of Lake Michigan and its various navigation. It is lighted with gas and warmed by steam and all the appointments and surroundings are tasteful and commodious." The school was intended to complete the education of the young lady students, as the College proposed in the original charter was intended to be for men only.

Ferry Hall was named after the Rev. William Montague Ferry of Grand Haven, Michigan, a Presbyterian minister, who had been a missionary to the Indians on Mackinac Island. A pioneer educator, he had established a school for Indian children with an enrollment of 150 students. Over a hundred were boarding scholars, clothed, fed and lodged by Mr. Ferry and his family. Many came from more than a thousand miles. The boys were taught mechanical trades and the girls, serving and house work, in addition to their scholastic work. Mr. Ferry was head of the school and pastor of the mission church. The project was discontinued in 1834. He then returned to Grand Haven, Michigan, a city which he himself founded. Here he gradually accumulated land and funds. When he died on December 30, 1867, he left $35,000 to Lake Forest University, $15,000 of which was for the erection of a building for a female seminary. His interest in a school for girls may have been due to his early teaching in female seminaries and having been a principal of one in Massachusetts. Mrs. Ferry was a close friend of Mary Lyon, the founder of Mount Holyoke College.

The original Ferry Hall building cost $60,000. It was 120 feet long and 54 feet wide with a basement and four stories of classrooms and dormitory space. The school opened with 66 students, some from as far as Maine and Massachusetts. The first Principal was Edward Payson Weston of Maine, who served until 1876. The lady Principal was Miss Emily M. Noyes. Ferry Hall replaced the Dickinson Seminary for Young Ladies. The curriculum embraced a four year course. The references in the first catalogue included several Lake Foresters, also James G. Blaine, Hannibal Hamlin and L. M. Morrill of Washington, D.C. The catalogue also envisioned a four year college course for women in addition to the preparatory school. All extravagance in dress was discountenanced. The simple and tasteful were encouraged. It was specified that "clothing should be plain, without puffs, rufflings or elaborate trimmings." During Miss Sprague's incumbency, Ferry Hall Bible classes were conducted by Mr. D. R. Holt.

ON MARCH 11, 1869, the City Charter was amended and approved. The new charter contained 16,000 words, while the 1861 charter had consisted of only 6,000 words. It was an expanded and more detailed version based on eight years' experience in city government. New city officials were created: A City Surveyor and Engineer, a City Clerk, a City Attorney, a City Treasurer, a City Assessor, a City Marshall and Collector, a City Supervisor and a City Sealer. Duties of all officials were defined in detail.

The two wards were expanded to three, giving the City Council the authority to "create additional wards" as the need arose. The Mayor's Court was discontinued. The mayors from 1861 to 1869, Harvey M. Thompson, William S. Johnston (Jr.) and David Lake being Chicago business men, had been too busy with their occupations to devote sufficient time to the conduct of a court, nor were they qualified to pursue legal justice, having had no legal training. Instead, the City Council, with the advice of the new City Attorney, was empowered "to enforce the observance of all rules, ordinances and police regulations, and to punish violations thereof by fines, penalties, and imprisonment . . . but no fine or penalty shall exceed five hundred dollars, nor the imprisonment, six months, for any offense."

The City Council members became "ex-officio, fire wardens and conservators of the peace within the city." The four stated meetings were changed to twelve, one in each month. The 1861 Charter had stated that "no tract of land exceeding ten acres within the territory (of the City of Lake Forest) shall be taxed for general city purposes." This was amended, as ten acres were changed to thirty acres, and it was added that "the same shall bear a proportionate share of taxes for school purposes." The sale of intoxicating liquors was prohibited within the city. Defaulters to the City or State were made ineligible to hold office in the City of Lake Forest. Apparently one or more city officials had failed to meet their tax obligations, but there had been no machinery set up to deal with such delinquencies. Punishment for illegal voters was prescribed.

The Mayor was authorized "to call upon any and all white male inhabitants of the city or country, over the age of eighteen (18) years, to aid in the enforcing of the laws of the state or the ordinances of the city." All residents over twenty-one were required to perform street labor for three days in each year or to forfeit 75¢ per day for each day so neglected or refused. Soon Aldermen and Firemen were exempted from this service and the forfeit price was left to the discretion of the City Council. No doubt the rising prices during and after the Civil War made it impossible to secure substitute labor for 75¢ per day. The 1861 Charter had provided that the City of Lake Forest would "erect and keep in repair hay scales," so that farmers and purchasers alike would be protected. Now the rule was made all inclusive requiring: "all traders and dealers in merchandise or property, which is sold by measure or weight, to cause their measures and weights to be tested and sealed by the city sealer, and to be subject to his inspection."

By the end of the decade (1870), Lake Forest had grown to be a quaint little town, with a few rickety bridges, across a few of its many ravines, or roads that detoured around others. There were board walks on several streets, and residents carried lanterns when they went out at night. One man who failed to carry a lantern, suddenly found himself deep in the Farwell Pond. Many of the villagers owned cows, which were gathered each morning by an enterprising young man and pastured in the vicinity of the McCormick estate, at the southern end of town. For this service the lad received fifty to seventy-five cents per week per cow. Lake Forest was proud of its "natural beauty and healthfulness. Here the annoyances of the great city could be avoided; at the same time the metropolitan advantages were only thirty miles distant. The community boasted of religious toleration and brotherly love."

VII

ORDEALS BY FIRE

1870–1880

UNDER an act of the Illinois Legislature a group of Chicago investors bought three hundred acres of land just south of Mayflower Park on March 5, 1867. They paid $80,000 for the property and erected an "elegant" Hotel in keeping with the traditions set during the previous ten years of Lake Forest's existence. It was called *The New Hotel* to distinguish it from the Lake Forest Hotel which was now called *The Old Hotel*. This new structure, completed on November 18, 1870, had everything. Overlooking the high bluff above the lake, it commanded a superb view. It was located just south of Ferry Hall, on what is now the Schweppe estate. It was a six story frame structure with sixty rooms, capable of accommodating one hundred and twenty guests. It boasted gas, hot and cold water, bathrooms, and all modern improvements of the period, including telegraph wire service. Its auxiliary buildings included an ice-house, laundry, stables and sheds. It enjoyed the shelter of forest trees and provided drinking water, second to none, from an artesian well. The New Hotel traffic to and from the station necessitated the installation of the first twenty-four oil street lamps "upon avenues and principal corners throughout the city."

The New Hotel had the advantages of a happy combination of hotel and a modern country club, one of the earliest to achieve such forms of luxury. But it lacked one thing: safety. It was a firetrap. An attempt to build a fireproof building had been made in the Lind Block in Chicago, but generally, no serious effort was made to fireproof any homes or public buildings in Chicago or Lake Forest.

At this time a list of twenty Lake Forest residents was published, containing names which were familiar in Chicago but intimate in Lake Forest. The list included these:

AMZI BENEDICT, *of Field, Benedict & Company*
J. V. FARWELL, HON. C. B. FARWELL, *of J. V. Farwell & Company*
T. HELM, ESQ., *Attorney*
W. V. KAY, *Banker*
T. J. KIRK, *of T. J. Kirk & Company*
COLONEL WILLIAM S. JOHNSTON, *Capitalist*
D. J. LAKE, *Real Estate*
SYLVESTER LIND, *Real Estate*
SIMON REID, *of Reid Murdock & Fisher*
HENRY C. DURAND, *of Durand & Company*
JOHN BUCKINGHAM, *of J. & E. Buckingham*
WILLIAM WARREN, *of London Liverpool and Globe*
H. M. THOMPSON, *of the Brevoort House*
E. S. WELLS, *of Wells & Faulkner*
E. J. WARNER, *of Sprague, Warner & Company*
HON. WILLIAM HENRY SMITH, *of the Associated Press*
WILLIAM H. FERRY, *Capitalist*
SAMUEL D. WARD
E. S. SKINNER

The topic of conversation revolved around the Franco-Prussian War which began in 1870. With Europe three weeks away there was little personal interest except for the fact that Norman Judd had served as Ambassador to Prussia during the Lincoln administration and his family now resided in Lake Forest.

On Sunday, October 8, 1871, a fire broke out in Chicago which burned out the heart of the city and seemed to put an end to all her future hopes and dreams. Following an extended dry spell, the fire began in the southwest section of the city, and swept across the river, north and east propelled by a strong southwest wind. The present area of the Chicago Loop burned completely, leaving only a little more than the Lind Block intact. The fire extended northward to Fullerton. The southern boundary was Taylor Street. In the west it was generally arrested by the Chicago River. Mayor R. B. Mason sent frantic calls to outlying fire departments, but nothing availed. Thousands saved their lives by taking shelter in the waters of Lake Michigan. Some three hundred died attempting to save something or somebody. Chicago had been built too fast and too cheaply. The fire cost $200,000,000 with the loss of 18,000 buildings.

When the fires had abated, looting, lawlessness and violence raised their ugly heads. The Mayor issued a proclamation stating that "The preservation of the good order and peace of the city is hereby entrusted to Lieutenant General Philip H. Sheridan, U.S. Army." General Sheridan did his duty quickly.

Both of the Presbyterian Churches, First and Second, in the latter of which the idea of Lake Forest had been conceived and planned, were left a mass of rubble. Only the stone walls of the Second Presbyterian Church stood defiantly. The Chicago homes of many of the backers of the Lake Forest Association were destroyed.

Mrs. David Fales wrote her mother to assure her that she and David were safe. She wrote:

Sunday night a fire broke out on the West Side, about three miles southwest of us. The wind was very high, and David said it was a bad night for a fire. About two o'clock we were awakened by a very bright light, and a great noise of carts and wagons. Upon examination, David found that the fire was not at all on the North Side, but was burning so furiously on the South Side that the whole sky was bright. They thought it would stop when it came to the river, but it proved no obstacle, and the North Side was soon on fire, and Wells and La Salle streets were crowded with carts and people going north.

We saw that with such a wind it would soon reach our neighborhood, and David told me to pack what I most valued. It seemed useless to pack in trunks, as every vehicle demanded an enormous price and was engaged. Several livery stables were already burned, and loose horses were plenty. One of the Wheeler boys had a horse given him for nothing. He took it home and tied it in their yard. Having no wagon, it was no use to him, so David took it, and after a while succeeded in finding a no-top buggy. David packed it full, set me and himself on top, and started off to the Hutchinson's.

Everybody was out of their houses without exception, and the sidewalks were covered with furniture and bundles of every description. The middle of the street was a jam of carts, carriages, wheelbarrows, and every sort of vehicle—many horses being led along, all excited and prancing, some running away. I kept my seat by holding tightly to the trunk. The horse would not be restrained, and I had to use all my powers to keep on. I was glad to go fast, for the fire behind us raged, and the whole earth, or all we saw of it, was a lurid yellowish red.

David had taken everything out of our house, and buried the piano and books, together with the china, in Mr. Hubbard's grounds. The Hubbards thought they were safe in a brick house with so much ground around it; but wet their carpets and hung them over the wooden facings for additional safety. It was all to no purpose. David saw ours burn and fall; then theirs shared the same fate.

The West Side was safe; but to get there was the question. The bridges were blocked and some burned. Some carts had broken down, horses had given out, and many people were walking and pulling big things, and seemed almost exhausted. Furniture and clothing lay all along the road. After a ride of two hours and a half we reached Judge Porter's at dusk, and found a warm welcome.

I never felt so grateful in my life as to hear the rain pour down at three o'clock this morning. That stopped the fire. David says the piano burned under the ground. The North Side is level, as is the burned part of the South Side, so that the streets are not distinguishable. People in every class of life are out of doors. The churches are full, and food is sent to them, but hardly anyone has any to spare.

William Bross, ex-Lieutenant Governor of Illinois and President of the Board of Trustees of Lake Forest University, wrote a description of the Chicago fire which was published in *The New York Tribune* of October 14, 1871. He said:

I reached the (Chicago) *Tribune* office, and, seeing no cause of apprehension I proceeded to the Nevada Hotel, my property, on the corner of Washington and Franklin streets. I remained there for an hour watching the progress of the flames, and contemplating the destruction going on around. The fire had passed east of the hotel but it soon began to extend in a westerly direction, and the hotel was quickly enveloped in flames. I became seriously alarmed, and ran north on Franklin street to Randolph to get back to my house which was on Michigan Avenue, on the shore of the lake. My house was a part of almost the last block burned.

At this time the fire was the most grandly magnificent scene that one can conceive. The Court-house, Post-office, Farwell Hall, Tremont House, Sherman House, and all the splendid buildings on La Salle and Wells streets were burning with a sublimity of effect which awed me; all the adjectives in the language would fail to convey the intensity of its wonders. Crowds of men, women, and children were huddling away, running first in one direction, then in another, shouting and crying in their terror, and trying to save anything they could lay their hands on, no matter how trivial in value; while every now and then explosions, which seemed almost to shake the solid earth, would reverberate through the air and add to the terrors of the poor people.

I crossed Lake Street bridge to the west, ran north to Kinzie Street bridge, and crossed over east to the North Side, hoping to head off the fire. It had, however, already swept north of me, and was traveling faster than I could go, and I soon came to the conclusion that it would be impossible for me to get east in that direction. I accordingly re-crossed Kinzie Street bridge, and went west as far as Des Plaines Street, where I fortunately met a gentleman in a buggy, who very kindly drove me over Twelfth Street bridge, to my house on Michigan Avenue. It was by this time getting on toward five o'clock, and the day was beginning to break. On my arrival home I found my horses already harnessed, and my riding horse saddled for me. My family and friends were busily engaged in packing, and in distributing sandwiches and coffee to all who wanted them. I immediately jumped on my horse, and rode as fast as I could to the *Tribune* office. I found everything safe; the men were all there and we fondly hoped that all danger was past. But a somewhat curious incident soon set us all in a state of excitement. The fire had crawled under the sidewalk from the wooden pavement and caught the woodwork of our basement. We believed that the building was fireproof. My associates, Mr. Medill and Mr. White, were present and, with the help of some of our employees we went to work with water and one of Babcock's fire-extinguishers. The fire was soon put out. Many kind friends gathered around the office and warmly expressed their gratification at the preservation of our building.

Believing all things safe, I again mounted my horse and rode south on State Street to see what progress the fire was making, and if it were moving eastward on Dearborn Street. To my great surprise and horror I found that its current had taken an easterly direction, nearly as far as State Street, and that it was also advancing in a northerly direction with terrible swiftness and power.

I saw that some wooden buildings and a new brick house west of the Palmer House had already caught fire. I knew at a glance that the *Tribune* building was doomed, and I rode back to the office and told them that nothing more could be done to save the building. In this hopeless frame of mind I rode home to look after my residence and family, intently watching the ominous eastward movement of the flames. I set to work, with my family and friends, to move as much of my furniture as possible across the narrow part east of Michigan Avenue, onto the shore of the lake, a distance of some three hundred feet. Never did friends toil more loyally than ours did for us. They saved most of our books, furniture, pictures, etc., that were left to us. Some that were not friends helped themselves to whatever struck their fancy when opportunity offered.

My coachman filled my buggy with some harness, a bag of coffee, and other articles, and left it with his friends on the lake shore. That was the last I heard of the buggy or anything that was in it. My daughter supposed that I had hired an express wagon that stood at the door, and I supposed that she had. We filled it full of goods and furniture. The driver slipped off in the crowd, and that was the last we heard of any part of the load. These were slight affairs compared with what many others suffered by the thieving crowd. I sent my family to the house of some friends in the south part of the city for safety.

For six or eight hours Michigan Avenue was jammed with every description of vehicle, containing families escaping from the city, or baggage wagons laden with goods and furniture. The sidewalks were crowded with men, women, and children all carrying something. One woman was carrying an empty bird cage; another some dirty, empty baskets. Anything that could be hurriedly snatched up, seemed to have been carried away without judgement or forethought.

In the meantime the fire had lapped up the Palmer House, the theatres, and the *Tribune* building. We saw by the advancing clouds of dense black smoke and rapidly approaching flames, that we were in imminent peril. Having got out all we could out of my house, about 11:00 a.m. on Monday, the 9th, I sat down by my goods, which were piled up indiscriminately on the lake shore. Soon I saw the angry flames bursting from my home. Quickly and grandly they wrapped up the whole block, and away it floated in black clouds over Lake Michigan. Early in the afternoon we began to send our goods south by teams, and by sundown all that we had been able to save was distributed among friends south of Twelfth Street.

The next morning I was out early, and found the streets thronged with people moving in all directions. To me the sight of the ruin, though so sad, was wonderful—giving one a most peculiar sensation, as it was wrought in so short a space of time. It was the destruction of the entire buisness portion of one of the greatest cities in the world! Every bank and insurance office, law offices, hotels, theatres, railroad depots, most of the churches, and many of the principal residences of the city, a charred mass—property almost beyond estimate gone.

While Mr. White and I were saving our families, on Monday afternoon, Mr. Medill, seeing that the *Tribune* office must inevitably be burned, had sought for and purchased Edward's job printing-office, 15 Canal Street, where he was then busy organizing things. When I arrived, Mr. Medill was among the printers, doing all he could to get ready to issue a paper in the morning. On Halsted street I located four stoves which I wished to purchase for the *Tribune* company, but the owner required 'de money for dem stoves.' On Saturday our note would have been good for $100,000, and on Tuesday we could not buy four stoves on credit. Messrs. Edward Cowles and E. S. Wadsworth furnished the cash with which the stoves were bought and the *Tribune* was printed, the day after the fire. But money soon began to flow in.

By 4:00 p.m. the stoves were up, the clerks were taking advertisements, arrangements were made to print on the *Journal* press, next door. A council was called and it was agreed that I should start for Buffalo and New York that evening to get needed materials for the print shop. About 8:00, I took the middle of Canal Street, south to Twelfth, east to Clark, then south to Sixteenth and just saw the cars (train) moving away. Nothing was to be done but to return to 607 Wabash Avenue. This was one of the most lonely and fearful tramps of my life. No street lamps, few people in the streets, and there were good reasons to give them as wide a berth as possible.

Another sleepless night; and in the morning as I sat sipping my coffee over some cold ham, I saw Sheridan's boys, with knapsack and musket, march proudly by. Never did deeper emotions of joy overcome me. Thank God, those most dear to me, and the city as well are safe; and I hurried away to the train. Had it not been for General Sheridan's prompt, bold, and patriotic action, I verily believe what was left of the city would have been nearly, if not quite entirely, destroyed by the cutthroats and vagabonds who flocked here like vultures from every point of the compass.

The Manierre home stood at the southwest corner of Michigan Avenue and Jackson Boulevard where the Continental Assurance Building now stands. George Manierre "used to shoot wild pigeons out of the locust trees in his father's front yard. The lake then extended to the middle of present Michigan Avenue. The Illinois

Central came in on a viaduct from the south to Randolph Street, some few hundred yards from the shoreline."

During the Chicago fire he sent his mother and three younger brothers in the family carriage to the Atteridge farm in Lake Forest as being his only thought of refuge for them at that time. When he saw the flames had engulfed his father's house, he went in his rowboat to the Illinois Central viaduct and tied up, to see if he could get a needed rest. The viaduct was crowded with refugees and he heard some rough masculine voices whispering: "Let's dump that boy out of his boat and take it and get out of here." George Manierre beat them to it and high-tailed it for Lake Forest where he arrived in the morning, having rowed all night. He came through the woods in the morning with a few of his books, his hunting dog and gun, his sole possessions he had salvaged from the Chicago fire. Miss Fanny Atteridge said he arrived at the Atteridge farm "black with soot and had had nothing to eat for two days and two nights."

Years later when he told this story to his son, Francis thought that was quite a row. "No," replied the father. "It wasn't, when you had no other choice and when you were young and husky. And besides I could land on the beach pretty nearly anywhere then for a rest, which you couldn't do now, with all the forbidding breakwaters."

Miss Fanny Atteridge added that the Manierre carriage which had carried many notables in its day, rotted and fell to pieces in the Atteridge barn. The only useful purpose it served in the barn was to provide a nest for the mother cats and their kittens.

THE PEOPLE of Chicago were faced with the decision of whether to start life over amid the charred rubble or to join friends who had moved north along the railroad. To help people make up their minds, several attractive advertisements appeared describing the virtues of Lake Forest. One of these was in the *North Chicago,* in 1873, which said:

At Lake Forest the ideal of suburban beauty is certainly reached. There is probably no place in the United States which combines within itself such a culmination of landscape beauty as has obtained here.

The rolling and diversified country, which has been gathering and swelling at this point, now masses in a grand effect, which is as beautiful as it is remarkable. The features of scenery which prevail here are of all kinds—the level and placid, the gently undulating, the vigorous and wild, with gorges almost similar in depth and grandeur to those observed in mountainous countries, and looking, therefore, peculiarly unique and beautiful in this land of level prairie. At this point one is justified, if ever, in becoming poetical, for it does seem, that nature having here exhausted her generous mood, and having become wildly prodigal in her gifts, has flung down upon the whole her wreaths of flowers and her evergreens, and proclaimed this her ideal.

We need such a natural prodigy near Chicago, and here it is. The limits of this domain have, fortunately, come into the possession of a cultured and wealthy people, and nature has been supplemented by the art of cultivated men. The residences erected here on the commanding sites are unsurpassed in architectural beauty and costliness, while the grounds and ravines have been adorned by every variety of horticulture and floriculture of which it is possible to conceive.

Another enthusiastic promotion appeared in *Our Suburbs* (1873):

This is one of the oldest and altogether the *par excellence* of Chicago's suburbs.

The village at present numbers about 1,200 inhabitants, representing more millions than probably any other equal number of people similarly situated in the west.

Lake Forest, it is safe to predict, now that it has a place to put people, will ere long become one of the favorite summer resorts of the country. Long Branch (N.J.) is a mud puddle beside it. Parties locating here will secure unexceptionable society, if they are worthy of entrance.

A distant observer in the early 1870's wrote somewhat less enthusiastically in the Portland, Maine, *Transcript*:

Not after the fashion of any other city is it built; it can never have been triangulated or quadrangulated; there is nothing rectilinear or rectangular about it. A man must be very upright, he must be, to live here, and very orthodox too, if he would have peace, but he can do nothing "upon the square"; he cannot even walk straight to his neighbor's house, his ways will certainly be winding and tortuous. Hogarth's "curved is the line of beauty" is drawn here with a free hand. If any one desires to make a visit for the first time on a friend residing here, let him not think to surprise him by dropping in upon him unawares, for he is himself in danger in this labyrinthian place of being surprised by nightfall in the midst of his search through these meandering courses.

Another group of articles praised Lake Forest Academy. The *Chicago Daily Tribune* in a June 1873 issue wrote:

The opinion which we hold of Lake Forest Academy cannot be a subject of doubt. We can but recommend it to all interested in educational matters, as one of the best managed and most prosperous in the West—or in the land.

The *Chicago Daily Post* reporting on the same date wrote:

The growth of Western scholarship, and the degree of excellence which can be attained was finely shown in the closing exercises at Lake Forest Academy, which has long had so enviable a reputation.

Sylvester Lind who had lost one fortune in the panic of 1857–1858 had made a strong recovery by entering the field of fire insurance and real estate. Now that the Chicago fire had wiped away his second fortune, he devoted himself, undaunted to public service and became the Mayor of Lake Forest for four terms in the 1870's. His election to this office was a great tribute to the citizens of Lake Forest as they respected him when he was wealthy and loved him when he had lost his fortune. In May 1872 Sylvester Lind requested of the City Council to borrow the "City screws for one day for the purpose of raising (his) house." As Mayor he spent much time rebuilding the many bridges across the ravines. Ezra Barnum was another Mayor of the period who devoted himself to local improvements.

In 1872 Henry Horton was City Assessor, Luther Rossiter was again Superintendent of Schools, Timothy Howe was City Marshal, Thomas Polan was City Supervisor, and George Frazier was City Clerk. William S. Johnston complained to Mayor Barnum that: "Lake Forest people are close fisted and wanting in public enterprise. If it had not been for my persistent and untiring efforts we never would have had any parks." Many names involved in the Chicago fire began to appear in Lake Forest lists, as permanent or summer residents, students, or supporters of Lake Forest institutions. The list included Bross, Chatfield, DeKoven, Fales, Hubbard, McCormick, Medill, Ogden, and Rumsey. D. R. Holt wished to purchase a large part of College Park, but the Lake

Forest Association turned down the requests. He must have reasoned that since the idea of a college in Lake Forest is dormant, the property set aside for the purpose might well be used to raise money for the Association.

Among the most cherished memories of many older residents are those of days spent in the public school which was taught by Miss Fanny Atteridge for several decades. She graduated with the first class of Ferry Hall in 1872. She began her teaching career that fall in a schoolhouse on Noble Avenue just west of Western on the site of the present Griffis Shop.

Miss Caroline Benedict was another early graduate of Ferry Hall who taught in Lake Forest for many years. She was a daughter of Amzi Benedict, one of the founding fathers of Lake Forest. She was known as a friend and confidant of scores of youngsters. She took care of decorations and refreshments at many social functions. It is interesting to note that in the early 1870's, Miss Caroline, together with Allie Smith and Anna Farwell, were summoned by D. R. Holt before the Session of the Presbyterian Church and rebuked for undue levity with Academy boys. There is no record of this incident in the Session records, as Amzi Benedict, who was Clerk of the Session from 1868 to 1893, omitted it.

Colonel William Sage Johnston came to Lake Forest with his family in 1865. He is described as a business man with a high sense of honor, courteous, quiet and generous. He built a house on Illinois Road on the site of the Gorton School. He died, before his house was finished, at the age of 78. His family, surviving, continued to live in this house until about the late seventies. For a while it was rented by the Ezra J. Warners and here Ezra J. Warner, Jr., was born in 1877. The latter loved to tell his friends he was born in the Deerpath Inn. When the Gorton School was built in 1894, the Johnston house was moved directly north to the south side of Deer Path, to make room for the new school which was at first called the Central School. In this new location, the Johnston house changed hands several times but served generally as the only hotel in town. At one point it was owned and operated as a hotel by a family named Brewster and called the Brewster House. The Brewster yard was noted for its many fruit trees and gooseberry bushes. The yard also served as a home for a private kindergarten which was taught by a Miss Grace Taylor. In 1906

M. H. Patterson was the hotel proprietor when the house was called the Deerpath Inn. The Inn prospered until 1930 when the new Deerpath Inn was completed on Illinois Road. The old Inn was torn down, and the whole property became the playfield for the Gorton School.

Several other homes were erected in the 1870's. Mr. and Mrs. Simon S. Reid came to Lake Forest in 1869 and opened their home on Sheridan Road, "The Lilacs," in 1872. It cost $24,000. Just south of the Reids and across the ravine a small cottage was built for Sarah Jane Rhea, in 1873. She had been a missionary in Tabriz, Persia, until the death of her husband. She returned with her three children and became the first field secretary of The Presbyterian Mission of the Northwest. Her influence became so pronounced that many local Lake Forest names began to appear in her special mission field, such as Ferry Hospital in Tehran, and Lily Reid Holt Hospital in Hamadan.

Most of the children in those days remember Mrs. Rhea for the missionary society which she started in the Lake Forest Presbyterian Church known as "Steady Streams." This society continued for fifty years and became a model for the "Lightbearers," a similar group of organizations throughout the Presbyterian Church. Children held all the offices except that of the presiding officer, who was a young woman especially interested in missions and in children. For many of these children Steady Streams provided them with a substantial knowledge of geography and foreign customs, and several became missionaries.

Other homes were built in this period. Ezra J. Warner built "Oakhurst" on North Washington Road, just north and east of Triangle Park, in 1873. In 1875 Calvin Durand built "Merrie Meade" on Mayflower Road on the center of a lot occupied (1961) by the new houses of the Kenneth Templetons, Hixon Glores, John O. Giles and Arthur Dixon. Until this house was finished the family boarded at the Old Hotel. Mrs. Calvin Durand designed a formal garden with beds symmetrically laid out in crescent, circular and other geometric patterns divided by narrow gravel paths. The house itself, surrounded by a spacious porch, was built to afford comfort and durability.

The C. G. Wenbans came from Diamond Lake in the 1870's because of the educational advantages of Lake Forest. They rented homes but built their own house in 1890. Mr. Wenban started a wholesale candy wagon with headquarters at the corner of Illinois Road and Oakwood. The Wenban boys attended the Academy. One son, Albert, returned to teach at the Academy for three years.

Charles Pratt, son of the pioneer Francis N. Pratt, built his home at 360 E. Westminster in 1876. This house is occupied (1961) by the A. Allen Bates family. The William Taylors built an imposing home on the southeast corner of Deer Path and Green Bay, the present Graham Aldis house. In 1874, William Metzger was born on the Hubbard farm in Lake Forest, the present property at the north end of Lake Forest and just east of Green Bay Road. Still living during the Centennial year, he ranks as the oldest Lake Forest resident who was born here.

In September 1875 Father James J. McGovern built St. Mary's Catholic Church and also served both at St. Patrick's and St. Mary's. John Birmingham and Timothy Howe helped to select the site. This frame church was organized and built at this time, but for some months previous to its completion, worship was conducted in the public school house. The August 28, 1875 issue of the *Waukegan Gazette* published a list of Lake Forest Protestants who had subscribed "liberally" to the new St. Mary's church edifice. The names included Senator C. B. Farwell, Ebenezer Buckingham, Sylvester Lind, William H. Ferry, Colonel William Johnston, Hugh Samuels, J. P. Manchester, Ezra J. Warner, Amzi Benedict, A. R. Sabin, and Simeon Williams.

THE horse and buggy or sleigh were necessary transportation during the 1870's. One was compelled to use the horse-drawn vehicle to avoid mud and dust in the summer, and deep snow or ice in the winter. During the winter of 1871 the John Baldwins drove their sleigh to a church social. They became lost driving home in a heavy blizzard. When they gave the horse his head, he turned in the opposite direction and got them safely home.

Fourth of July celebrations included "rural sports." People played lawn tennis, croquet and took part in archery competitions. Archery was especially popular at Ferry Hall. Dances conducted by a leader and called "A German" occupied the youth, and continued into the 1920's. There were also private theatricals, impromptu charade parties, concerts and receptions.

Baseball was a popular and well organized sport. James Lamb and J. V. Farwell, Jr., induced A. G. Spalding, owner of the Chicago White Sox professional team, to bring his team to Lake Forest for a game with the Academy in the spring of 1876. The score was 31 to 1. The lone Academy run was scored by E. J. Bartlett, a graduate of the Academy and at this time an Academy instructor. He lived to be the Grand Old Man of the Dartmouth College faculty.

Robert Davis Samuels related that about 1876 he was one of several who were privileged to listen to Dr. Alexander Graham Bell's first message, through Highland Park to Ferry Hall. This may have been from the Philadelphia Centennial Exposition which occurred on June 25, 1876, or soon afterwards. Mr. and Mrs. F. N. Pratt of Lake Forest attended the Exposition.

IN THAT SUMMER of 1876 Mrs. C. B. Farwell, backed up by the Lake Forest Association, finally succeeded in organizing Lake Forest College as a permanent institution and on an unexpectedly co-educational basis. She wished to realize the provisions of the original Lind University charter of 1857, but she had a personal interest as well. She herself was an educated and cultured woman, a former teacher who wished to make liberal education available to all, especially to young women. Her daughter Anna was about to graduate from a Chicago high school and talked of going to college. Mrs. Farwell wished to have her at home during her college career to get her acquainted with the people and places of what she hoped would be her future home. Besides, she was partial to co-education, which was not provided generally in the eastern colleges.

Anna Farwell was happy to stay in Lake Forest and several of her classmates expressed their desire to join the first class of the new institution. Dr. Robert Patterson of the Second Presbyterian Church of Chicago consented to become the first president. Several of the students received substantial financial aid from Mrs. Farwell. She continued her interest in the College during the early critical years, until the school was on a firm foundation. Her gifts are said to have totalled $300,000. Lake Forest College could not have started without her nor could it have continued without her support.

The idea of a coeducational college was unusual at the time, in spite of nearby Northwestern University which had just become coeducational in 1873. Mrs. Farwell was therefore a pioneer educator in a real sense. One school of thought believed in college education for women but not in coeducation. Another group thought that young ladies with college educations lost their charm and femininity. Very few girls attended college in those days.

The New Hotel had been operating at a continual loss for the past five years since it functioned chiefly for summer guests. In the fall of 1876, when a $40,000 indebtedness to the Lake Forest Association could not be raised by the hotel company, the New Hotel was turned over to the newly created Lake Forest College, together with twelve acres of land, and for a year and a half this building afforded dormitory and class-room space to the new institution. Classes were begun on September 7, 1876. The first faculty consisted of three members.

Since the Hotel had been built without a heating system "the students shivered during the long winter months. Inexplicable fires began to break out. A watch was organized and the building was nightly patrolled. On the morning of December 16, 1877, after the watch had retired and all was quiet, suddenly at about two o'clock a single cry of 'fire' echoed down the halls. The little class hurried out upon the lawn, and saw that for the last time the nest of their Alma Mater had been attacked by flames. The conflagration had started in the cupola, surely an odd place under the circumstances of its being three vacant stories above any firing influence. Only a few moments were necessary to afford the fire uncontrollable headway, due to a fanning wind from Lake Michigan. In three hours the ravenous flames had devoured the hotel and licked up every shred, board and shaving about the place; the ashes were strewn far about, and a cloud of brown smoke hung over the lake until the wind scattered it."

The College survived this baptism of fire. Classes were held in the Old Hotel. Plans were made, soon after the ashes had cooled, to erect a college building in College Park, the area which had originally been intended for the college. There was feverish activity as kilns were set up in the area of the old Gym and clay was dug from which the bricks were baked on the spot. Loads of lumber and other building materials were brought in, day and night, despite the mud and dust of the approaching streets. It was a hot and dry summer. The result was that College Hall was finished for occupancy in 1878, the fruit of great faith and dedicated labor. Where the clay was dug, a deep hole was formed known as the Gym Pond until 1930, when it was drained to form the girls' hockey field.

College Hall was built in the architectural custom of the period with a "stoop" entrance. A high and wide flight of stairs rose to the main floor. It was graced with a mansard roof and an extensive open porch on the west side of the main floor. At the north end of this floor was the library with some 6,000 volumes. Newell Dwight Hillis, as a Lake Forest College freshman, was assistant Librarian for a year, and he said he read or looked over every volume in this library. He became a well known preacher and lecturer after the turn of the century. The Library racks were ceiling high, and in the center of the room was a reading table with a half a dozen chairs.

Adjoining the library on the east was the reading room, a student enterprise with a large table and a dozen chairs in the middle. Around this room were wall stands to which the magazines were firmly chained and locked: *Harpers, Scribners, Century, Atlantic Monthly, Munseys,* and the much read *Outing,* the sport magazine of those days. Also there the student could read *Puck* and *Judge,* the two weekly funnies of those days, *Youth's Companion, Leslie's Illustrated, Harper's Bazaar,* and occasionally *War Cry.* The daily newspapers included *The Chicago Daily Times* and *Chicago Inter Ocean;* the latter was published by H. H. Kohlsaat, a well known Chicago restaurant man.

Across the hall from the reading room was the President's Office, overlooking the campus. This office was the "holy of holies." A call to go there was either an acolade, like a call to the White House, or a disgrace, like a summons before a Senate investigating committee. Adjoining the reading room was the modern language classroom and on the other side of the hall was the Latin department. At the south end of the Hall was the chapel, which could crowd in about 150 students. It was used as a classroom at times, but since chapel was compulsory it served as a main meeting place once a day.

In the basement, under the library, was the coal bin, and, under the reading room the boiler room. Adjoining the boiler room was the chemical laboratory. Under the chapel was the physics and higher mathematics classroom, complete with Scottish born Prof. Malcolm MacNeill, whom the students called "Little Mac." Then came the Biology room. This and the chemistry room were closely guarded, lest some inquiring numbskull pour water into sulphuric acid in its raw state, or disturb some biological experiment which had taken days to prepare. Directly under the entrance hall was the book store. The three upper stories were dormitories.

THE REPUTATION of the Academy had spread far enough to bring a student from Constantinople. Hovhannes Nergararian was the first recorded overseas student, entering the Academy in 1877, knowing no English. His father was the eastern European representative of Chicago's famed McCormick Harvester Company, manufacturers of all kinds of farm equipment. Since that time and especially since the turn of the century, probably not a year has passed without several students coming from other continents to Lake Forest schools. Soshichi Asida of Japan graduated from the Academy in 1902 and then graduated from Lake Forest College.

THE Lake Forest Association continued to operate until April 13, 1878, when it was dissolved and its affairs concluded by the consent of the stockholders. The lands then held by the trustees of the Association were sold and the debts paid. Lake Forest University, composed of the College, Academy and Ferry Hall, then became the heir of the Association.

IN SEPTEMBER 1878, President of the United States Rutherford B. Hayes with Mrs. Hayes came to Lake Forest. This was the only Presidential visit to Lake Forest during the first century of its existence. They were the guests of Mr. and Mrs. William Henry Smith. Mr. Smith was president of the Associated Press at the time. The whole town, including all the students, gathered at the station to greet the President and the first lady.

The President's party also included Lieut. General Philip H. Sheridan, Colonel Albert J. Myer and U.S. District Judge Henry Blodgett. The entire party came by special train from Chicago, and received a loud welcome. Crowds lined Deer Path almost to the lake, to watch the procession pass. The Smith home, just south of the C. B. Farwell's was decorated with many floral gifts. One was a large American flag, skillfully fashioned in flowers, and presented by Mrs. Henry Durand. Another was a large "Welcome," written in lilies, heliotropes and tuberoses, a gift of the employees of the Custom House in Chicago. Jane Durand (Allen) a very tiny girl was held up by her father, a former member of General Sheridan's army, for General Sheridan to kiss. She remembered vividly how she disliked the General's prickly moustache. In the evening, a reception was held at the Smith residence, at which many guests were present. A large brass band played throughout the evening.

The Chicago Tribune described this visit as:

One of the most complete affairs of the presidential trip. It was the subject of frequent remarks that the proportion, not only of well-dressed, but positively handsome ladies was much greater than is usually seen on similar occasions. And then, the reception being a general one to the citizens of Lake Forest, and there being but few guests from abroad, the occasion partook more of the nature of a social party than a state affair. Add to this a fine brass band, playing at intervals on the lawn, a quartet from Lake Forest of Messrs. Sabin, Sprague, Barnes and Powers, elaborate floral decorations and a roomy and handsome mansion entirely at the disposal of the company, and little more could have been desired.

Mrs. Hayes was most becomingly attired in a gray silk skirt with brocaded overdress, relieved in blue and shell trimmings. Mrs. William Henry Smith wore a heavy black grosgrain with point-lace trimmings. Miss Abbie Smith blushed in pink brocaded silk, relieved with black velvet, and Mrs. J. N. Jewett wore an ecru silk and velvet mixed.

In 1878 the D. R. Holt boys, Arthur, George, Charles and Alfred, went around the world—an almost unheard of accomplishment. Their letters home were circulated for all the neighbors to read. When they returned to Lake Forest, flags were displayed all over the town. The gate of the Holt residence was gaily decorated. For a small suburb, Lake Forest had unusual contacts with and interest in the world at large.

In September 1878, James Anderson imported six black Aberdeen Polled cattle from Scotland. Alexander Kelley accompanied them from Scotland through Canada to Lake Forest. This is perhaps the first shipment of its kind to the United States. The oldest was nineteen months, and weighed 1,100 pounds. Soon after this Kelley brought another shipment for the Farwell brothers.

Many nationally known figures visited in Lake Forest at this period: Whitelaw Reid, the distinguished Civil War correspondent, editor of the *New York Tribune* and Ambassador to Great Britain; Senator W. B. Allison of Iowa; Senator John J. Ingalls of Kansas; General John A. Logan, the founder of Memorial Day, three times president of the Grand Army of the Republic and the acknowledged head of the Republican Party in Illinois; Robert G. Ingersoll, the celebrated agnostic and one of the great orators of the day; General W. T. Sherman and General Philip Sheridan of Civil War fame.

In 1878 someone entered the Academy dining room to announce that there had been a serious railroad accident at Glencoe. The news soon spread over town, and everyone who had a carriage and a team of horses, and most people had, drove to Glencoe and brought back passengers to Lake Forest. The Kenosha train had run off the track. One of the cars rolled down an embankment and the stove had tipped over on a passenger, burning him to death. The other passengers had been piled up in the aisles on top of one another, and had escaped with a few broken bones. There were several Lake Foresters on the train.

The first Chicago-Milwaukee & St. Paul train came through west of Lake Forest in 1872. The first Northwestern Sunday train Chicago to Milwaukee made the trip in 1879. An automatic block signal system was installed on the Northwestern from Chicago to Waukegan in 1903.

On MARCH 1, 1879, occurred the fire which destroyed the original Academy building. On that Saturday some of the boys were out enjoying the fresh promise of spring. Snow was still on the ground. Some boys were collecting sap from the maple trees. Two college students driving a sleigh along what is now Sheridan Road saw flames issuing from the roof of the Academy building. Rushing into the dining room, where faculty and boarding students were having their noon meal, they gave warning. Old "Guv" Marshall, the colored janitor, ran to ring the Academy bell and stayed at his post for some time, keeping his head out of the window for fresh air. Soon the park was filled with students and townspeople. A strong north wind kept the fire from the north end of the building, and students threw out everything they could lift. When the south end had been burned out, the fire moved slowly back north again until the whole building was consumed. The entire roof caved in, but the first floor for a short while remained untouched. Henry Ware, a student, stood in the window of the Principal's office and held up a placard reading: "God bless our school." The woodsheds behind the Academy then caught fire from the intense heat of the main structure, but the barn and the immense piles of firewood in the back yard were saved. Soon the smouldering ashes were all that was left of the building.

Miss Ellen Holt, who died in 1961, was a little girl at the time, and not allowed to go with her brothers, but she watched the whole panorama of smoke and flames from the roof of their house. She heard the shouts of students and townspeople striving to save furniture and personal belongings. John Birmingham was also too young to be allowed to go to the Academy fire. His mother permitted him to watch from the top of a hay stack. He later attended the school as did all Lake Forest boys until the turn of the century.

According to Mrs. Robert G. McGann, one of the C. B. Farwell daughters, the fire was set by two students, Edward Pritchet and Charles Dole. They had soaked the floors with kerosene and had then applied a match. The building was insured for $10,000. The contents were also insured.

The furniture and other articles which were saved were carried to the Old Hotel, and school continued in the Dickinson house as temporary quarters. In 1880 a brick building, known as North Hall, was erected on the College campus, a gift of the C. B. Farwells. In September of that year, school opened in that building.

VIII

COLLEGE TOWN

1880–1890

In collecting photographs of early Lake Forest one is impressed with the family groups of the period, which tell an eloquent tale. The background is the family homestead. In the center, on the lawn, the father of the family is seated. He has originated in a simple environment on an Eastern farm, in Connecticut, Massachusetts or New York, and is proud of it. In the Mid-west he has prospered through selling lumber, real-estate, food or clothing. His wife sits close by on another chair. Their children are carefully placed at intervals so that the photographer can include as much of the grounds as possible. The family circle is often completed with two cows, horses, and the help. Sometimes there is a colored man holding the animals still. In the background is an orchard and a barn. It is almost a farm scene, but not quite. The garden, elaborate with geometric patterns and designs, and the long gravel driveway in front and around the house and on to the barn, suggest the fusion of the earth and sunshine of the country with the selected formalities of the city—this is the coming suburb.

In 1880 a Ferry Hall student, Nellie Durand, wrote about Lake Forest for a school assignment. She said: "Yesterday the population of Lake Forest was 1000, but last night I had a baby brother, so now the population is 1001." Years later she recalled how her pet lamb followed her to Sunday School across the old wooden bridge at Sheridan and Deer Path, after she had carefully said good-bye to it.

In those days, it seemed as if Lake Forest would remain a village forever. People did not want streets lighted, marked, or paved. Everyone preferred to contend with mud and dust continually. The only remedy was for people to go down to the lake shore and load wagons with gravel to put on the streets in front of houses, and on driveways. Going about at night could only be safely accomplished by carrying an oil lamp. Lake Forest might have been called a "one horse town," except that there happened to be some three hundred horses in the village. There was, however, only one Protestant and one Catholic Church, and one doctor. Dr. Alfred C. Haven came in 1882 and served the community until his death in 1925. He practised medicine and some dentistry. His first office was in the Lake Forest Hotel. He built his home on Washington Road a few years later, the present Paul Curtis residence.

The unmarked streets and their convolutions caused strangers to inquire their way as they do even now. One day a stranger asked the location of a certain house, and when he was told, inquired: "Why don't you have your streets marked?" A youngster replied: "They *are*, on the map." Another newcomer asked for directions to the railroad station. When he was asked: "Are you going away?" He answered: "No, I want to get back there so I'll know where I am."

Basic transportation was provided by the horse. When the father of the family left home to take the eight o'clock train for Chicago, it was a great occasion for the children who loved to go along in the family carriage. One pet horse would trot leisurely until he heard the train whistle, then nothing could hold him back. The Samuel D. Ward family's horse was deliberate and slow. When they offered a ride to a pedestrian, he replied: "No, thanks, I want to make the train; I prefer to walk."

The Northwestern ran about ten trains daily each way. The line was single track. There was a cut-out switch north of the Station, where two trains could meet and pass. This frequently occurred. The usual trip to Chicago took about an hour and twenty minutes, with a couple of express trains doing the trip in 58 minutes. Some Milwaukee trains stopped at Lake Forest, and then continued to Chicago, non-stop. It was rumored that the railroad extended special courtesies to Lake Forest because of Senator C. B. Farwell. A few years later Marvin Hughitt, President of the Northwestern Railroad, built a home in Lake Forest, as did his son-in-law, Hugh R. McCullough, General Passenger Agent of the line. During their residence in Lake Forest, train service was even better. One record trip from Chicago was made in 28 minutes for a group of stranded students. Another time a special train brought only one person, a doctor from Chicago to Lake Forest.

Lake Forest was a paradise for children, who enjoyed the simple pleasures of ponies, dogs, barnyard pets and bicycles. Many youngsters had old fashioned bicycles with a 52-inch wheel in front, a saddle on top and a little wheel behind. Charles Durand had one of the first "safety" bicycles, with wheels of equal size: the forerunner of those of the present day. A dozen of these were introduced within their first year of introduction.

During the 1880's there was a Lake Forest Bicycle Club, which was issued a booklet with a detailed map of all the usable roads in northern Illinois and southern Wisconsin. The members of the club included E. A. Barnum, Cyrus Bentley, Jr., Frank Douglass, Albert L. Farwell, Frank C. Farwell, F. J. Peabody, L. L. Spruance and Simeon L. Williams. The group rode to Geneva Lake "which never had so many people around it, but there is still room for more." They watched a "yacht race for a large purse" before pedaling back to Lake Forest.

Other neighborhood activities were recalled by Miss Ellen Holt. Children would collect on the front steps of the Reid porch. Among them were the Reid girls and the Holt boys, who were always rather cross when an early supper hour interfered with their play. Grandfather Reid insisted that all must be home by four o'clock, even when they had been out in the country on an overnight trip. "A crowd of us went out by carriage to Deep Lake, including the Reids, Maud Warner, the Ward family, and the Holts. I'll never forget how upset the farmer's wife was when she saw so many of us arrive at her farm, and said there wasn't room for us. But we stayed and had a great lark, three children to a bed, and Alfred (Holt) and Mr. Ward in a room behind the kitchen stove."

Another youngster related that "overnight trips were quite popular. When I was about twelve, we took a trip, by hayrack, way out to Round Lake to spend the night in hammocks on a pavilion. It was on a very hot day and one of the team of horses dropped dead in the harness. Fortunately we were near a farm where we could secure another horse. It was quite the thing for young married couples to take weekend trips in phaetons. These were one-seated, four wheeled rigs with folding tops. A 'sporty' weekend out at Diamond Lake might include hickory nutting, fishing, or just driving about the country. Since there were no paved roads, plans were made according to the weather to avoid deep mud."

COMMENCEMENT DAY, June 1880, was a significant one for Lake Forest. On that day the first Lake Forest College class graduated two girls and five boys. The board of trustees of Lake Forest University held a meeting; then the academic procession formed, led by the Academy band, and marched to the Presbyterian Church. The Church was soon filled with townspeople and three carloads of Chicago Presbyterians. The services lasted nearly four hours. The seven graduates were:

ANNA FARWELL	Lake Forest
JOSEPHINE LOUISE WHITE	Chicago
PAUL DAVID BERGEN	Iowa
FRED LEVI FORBES	Indiana
WILLIAM O. FORBES	Indiana
JOHN E. TARBLE	Florida
CHARLES FARWELL WARD	Chicago

The two honor prizes were won by the two young lady graduates who "presented essays which would have done credit to the ablest male graduates of any college in the country," according to the *Inter Ocean*, a Chicago newspaper. "It was practical proof of the success of the co-education theory, so well illustrated in these scholarly and accomplished young ladies." Miss Anna Farwell, who was vice-president of the class, delivered her essay on: "The position and opportunities of women in America." Miss Josephine White spoke on: "Alexander Hamilton's Financial Policy."

Anna Farwell became the wife of a prominent musician, Reginald de Koven, and wrote the authoritative life of *John Paul Jones,* and *The Count of Gruyère.* Josephine White became Mrs. Lindon W. Bates. Paul David Bergen was later the president of the Presbyterian College in Wie Hsien, in Shantung, China. The two Forbes were ordained as Presbyterian clergymen. Charles F. Ward became a musician, and died in 1883. John E. Tarble died in 1882.

For three decades, after this first commencement, Lake Forest centered in Lake Forest College. The townspeople were eager and proud to build up their new and unique institution. New buildings were donated in quick succession. Some of the children gave a play and a concert at Ferry Hall to raise money for the college bell. The bell was installed about 1882 and announced services at the Presbyterian Church as well as 6:30 student rising hour and classes. Lake Forest was once more on a sound basis after the Academy fire silenced the only bell in town. The President and faculty members were admired and entertained as the first citizens of the city. The Academy and Ferry Hall were to provide students for the college. Ferry Hall graduates were now encouraged to complete their education there until Ferry College for Young Ladies could be established late in the decade. This institution was likewise a part of Lake Forest University but differed from Lake Forest College in that it was for girls only. A unified and coordinated educational program was now offered from the primary grades on up.

One of the faculty members of Lake Forest College kept a record of the average term grades of students during the two school years 1887–1889. The grades were: Sidney Benedict 97.87, Grace Reid 89.8, Juliet Rumsey 89.69, Rose Farwell 89.6, A. G. Welch 89.53, E. S. Wells, Jr. 88.73, Kate Stroh 82.5, H. C. Durand 75.93. Garcia G. Sickels was first in the class of 1890 with a four year average of 90.31.

In 1880 a Republican political rally was held in the Academy Hall, on the College campus, which seated more people than any other building in the village. Charles B. Farwell was a candidate for the U.S. Senate, and he and his brother, John V. Farwell, Sr. addressed the meeting. Great enthusiasm was aroused among the boys, most of whom preferred the Republican party and held the Farwells in high esteem.

These two Farwell brothers were born in New York state, came to Mt. Morris, Illinois, as youngsters, in a covered wagon, then to

Chicago. In due time they became leading citizens in the Chicago area, then nationally and in England. Charles B. Farwell was distinguished-looking, with thin gray hair, moustache and chin whiskers. He was a member of the House of Representatives or the Senate of the United States on and off for thirty years, beginning with 1870. He and his family were staunch supporters of Lake Forest University and every civic and religious project in Lake Forest.

His younger brother, J. V. Farwell, the original *Merchant Prince,* was clean shaven and wore glasses. He had the appearance of a scholar rather than a business man. He organized J. V. Farwell & Company, the leading wholesale dry goods firm in Chicago, in 1850, where Marshall Field received his early training in merchandising. For a while the firm was called Farwell, Field & Company. The new building in which the business was housed was burned in the Chicago fire of 1871.

J. V. Farwell was interested in the Dwight L. Moody religious revivals of 1857–1858, and was instrumental in the erection of the first Y.M.C.A. building in the world, in Chicago. He donated the land and a considerable sum of money besides. During the Civil War he visited the battlefields to promote religious services. After the War he followed Moody to England in 1867, and continued to support his efforts with substantial financial aid. Through his influence "Billy" Sunday later received his first religious assignment, working in the Chicago Y.M.C.A.

The two Farwells undertook a pioneer project in 1875 for which they received 3,000,000 acres of land in ten counties, in the Texas Panhandle, for financing the erection of the Capitol building in Austin. The gigantic XIT ranch became a model for organization and operation of many other famous Texas ranches. Aberdeen-Angus, Durhams, Shorthorns, Herefords and other fine breeds were stocked. In 1885 Ranch Rules were distributed, in which the use of small firearms, card playing, and Sabbath-breaking were forbidden. At that time a British syndicate was formed to promote the development of this vast acreage.

A strong advocate of temperance, J. V. Farwell once discovered his Lake Forest help drinking beer in the ice house, gave them a lecture on the evils of drink, read the Scriptures to them, prayed over them, and then announced he would give them a second chance. They were soon caught drinking again, and fired on the spot.

J. V. Farwell served as the sixth mayor of Lake Forest. Three members of the Farwell family have been mayors. Farwell Winston, a grandson of C. B. Farwell, Albert Farwell, a grandson of J. V. Farwell, and Kent Chandler, the husband of J. V. Farwell's granddaughter, Grace Tuttle Chandler.

DURING the 1880's the idea grew that the whole town of Lake Forest should become one big beautiful park, without fences or walls. This brought many problems. Student groups cut through private property to make more direct routes to the business district, the station or the lake. In fruitful seasons orchards became a worse temptation to these students. Stray cows visited strange lawns and flower gardens much to the dismay of citizens who did not appreciate their uninvited presence. Joseph B. Durand was elected mayor, in 1886, because he promised to keep cows out of people's yards. He must have succeeded since no complaints deface the records of his term as mayor. At this time, in the dry town of Lake Forest, there was a real crisis when whiskey was prescribed for an injured man. Where could any be found? The sheriff knew the only place in Lake Forest where it could be secured: the home of the mayor, Joseph B. Durand.

There was a furor over locating the cemetery. Some wished to continue it where one had existed before Lake Forest had been chartered as a city, east of Green Bay Road near the Lake Bluff border. Others wished to maintain the site originally planned as a part of the earliest Lake Forest plat. The city became divided over the issue. A bare majority voted to maintain the latter site, the present one at the north end of town between Sheridan Road and the lake. Those who had opposed this location hoped for a future highway along the lake shore, from Chicago to Milwaukee, which the present location makes impossible. One of these, hoping to enlist the support of John S. Hannah, who lived near the cemetery on Lake Road, asked if he didn't object to the neighborhood in which he lived, received the reply: "Not at all. They are the quietest neighbors we have ever had."

Once the new cemetery ordinance was passed, a new plat was made and new prices were fixed. In 1882 Henry C. Durand made a gift of $4,000 for "ornamenting and improvement of the cemetery grounds." By 1901, his gifts for this purpose had increased to $10,817. On May 1, 1883, the City of Lake Forest set aside the western portion of the cemetery for the use of St. Mary's Roman Catholic parish.

Another ordinance involved the Sabbath. Baseball and other games were forbidden within the city limits, and it was declared unlawful to sell or expose for sale on any street or public ground, any newspaper or other article. The penalty for disobedience was $5.00. Other ordinances set penalties for killing birds, or for discharging firearms of any description. The mayor was empowered for such length of time has he might think proper, to order all dogs within this city to be muzzled. A dog license fee costing $1.00 for males and $2.00 for females was required. Metal tags were provided and fines were set for shooting dogs, or for stealing their tags.

The City Seal was adopted by an ordinance on June 5, 1882, which made the motto: "Natura et Scientia Amor." In the center was represented natural scenery. Another ordinance on the same date forbade anyone to "dig, remove, or carry away, or cause same to be done, any soil, sod, earth, sand or gravel from any street, alley or public grounds in this city." The fine was set for $10 for each offense. Another ordinance stated that "Beginning May 1, 1883, the salary of the Mayor (shall) be fixed at $400, and thereafter no salary be paid to any Mayor of the City until further order of the Council." On August 2, 1886, it was decreed that: "Every person, not a citizen of Lake Forest, who shall offer for sale any goods, wares or merchandise, in or along any streets or Avenue, or from house to house, or in any public place in the city, shall be deemed a peddler, and shall pay a license of $2.00 per day. This does not apply to farmers coming in from the country with produce for the market."

During the winter of 1881 there was an unusually heavy snow storm, with high winds and drifts. The drifts were so high that they threatened to interrupt railroad traffic to Chicago. The Northwestern used a four-engine tandem to plow the snow. At the same time fifty shovellers worked day and night to keep the tracks open.

People were beginning to have indoor plumbing. The Holt family had one of the first installations. One day a corpulent farmer lady was visiting Mrs. Holt. She was being shown over the house, when Mrs. Holt said: "And here is the bath." The lady remarked: "That must take off a lot of fat!"

Water for the bathrooms was carefully stored in tanks in the attic after each rainfall. Mosquitoes gathered on the ceiling above the tanks, and people destroyed the pests by putting cans of kerosene on ends of sticks and pressing them up against the ceiling.

Every home had its well, in some cases artesian, with its own pressure. That of the I. P. Rumsey's, on the original Quinlan property just east of the present Public Library, was required to be kept available to everyone in the city, according to its deed. Some houses had windmills, but other wells were pumped by hand as was the one on the University campus. The main well on the campus was next to the frame building called Academia. When independent thinkers became objectionable to the conservative upper classmen, the former were put under the pump for purposes of correction and general character improvement.

On a Sunday night in the summer of 1882, fire demolished a large part of the business district of Lake Forest. No fire department had been developed. There now grew up an agitation for a water system which was first necessary before a fire department could be effective.

Joe O'Neill built the first brick building after the fire and expanded his hardware store. His brother, William, presided over the tin shop which soon became famous in the Chicago area by supplying all the tinware sold at the Columbian Exposition in 1893. In 1885 C. George Wenban organized the Lake Forest Livery Boarding and Sales Stables, at the corner of Oakwood and Deer Path. By 1890, Fred and George, his sons, entered the business which now included undertaking. Since 1909 George Wenban, Sr., has been a Buick dealer as well.

In May 1884, "Fairlawn," the C. B. Farwell home, was the scene of the marriage of Anna Farwell and Reginald de Koven, which set a pattern for many Lake Forest weddings. Reginald was the composer of some fifty compositions and the light operas *Robin Hood* and *The Canterbury Pilgrims*, the music for Kipling's Recessional, and the ever-popular *Oh, Promise Me.* He was an Oxford graduate, a rarity in the Mid-west, and had an English accent which is said to have endeared him to the ladies, though the men did not quite know what to make of it. His uncle was a well known

Chicago banker, but Reginald had little interest in business. His father, the Rev. Henry de Koven, had moved to Florence, Italy, where Reginald was brought up in an artistic environment and developed his musical talents.

The Chicago guests arrived at the Lake Forest station in four packed railway cars. Nearly all the carriages in town met them and drove them to "Fairlawn." The house was decorated with plants and flowers, many of them from the Farwell and neighboring greenhouses. Smilax was draped about the chandeliers.

The wedding ceremony took place in the bay window of the parlor where an altar had been erected against a background of plants and roses. The bridesmaids were Grace and Rose Farwell, the bride's younger sisters, Fannie Farwell, her cousin, and Louise de Koven, a cousin of the groom. The bride wore a gown of white satin, trimmed with Flanders lace, complete with a veil and diamonds. The bridesmaids were in white muslin, over silk.

The ceremony was performed by Dr. Bebbert, rector of St. James Episcopal Church of Chicago, assisted by Rev. James G. K. McClure, pastor of the Lake Forest Presbyterian Church. After the reception the couple sailed on the *Bothnia* to visit the parents of the groom in Florence, Italy, where they finally made their home.

PRIOR TO 1880 an idea was quite prevalent that the lake shore was a poor place to build a home. It was damp. The early families had built inland in all directions, but had avoided the bluff above the lake. Now that the newcomers were compelled to choose new properties on which to build their homes, many of them preferred the unoccupied lands along the lake front. The prejudice against these lots gradually vanished so that today they are considered among the most desirable. By 1880 people began to talk about the grand view of Lake Michigan, beautiful sunrises, and easy access to the beach.

In 1883, Walter Larned built one of the first houses on the lake, "Blair Lodge." This house stood just south of Ferry Hall, where the New Hotel had stood. He installed a rustic gate at the south end of his property, and the driveway to his house was bordered by a high hedge of Japanese quince, which when in blossom, was a sensational sight to visitors. The house contained a secret room. Mr. Larned was a lawyer, the art critic for the *Chicago Daily News,* the author of several books, and an inveterate traveller. He started the Chicago Art Institute Club in Lake Forest for which Durand Art Institute was built. It was referred to as "our cultural high-light." He and his family frequently entertained famous guests from all over the country, some of whom remained for a month or more. One of these guests was the Rev. Zephaniah Humphrey, whose daughter Zephine became a well known author.

The Larned house had one drawback—the family had to warn guests not to look at the beach below as frequently nude bathers appeared there. This condition was corrected after August 5, 1895, when an ordinance stated: "No person shall swim or bathe at any hour of the day between sunrise and sunset in Lake Michigan, in a state of nudity within one mile of that part of the shore of said Lake which is within the corporate limits of the City of Lake Forest. Fine $10."

Another early home on the bluff was built by Abram Poole, in 1884. He named it "Elsinore." This was the property now known as the Stanley Keith place at 1315 N. Lake Road. All the Pooles were immersed in literature and the arts: one of the most interesting families of the period. Mr. Poole was a member of the Chicago Board of Trade and a veteran of the Civil War.

In the eighties there was much talk about the problem of prohibition and local option. A crusade was developing throughout the North Shore, and children helped circulate petitions and pledges, which people signed, promising never to touch liquor. There was one particular young man about whom many were concerned. He used to ride by unsteadily, on his bicycle with the large wheel in front and the little one behind—very much the "dandy." One day three children, Alice Reid, Lily Ward and Ellen Holt hid in the bushes and as he came along they dashed out from behind the hedge shouting: "Sign a pledge and be a blessing!"

In 1881, the Presbyterians installed the church's fourth pastor, the Rev. James Gore King McClure. Lake Forest was a conservative, church-centered community in those days, whole families attending Wednesday evening prayer meeting carrying lanterns along the dark streets. The older people in Lake Forest took the new minister under their wings and affectionately referred to him as: "The Little Minister." Dr. McClure was a favorite of town and gown, especially since there was no other Protestant church in the "village." He was genial, quiet, modest, and an unusually fine preacher. His message was full of vitality. During the twenty-three years of Dr. McClure's pastorate, he was twice President of the College, and the love and confidence which he inspired caused gifts to flow into the church, the schools, and the city. In 1887, Rush Medical College was attached to Lake Forest University. In 1890, the Chicago College of Dental Surgery was annexed. This school was founded by the world-famous Dr. Truman W. Brophy, who devised an operation for cleft palate and harelip. Because of its close association with McCormick Theological Seminary, it was thought that the European conditions of a University having four faculties had been fulfilled by Lake Forest University.

An unknown Academy boy has left this description of Dr. Mc-Clure in the Presbyterian Church: "The different people come in, the students all go up in front in the left and the right wings— well, all except myself, who take a back pew. They allow me the privilege because I am an Academy Vigilance Committee. He is a saintly man as ever lived—small and half shy like a school boy, but he has hold of every heart string in that congregation. Even the wicked 'Cad' (nickname of the period for Academy students) listens with sympathetic gaze. He is so pleading, pure, earnest and simple-mannered, and tells the story of Christ in so childlike a way that congressman (Hon. C. B. Farwell) and 'Cad' alike give their whole attention."

In 1886 the Presbyterian congregation began to build a new church out of stone. Dr. McClure raised every cent by personal subscription. He collected as little as 50¢ and as much as $5,000 from different donors. Henry C. Durand headed the building committee. "He watched every detail of construction, he knew almost every stone and every beam, he was here early and late. At the same time the Manse was built." Simon Reid and D. R. Holt were the other members of the building committee. The architect was Charles Sumner Frost, a son-in-law of Marvin Hughitt. Frost was in the office of Henry Ives Cobb at this time. He used the stones from the Second Presbyterian Church of Chicago, "The Spotted Church," which was most appropriate since the Lake Forest dream had come from this Chicago Church. These stones had been assembled after the Chicago fire and taken to Winnetka, where they were sold to Hall McCormick, who in turn sold them to the Lake Forest church.

Among the important documents included in the cornerstone were the papers freeing from slavery a beloved town character, Samuel Dent. Mrs. William Sage Johnston's six children provided the church tower bell which is inscribed: "In loving memory of Jane Butterfield, wife of William Johnston, died January 5, 1875." The work on the interior of the church was supervised by Mrs. Simon S. Reid and Mrs. Ezra J. Warner. Construction was completed in 1887.

The church was dedicated free of debt in June, 1887. Dr. Robert W. Patterson preached the dedicatory sermon. Mr. Frost, who designed all the Northwestern railway stations from Waukegan to and including Chicago, added the Sunday School wing some years later, and found matching spotted stones in a south side church that was being dismantled. The first wedding in this church building was that of Miss Jane Durand and Hubert Allen.

One youngster wrote a school composition which said: "There are two important men in Lake Forest—Dr. McClure and Mr. Dent." At the time, Samuel Dent had a livery stable and provided most of the transportation for those who did not have their own horses and vehicles. He was allowed to drive through the various estates with his carriage filled with sight-seers. He would tell something about each estate. It was not easy to run accurately over the wicket that opened the Cleveland gates at the entrances.

One winter day Samuel Dent drove George Holt home from the station, upsetting the sleigh in a snow drift, and refused to accept the 25¢ fare because of the catastrophe. He said: "Tip over enough, Mr. Holt." Samuel used to enjoy giving rides to all the youngsters in town. Once when he was surrounded by a group of children, he said: "I feel just like a fly in a pan of milk." The children had a riddle they liked to repeat: Why is Lake Forest like an old tea kettle? Answer: Because it has a Dent in it. The children in town were an important part of the Lake Forest communications system. Before the coming of the telephones, youngsters were asked to deliver messages, to Dent or to anyone else, which they did very proudly.

Someone has left another description of Dent which bears

quoting: "That noise you heard on the platform just as the train started from the Lake Forest station was Dent laughing. Dent is the best darkey that ever grew. He is the Lake Forest mascot. He can neither read nor write, but he can tell a bogus quarter in the dark. He runs a livery establishment, and will do anything, night or day, for you, up to Saturday night; then he shuts down till Monday. If a sick woman wants him to get up a rig to take her to Church, he won't do it without an affidavit that she isn't able to walk. He thinks that anyone who has to ride Sundays had better not come to Lake Forest to live. The Northwestern Railway people talk of putting Dent's picture in a panel on the station house, instead of the LAKE FOREST sign. He is a firm supporter of the African Methodist Episcopal Church and can get more big words in a prayer of the same length than any Andover professor. If doing kind things and leading an honest life make a good citizen, few towns have a better one than S. Dent."

There is a gravestone in Lake Forest Cemetery which bears this inscription:

IN MEMORY OF
SAMUEL DENT
BORN IN TUSCUMBIA, ALABAMA
ESCAPING FROM
SLAVERY HE ENTERED THE UNION
ARMY IN 1862.

DIED AT LAKE FOREST, JUNE 9, 1898.

"IF THE SON SHALL MAKE YOU FREE
YOU SHALL BE FREE INDEED."

THIS MONUMENT
IS ERECTED BY THE
CITIZENS OF LAKE FOREST
IN TOKEN OF THEIR
ESTEEM FOR A LOVEABLE
CHRISTIAN, DEVOTED
CITIZEN AND FAITHFUL FRIEND.

The Negro district was in the vicinity of the Washington and Illinois Roads intersection. College and Academy students attended the meetings of the African Methodist Church and enjoyed especially the fervent prayers and the melodious singing of the congregation. There was an added attraction when a college boy preached the sermon and many students attended to give the speaker moral support. The town young people were often involved in projects to raise money for this church.

THERE WERE many parties in town to occupy the youth of all ages. Grace Reid gave one large St. Valentine's party. Rose Farwell, a queenly beauty, gracious, athletic and truly democratic, gave parties which young men of her age were especially eager to attend. Mrs. Simon Reid entertained dozens of Academy and College boys at her home. She kept many of them busy doing odd jobs and paying them most liberally, to help them in their education. Mrs. Calvin Durand entertained groups of boys at her home for Sunday dinners and permitted Ferry Hall girls to tramp across her cow-pasture for a short-cut in going uptown. Caroline Benedict presided at the many social functions for the entertainment of school and college boys and girls. Singing was an integral part of all entertainments as people gathered around the piano, while Charlie Holt or some other person led them in soulful melodies. Everyone enjoyed debates, oratorical contests, band concerts, chamber music, and sport events.

In the 1880's Ferry Hall was called "The Seminary." Many period jokes revolved around this name. Charlie Fletcher was asked by a visitor where the Seminary was. He said: "Which do you mean, the girls' school or the burying ground?" Arthur Reid and Harry Durand took delight in calling themselves alumni of Ferry Hall. They had attended a primary school there which was coeducational. Fanny Atteridge, one of the first Ferry Hall graduates, taught several decades in the second public grade school of Lake Forest which was at the north end of town, west of the tracks, near Noble Avenue. The public schools were crowded with 140 pupils and only three teachers presided over them—the Misses Atteridge, Bonner and Marvin. One of the nagging problems for the Super intendent was securing board and room for the teachers.

CHICAGO at this time was absorbed with problems involving labor discontent. The city had made an amazing recovery after the Chicago fire, but now the whole country was in the depths of a severe depression, with falling prices and wages. Many were losing their jobs. At the McCormick plant, at Blue Island and Western, when workers were discharged because "they were not needed," there was considerable strife and violence. The *Arbeiter Zeitung,* considered an anarchist newspaper, published increasingly bold and incendiary articles. Inflammatory speeches were reported. There were threats to life and property. Armed groups drilled nightly and were reported to be practicing with dynamite, bombs, rifles and small arms.

On May 1, 1886, the original May Day, 25,000 people gathered at the Haymarket Square, two blocks west of the present Northwestern Railway Station, to be harangued by anarchist-socialists, following the McCormick strike. This demonstration had been carefully planned for six months, but no riot developed as the leaders had hoped.

By Monday, May 3, the strike spread over the city. Many businesses were affected. Red banners and flags were displayed in the loop area. Some struggled to take these down as others fought to display more and more bunting. Crowds gathered at the McCormick factory and more violence resulted. Captain Ward of the Desplaines Street Police Station, alerted by Mayor Carter Harrison, and alarmed by the reports, increased his force to 100 police officers.

On Tuesday May 4th a new mass meeting gathered force at the Haymarket where farmers brought hay for the horse-drawn transportation of the city. The square was large enough to accommodate a large crowd. Spies announced that "we'll be masters of Chicago before morning." The meeting soon moved from the Haymarket ½ block North on Desplaines Street. Speeches followed in quick succession.

All was comparatively peaceful until about 9:30 a.m. when Fielden took the stand. He advised the crowd to "exterminate the capitalists and do it tonight." By 10:00 a.m. the crowd got excited and very noisy.

Captain Ward and his 100 police left the Desplaines station toward the meeting, marching in column. Fielden was still talking when they arrived on the scene. Amidst jeers and shouts Captain Ward ordered the crowd "to disperse peaceably," when suddenly a dynamite bomb exploded in the midst of the police formation. Many officers were thrown to the ground, then reforming, they charged the crowd with pistols blazing. Their fire was returned, then the unruly crowd dispersed as their leaders fled, under fire.

In all 7 police officers were killed and an uncounted number of civilians. The police station was filled with the wounded and dying. The city experienced deep anxiety for several days and nights until federal troops arrived from Fort Laramie, Wyoming, to restore order. Nearly all the leaders of the riot were apprehended and convicted.

In ensuing discussions, General Philip Sheridan suggested a federal military post close enough to be of immediate use, instead of depending on Fort Riley, Kansas, or Fort Laramie, Wyoming. The Farwell brothers had returned from a hunting expedition out west on the troop train which brought federal troops from Fort Laramie. These two were especially impressed by the effect of these troops on the strike and the riots. Senator C. B. Farwell now pressed the issue in Washington. A small committee of Chicago business men raised money and chose the site of Chicago's own federal military post, just south of Lake Forest. The movement was backed by the Commercial Club and the Board of Trade. In 1887 six hundred and thirty-two acres were bought by the government for a total of $10.00, and construction had proceeded far enough so that two companies of the 6th Infantry were stationed in Camp Highwood, as it was called at first.

On February 27, 1888, the name was changed to Fort Sheridan. In September of that year Congress appropriated $300,000 for substantial construction. The barrack buildings were erected during 1888, but the tower construction posed a serious problem, when excavation for its foundations revealed quicksand. The army engineers finally solved the difficulty by pouring carloads of cement to establish a firm base for the foundations and to hold the enormous weight of the structure. The tower was completed in 1891, at a cost of $86,065.

Among the early prisoners in the Fort Sheridan guardhouse were several Indian chiefs taken in frontier uprisings. These included: Chiefs Sitting Bull, Plenty Wound, Come and Grunt, Take Shield Away, Hard to Hit, Know His Voice, and Good Eagle.

Sergeant Lawrence H. W. Speidel, a member of Company K, 6th Infantry, was an occupant of the first barrack to be completed. He, personally, raised the first flag over Fort Sheridan. His Company had been transferred from Ft. Laramie. In May, 1888, he married and like others from Ft. Sheridan, established his home in Lake Forest. When he was discharged from the Army he started an oil and gas business, had a barn on Western Avenue, and horses with which he delivered his gas for the Wellsbach lights which were used to illuminate the homes of those days. He also assisted Mary McLoughlin at the Post Office. He died in Lake Forest after 36 years as a well-known and respected Lake Forester.

BASEBALL was a firmly established sport in Lake Forest during the period after the Civil War, but now a new sport was initiated by Clyde Carr and James Harbert—football. These two gathered together a group that attempted to learn to play the game, in 1886. The following year "Prof." Billy Williams arrived to teach mathematics and physics at the Academy. He organized the first team in the Mid-West and became the first coach. He had learned the game at his alma mater, Williams College, in Massachusetts, and continued to play on the Lake Forest team which included both college and Academy boys. His team defeated the University of Chicago by three touchdowns; Burtis R. MacHatton, a former Academy student, scored two of the three. Northwestern was defeated 20–0. In those early years Billy Williams was considered the father of Western football. When the forerunner of the Big Ten was organized during the next decade, Lake Forest Academy was one of the charter members, according to Billy Williams, the only secondary school so listed.

Many graduated from Lake Forest schools and later achieved distinction in business and the professions. Charles H. Wacker came to Lake Forest to school because the Chicago fire had destroyed the high school he was attending. He later studied in Germany, and became a Chicago business executive. In 1909 he was chairman of the Chicago Plan Commission, which beautified the city by supervising the erection of public buildings, parks and boulevards. The resulting project included the Union Station, Shedd Aquarium, Soldier Field Stadium, Field Museum and many other buildings. Wacker Drive was named after Charles H. Wacker.

James H. Rogers graduated from Lake Forest, then specialized in study of the organ. His graduate studies included the famous teachers of the day, Clarence Eddy in Chicago, then Paris and Berlin under the famous masters of music, Loeschhorn, Rohde, Haupt, Guiliamant and Widor. Returning to the U.S.A. he became a prolific composer and writer on musical subjects. His greatest contributions to American music were in the field of organ and church music in which he published over two hundred works.

Paul Starret walked with his brother to Lake Forest Academy in the eighties, every Monday morning, returning to his Highland Park home, walking, every week end. He became a construction engineer and built the first skyscraper, the Flat-Iron building in New York, as well as the Pennsylvania Railroad Station, the Commodore and Biltmore Hotels and the Empire State Building, the highest in the world. He also erected the Blackstone Hotel in Chicago and the Lincoln Memorial in Washington.

From the day the Lake Forest Hotel was built, Lake Forest was a favorite spot for visitors from Chicago. Their reactions were those of the most recent visitors. Mrs. Israel Parsons Rumsey spent a half day on such a visit with her family on July 4th, 1887, which she described:

We drove from the station to the Lake Shore, where we had our lunch on the bluff overlooking the lake which I never saw so beautiful. Part of it a deep blue, like the sky, part delicate green and as smooth as glass, with four white sailing vessels floating slowly over it, and shadows from the passing clouds varying the tints. The children went down on the beach, and played in the sand and water. Mr. J. J. Halsey read to us, and we had the benefit of Mr. Farwell's horses and surrey to take some of us to the station about 6:00 p.m., driving around by some of the pretty places. Lake Forest is such a quiet restful spot to spend the 4th and it rather grows on us as a place to live in. The children take very kindly to the idea. But it looks rather dubious as to being able to find any place that we can afford to buy.

September of the same year found the family settled in the former Quinlan house, which for two generations was known as the I. P. Rumsey House: "The Evergreens," just east of the present Library. Mrs. Rumsey wrote of "all kinds of vegetables and melons and grapes every day" and "perfectly lovely rides around here: we went down through a ravine (McCormick's), on a road very narrow in some places, down onto the lake shore, and rode right along the water's edge for a long way. The country seems to agree with the horses as it does with the rest of us. We hate to go back to our Chicago neighborhood and be talked to and scolded. There is no telling when they will stop. But we don't care very much. At the Presbyterian Church Miss Davies sits two seats behind us and says our family has been a problem to them ever since we came. They wonder who we all are. Monday afternoon I put on a bold front and went calling all by myself. Made five calls and found all the people in. In the evening my husband and I called on the Benedicts and Durands. In all I have made thirteen calls and have nearly as many more to do. Lake Forest is not an easy place to live in, there are some things about the life which require constant adjustment, and don't stay put. In this place of young people there are all sorts of ideas."

In 1888 a property was acquired by the City of Lake Forest from D. R. and Ellen H. Holt on the corner of Deer Path and Oakwood. A four room school house was built on this property and named the West School. The former school on Noble Avenue and just west of the railroad tracks was discontinued and dismantled. Part of it became the Baptist Church on Oakwood where it still stands. Another part was moved to Deer Path and became a private dwelling. It is the present home of Charles Overall across the street from the Telephone building.

Miss Kate McMahon became the Principal of the new West School. Miss Alice Treffry, Miss Louise French and Miss Alice Poole were the other teachers. In 1912, after a fire, this school was rebuilt, enlarged, and renamed the "John J. Halsey School." When the West School was first erected, Superintendent Roy F. Griffin remarked: "Boys who ought to be in school, prefer to wander from place to place during the day instead of attending school. They acquire habits of idleness and often are led into vice. Your Superintendent sees no way of remedying the evil." Perhaps the new school was so attractive that students were eager to attend.

The new school inspired Miss Kate McMahon to ask for a salary increase to $50 per month. She said: "First, the labor is worth it, second, my experience entitles me to the increase, and other places are paying comparable salaries." She added: "Unless granted, Miss McMahon declines reappointment."

On April 13, 1888, at a meeting at the residence of the Rev. and Mrs. George R. Cutting, Principal of Lake Forest Academy, the Alcott School was founded, in honor of Bronson Alcott, a pioneer American educator and the father of Louisa May Alcott. Miss Alcott was best known as an author of a series of autobiographical children's books, the best known being *Little Women*. Among those present were Mr. and Mrs. Calvin Durand, Mr. and Mrs. John H. Dwight, Mr. and Mrs. David M. Fales, Mr. and Mrs. C. K. Giles, Prof. L. F. Griffin, and Moses L. Scudder. The result was another private school at the grade level. Allen C. Bell took over the institution in 1904. The name was changed to the "Bell School" about 1930. Another school had begun in 1927, called the "Lake Forest Day School." In 1958, after the retirement of Allen Bell, the two schools combined to form the "Lake Forest Country Day School."

THE Grand Army of the Republic, Lake Forest Post 676, was organized in 1889. Calvin Durand was the first Commander, B. F. Paullin was Post Adjutant. The year of its organization, the Post received the gift of a silk American Flag as a present from ten leading citizens of Lake Forest. The flag was unfurled for the first time on Memorial Day, 1889. In the 1920's, when the G.A.R. ceased to function, because of loss of membership through death, the flag was given to the newly organized American Legion. This flag was displayed in the Legion home until 1961 when it was placed in the Lake County Museum.

Commander Durand, who had been a member of the Chicago Board of Trade Battery, ambushed by Wheeler's cavalry near Atlanta and imprisoned in Andersonville and at Libby, made the annual Memorial Day address recounting the tribulations of the veteran and stressing the cost of liberty and democracy. Captain I. P. Rumsey, another leading member of the G.A.R. is remembered for his appearances on a beautiful white horse during patriotic occasions. His last public appearance was in April, 1916, on the birthday anniversary of General U. S. Grant, when he presented Lake Forest University an appropriate flag-pole, erected in front of the college library. The senior class of Lake Forest College supplied the flag. Captain W. A. Moffett, U.S.N., sent the Marine Band from Great Lakes. Lake Forest College's President,

John S. Nollen, made the speech of acceptance. The large gathering included the student body and many townspeople. Mayor William Mather Lewis, a graduate of Lake Forest College, made a speech of welcome. Captain Rumsey's son, Henry, became the builder and first President of the Chicago Board of Trade in the new building, in the late twenties, and served Lake Forest as Mayor.

IX

BUDDING CULTURE

1890–1900

In 1890 the United States census showed a population of 62,-622,250. Lake Forest boasted a population of 1,750, with an additional 250 students in the College, Academy and Ferry Hall. The city was without paved streets. The roads were in deep mud, and horses were continually in a lather from struggling through mire, often six inches deep. Most of the bridges across the ravines were about one hundred feet long. They were built of heavy timber trusses and floored with heavy planking. The roadbed of the bridges became a sounding board to the tread of steel-shod horses. It sounded like the beating of giant drums.

There were several stores in the 1890's lining the west side of Western Avenue and extending north about two blocks from Deer Path. These were generally brick structures replacing the frame buildings, which were burned out by the big fire of 1882.

James Anderson had the largest store in town. It was a general store and grocery, in a three story building where Walgreen Drug Store stands (1961). At this time oats could be purchased at 8¢ per bushel, corn 19¢, wheat 35¢, eggs 5¢ per dozen, milk at 1¢ per quart, and cream 6¢ per quart. Mr. Anderson was a fine, dignified, austere gentleman and a pioneer settler of Lake Forest.

Next in line was the Post Office in a little frame rented building. Miss Mary McLoughlin was postmistress for several decades.

The center of interest to the juveniles of those days was French's Drug Store, the predecessor of Martin's Drug Store. It contained a soda fountain offering three kinds of drinks: a phosphate was 5¢, an egg phosphate was 10¢, an ice cream and soda were 10¢. Mr. French introduced sundaes, first introduced by druggists in Evanston soon after the Chicago World's Fair. The press and pulpit fulminated and fussed over the degenerative effect of indulgence in such beverages.

O'Neill's Hardware held the greatest interest for the young men in town who admired the display of hunting equipment including firearms each autumn. Sam Blackler ran the meat market and before any bank was organized, it performed a sort of banking service for the town. There was considerable grumbling in those days because the price of round steak had gone up from 10¢ to 12½¢, and sirloin was raised to 15¢.

Wenban's was one of the most active spots in town. It included a livery stable, an undertaking establishment and the original fire department. Mr. Wenban and his sons, George and Fred, were the Czars of transportation in that age. One of them would act as guide or driver for hayrack rides and picnics to Diamond Lake or to Waukegan, by sleigh or by wagon at eventide or for an oyster supper at the old Washburn house. Sometimes when the roads were muddy, a four-horse team was used.

Frank Smith was the town barber, holding forth where the bank now stands. He was the only barber within eight miles. The standard fees were 10¢ per shave, 25¢ for haircuts. He was known to make special prices in wholesale lots. One family of four boys received haircuts for 65¢ provided they came at noon on Mondays. Frank was a student of human nature. He could tell whether a boy's allowance was 25¢ per week or a dollar. When it was the latter he tried for the whole dollar. Many a boy was talked into his first shave, and then persuaded to a tonic and a singe, and if Frank could go no higher, in services, he told of the real rugged he-men of the past, who always left a generous tip.

Another enterprising and versatile business man was Julian Matthews, who came from Virginia, riding in a box car loaded with fine horses. His first job was as coachman for Dr. William C. Roberts, President of Lake Forest College. In the 1890's Julian had a store on Western Avenue near the location of the present

Community Store. His family lived in the upstairs apartment. Downstairs he operated a restaurant and bakery, Mrs. Matthews presiding over the cooking and baking. Bread was sold to the Deerpath Inn when Mrs. Patterson was the proprietor. The waiters would eat the Matthews' bread themselves and serve inferior bread bought elsewhere to the guests. Bakery goods and ice cream, packed in ice, were delivered in Matthews' wagon. Bread was 6¢ a loaf, pies 20¢, doughnuts 12¢ per dozen.

Julian Matthews had a livery stable at the back of his restaurant. Livery charges were 25¢ to anywhere in town. For sightseeing, $2.50 per hour. He operated a "stake wagon" which he used to move summer residents from Chicago and back, changing teams in Evanston at the Butler Brothers Livery Stable. His stable burned to the ground, but the polo ponies and Matthews' own horses were saved, except two which insisted, by force of habit, on returning to the barn though it was in flames. There was danger that the Speidel barn nearby would catch fire. It would have been disastrous as kerosene was stored there.

Later the Matthews family moved to Illinois Road. During this interim Julian owned a spirited colt. One day the Matthews boys drove him uptown but forgot to weight him. A train standing in the station started up, as did the colt and his buggy. He raced south on muddy Western Avenue, without a driver, to the consternation of the passengers. He passed the train, then crossed the tracks turning east in front of the onrushing engine at Farwell crossing. Horse and buggy returned safely to the stable on Illinois Road.

Julian Matthews was a regular attendant at the horse shows at the Onwentsia Club with his ice cream wagon. When he went to the Academy football games, where the boys were partial to pie and ice cream, he soon learned not to leave the premises until he had carefully checked the harness and the traces because the boys were adept at practical jokes.

In August 1890 the double tracks of the Northwestern railroad were finished as far as Lake Forest. This improvement formed the basis of much comment, since it began as a left hand drive and has so remained for the first century. Many reasons have been advanced, including design by an Englishman and a larger commuting population on the lake side, but it must be noted that, after the Civil War, several railroads had left hand drives, including the New York Central, which was the only other large system to maintain the left hand drive for many years. The Northwestern began this system in 1890 and found it cheaper to maintain what it began than to build new stations on the other side of the tracks. Automatic block signals were installed to Waukegan in 1903.

A private water company was organized in 1890 to furnish water to the entire city. Bernard McGovern, who had come to Lake Forest directly from Ireland in 1887, was in charge of laying the first water mains. This led to the formation of the first fire brigade in Lake Forest in 1893 with William J. O'Neill, Sr., as fire chief. Claude Crippen was assistant chief, and Fred J. Wenban, captain. Other members included James King, C. T. Gunn, Joseph Anderson, George Anderson, John G. Hinge, William Lawson, and John E. Fitzgerald who was captain for many years. It was a volunteer organization with two small hose reels holding 350 feet of hose each, supplemented by picks, axes, and poles, mounted on carts and pushed by manpower. One of these units was housed at the Wenban Livery Stable, the other at College Hall, because town and University young men had volunteered for the formation of the hose companies. Soon more hose was added, and horses were used to transport the equipment.

An election for Mayor in 1891 pitted Mr. Calvin Durand against Mr. F. E. Hinckley. The former wanted cedar blocks for paving, the latter brick. Chicago had just installed cedar blocks in the loop area and they were proven to be quiet and well suited to horses and carriages. The brick pavement was recommended for its durability.

The major issue, however, arose after the sewer assessment of the previous year, when their estimates were found to be unequal. The issue had been fought out in court and the assessments levied by the City Council had been confirmed. Nevertheless the issue was kept alive in the election for Mayor. Mr. Hinckley of the "Reform Party" advocated reassessment. Mr. Durand of the "People's Party" advocated that the assessment promoted by the City Council be upheld. Newspaper articles appeared pro and con. The City Council issued hand bills stating that Mr. Hinckley's charges were unfounded due to his short residence in Lake Forest. There was feverish electioneering activity. Two hundred twenty-four votes were cast, the largest in the city up to that time. Mr. Durand won by 28 votes.

The sewer assessment was soon forgotten, but the cedar blocks were installed from the railroad station east on Deer Path and south on Mayflower Road to the Cyrus H. McCormick's. The blocks were cross sections of cedar logs, eight inches long, and varying in diameter from 6 to 10 inches. The foundation was about 15 inches, being one layer of slag, and two layers of crushed stone, and a course of sand, all watered down and rolled. The blocks were laid by hand and the chinks filled with tar poured by hand.

The result was a nice piece of pavement. It gave a good foothold for horses. A couple of miles were laid, which lasted about 20 years, though some patches remained until 1930. These new pavements were in keeping with the increasingly handsome equipages, lovely phaetons, the sprightly run-abouts, conventional closed carriages, and also for mounts.

Light sleepers could keep track of night life. One could hear a team leave the station and pound its way over the cedar block pavements to the Presbyterian Church, then across the bridge, on across the college campus and the Gym bridge, toward Ferry Hall and across the bridge there, beyond to the south toward McCormick's another large bridge, giving off a sound like distant thunder at night. Jules Knox took a job of unloading cedar blocks for 80¢ a day. On Sundays he and other young boys were invited to Sunday dinner at the home of the Mayor, where Mr. Durand would tell them tales of the Civil War. A few years later a cheaper pavement called water-bound macadam was introduced, and by 1900 there were probably ten miles of fair pavement in Lake Forest. The macadam roads were much quieter.

Board walks had been installed on the main thoroughfares even before 1860. In the 1880's the number of these increased so that nearly all the streets in and near the center of town were lined with these board walks. The college campus was adorned with its own board walks. They were purely utilitarian and ugly: two or three boards each twelve inches wide and two inches thick, but they were a comfort in bad weather.

The first cement sidewalk was laid by Henry C. Durand in

front of his house on Deer Path. He is said to have brought the idea from Pasadena, California. It was not supposed at that time that cement could stand freezing weather. Before the end of the decade all Lake Foresters became distinguished as sidewalk builders. The board walks of previous years were discarded. Cement was laid, everywhere, in any width the property owners chose. By the turn of the century the width was standardized, and the city built sidewalks, charging a special tax. E. Bailey, street commissioner, supervised an unusual amount of sidewalk construction.

Several college buildings were donated and erected during the 1890's. The Gymnasium, first in the Mid-west, containing that luxury of luxuries, a swimming pool, was erected in 1890, the gift of Senator C. B. Farwell. The following year the Durand Art Institute was built of the same red stone and by the same architect, Henry Ives Cobb, one of the leading architects in the country. It cost $50,000, a Romanesque building with brown stone walls and red tiled roof. The design was that of a central building with high, pointed roof and two gables projecting from it at right angles, the roofs of which are somewhat lower. This divided the building into three parts, one a gallery for pictures and statuary, one an auditorium with a capacity of 600, including a stage, a third part to house an art library and to provide rooms for the science department. This building provided a home for the Art Institute Club with many members from town and gown. Its purpose was to promote all the arts.

Lois Durand Hall, a dormitory for young women was built in 1897 after a wide study of dormitories used in various women's colleges. This, too, was the gift of Henry C. Durand in memory of his mother. The Lily Reid Holt Memorial Chapel and the Arthur Somerville Reid Memorial Library were built in the gothic style in 1899, the gifts of Mrs. Simon Somerville Reid. The Chapel and Library are connected by a cloistered colonnade and "have the effect of one structure, the tower of the Chapel crowning them both with grace." The material used in their construction was Bedford stone. Frost and Granger were the architects. The gifts for nearly all these buildings came as a result of Dr. J. G. K. McClure's requests for them. Several hundred vines, shrubbery and trees were planted on the college campus through the gift of Byron L. Smith.

The College and the Academy were growing rapidly, numerically and in prestige, causing congestion on the limited campus. Both used many of the same facilities: the Gym, the Library, the tennis courts and the other athletic fields. Football and baseball had their beginning on the old field, behind the original Academy building at the intersection of Sheridan Road and Deer Path. In 1890 Knowlton (Snake) Ames and Ben Donnelly, famous football players from Princeton came to show the Academy and College teams the finer points of the game. One of the great athletes of the Academy, then later at the College, was Marion Woolsey. He became a construction engineer for the New York Central Railroad. He returned to Lake Forest long enough to supervise the laying of water mains and sewers in Lake Forest. He also installed the first steam lines for the College, Ferry Hall and the Academy.

The sport mecca, throughout the winter months, was the Farwell Pond, fed by an artesian well. When the ice was good, it was crowded with dozens of merrymakers. The well was capped with a spraying fountain near one end, which kept a bit of water not frozen over. On frequent occasions some youngster would get too near this water and in he would go. Then it was a major operation to drag the victim out.

An interesting summer sport was practised by several groups of young men who secured coaches, each with a team of fast horses. With eight men in each coach all dressed up with vest and top hat, they raced around the "square." The starting point was the railroad station, west on Deer Path, north on Telegraph Road (Waukegan Road), east on present route 176 and south on Green Bay Road and back to the Station. The second coach reversed the route. The first coach back to the station was the winner. These were sometimes known as opposition coaches. One of these sportsmen was Dr. George Fiske, whose home was on Fiske Hill just north of Sacred Heart Academy. Sheridan Road at that point went steeply down to the ravine bottom and up at a very sharp incline; the early autos could hardly make this hill. Dr. Fiske was an eye, nose and "bridge" specialist. He played bridge at the University Club with his Derby hat on.

In 1892 the Academy was moved to a new campus, its third, a quarter of a mile south of the College campus, on Sheridan Road.

133

With the growth of both these institutions, the College and the Academy, on the same limited campus, with increased activities, the pranks and never ending horseplay of the Academy boys became a continual and increasing annoyance to the more mature college students and faculty. When the Academy moved, the two institutions began separate careers. Now the athletic teams were completely separated, and the two institutions maintained separate faculties. They did have the same board of Trustees until 1925, when these became legally separated.

On June 8, 1893, three new Academy buildings, on the new campus, were dedicated. Pond and Pond of Chicago designed the buildings. George H. Holt was the chairman of the building committee. Annie Durand Cottage was the gift of Henry C. Durand. Mrs. Durand furnished the building throughout with new furniture. East House, the second dormitory, was financed from funds advanced by members of the Board of Trustees of Lake Forest University and others. Reid Hall, the recitation-chapel-office building was the gift of the Simon Reids. The upstairs classroom windows were so high that a student could not be distracted except by the flight of occasional birds and the waving of the uppermost branches of the trees. This innovation was considered a very important advance in classroom construction. In 1894 another dormitory was completed, the Eliza Remsen Cottage, the gift of Ezra J. Warners, named for Mrs. Warner's sister who died during her college days. The Academy buildings were also the result of Dr. McClure's untiring efforts. The new Academy campus, in addition, contained a well drained football field, and three tennis courts. The entire area was planted with trees, shrubs and vines, through the generosity of Mr. and Mrs. L. W. Yaggy.

The separation of the Academy released the old Academy building and the building known as Academia which had been used for an Academy dining hall, for the use of the College. In 1893 Dr. A. C. Haven established the Haven Gold Medal for the best Academy Commencement Oration and Prof. A. C. McNeill established a prize of Fifty Dollars for the best essay in English.

The Rush Medical College building was finished in 1893, "a beautiful and commodious building." The corner stone of the Dental College building was laid and provided accommodation for "the most numerously attended Dental School in the world." Both these structures were a block west of the Presbyterian Hospital, in Chicago.

The center of all interest in 1893 was Chicago's Columbian Exposition. It celebrated the landing of Columbus in America. It came a year too late; nevertheless, it was a triumph achieved by the Chicago city fathers, affecting the city and its environs in many ways. The location was Jackson Park, and the dominating note was the classical architecture, comprising 150 buildings. It was called the White City.

One of the most popular buildings was the Columbian Museum, containing birds and beasts, ores and precious stones from all over the world, and a rare American Indian collection. Two permanent institutions may be said to have descended from it— the Museum of Science and Industry and the Field Museum of Natural History.

The cultural influence of the Fair was instantaneous. In Lake Forest, works of art began to adorn the walls and fringed mantle pieces. These were copies of famous European paintings and statuary of the period, some of which were created in Chicago on the spot and visitors purchasing them arrived home with proof that they had been at the Fair. French, Chinese, Italian and Japanese art objects, some useful, some ornamental, appeared in quantity in nearly every home. Rooms were rearranged, additions were sometimes built, to make room for these new acquisitions.

The younger generation was attracted by the mass of humanity, the teeming activity and the bizarre entertainment of all kinds afforded by the Fair. Many Lake Forest boys availed themselves of the opportunity to earn a few dollars. One boy, Johnathan J. Jackson, was a guide, at the princely and unheard of salary of $15.00 per week. He was also a conductor on a train which ran around the perimeter of the grounds, and occasionally an engineer and fireman on the little steam engine that hauled the four car trains. This railroad track was four miles long.

There was the famous "Streets of Cairo," with its "Little Egypt" and dancers. Here Billy Rose got his start as a circus man. In Igorote Village a group of untamed South Sea Savages spent the summer in peace. Buffalo Bill Cody's Wild West Show was especially attractive to the very young boys. There was the Ferris Wheel, Madam Farley's Wax Works, trained seals, Venetian glass blowers and gondolas, and Russian Cossacks and dancers. On a memorable day in October, the turnstiles checked in over a million people. The Fair was notable for its introduction of electric lighting. Strings of naked bulbs were everywhere.

Then there was the quick lunch, a new idea introduced by H. H. Kohlsaat, the Chicago restaurant man. From then on wheat cakes were to take their place in the American diet. A big stack of them with lots of butter and maple syrup for 10¢ furnished the sustenance of many a visitor to the Fair. Kohlsaat's first quick lunch restaurant was on Randolph Street, at the entrance to the Illinois Central Station where trains left every few minutes for the Fair grounds at Jackson Park, eight miles away.

MANY substantial business contacts were due to the Chicago World's Fair. It was here that Albert B. Dick, soon to become a Lake Forest resident, and Thomas A. Edison met to lay the foundations of a typically American small but successful enterprise.

A. B. Dick had a thriving lumber business in Chicago in the 1870's. Because of this, he wished to send out 50 letters per day to his customers, describing his merchandise and quoting prices. When printing proved costly, he devised a simple duplicating process which he called: "Autographic stencils." He soon discovered that the more letters he mailed, the more lumber sales resulted.

Thomas Alva Edison was contacted and a friendship grew between the two men. Gradually A. B. Dick abandoned the lumber business and devoted full time to the duplicating business. In 1893 the two men met at the Chicago World's Fair, where further progress resulted from the adoption of Edison's "electric pen," a small pointed steel shaft with a rapidly vibrating needle at the point driven by an electric motor which in turn was powered by galvanic batteries. It made 8,000 perforations per minute on a sheet of paper which now became a stencil. By rolling ink over the stencil, it was duplicated on the sheet below. Edison made the stencils more durable by coating them with wax. He released several of his patents for use to A. B. Dick. The result was essentially the present A. B. Dick & Company Mimeograph. On May 5, 1884, the first officers of the A. B. Dick & Company had been elected. After the Fair, the duplicating process was a successful new business. The objective of the Company has since been "the delivery of well-printed duplicates of letters and forms, easily, rapidly and inexpensively."

The railroad companies were among the first to accept the advantages of the new process. Other businesses followed. Gradually the new stencils were adjusted to the rotary Mimeograph, introduced in 1900, and to the typewriter. The discovery of long and soft fibers of a species of hazel brush, grown in Japan, improved the stencil. Then chemical stencils were introduced in 1924. Today, electrically driven Mimeographs duplicate 1,000 sheets in an hour.

IN MAY 1894 occurred the Pullman Car strike in the Chicago area. It started with the reduction of wages among the employees of the Pullman Car Company, but soon spread so that there were only a few trains operating between Lake Forest and Chicago. If one could take a train to Chicago there was no guarantee of returning. There was almost a complete tie-up of all traffic as far as the West coast. On July 3, out of 91 trains due at the Northwestern station, only 16 arrived. There was violence in Chicago and the southern suburbs; hundreds of people were injured and there was heavy property damage. On July 5, President Grover Cleveland sent out federal troops from Fort Sheridan to the south side, to restore order and to maintain the movement of the mails. Traffic was restored within a few days. Governor J. P. Altgeld of Illinois, a man of high ideals, a wealthy social and political reformer, but considered radical by nature, took sides with Eugene V. Debs, the labor leader, who had ordered the strike. Altgeld interpreted the President's action as an anti-labor and unconstitutional interference with states' rights, but Cleveland insisted he wished only to keep mail trains moving. Eugene V. Debs appeared in the First Presbyterian Church of Lake Forest, in overalls, which did not suit him, and attempted to justify the strike to the people of Lake Forest.

THE MARRIAGE OF Miss Nellie Durand of Lake Forest was an important social event in 1894; but it caused a considerable amount of misgivings to her parents, since the groom was a Democrat. Some of the ushers and the best man were entertained at the

Holt's home, "The Homestead," just south of the home of the bride. At this time smoking, drinking, and card playing were frowned upon by all the Presbyterian families. When the best man could wait no longer to have his smoke, he and his ushers from Milwaukee retired to their bedroom fireplace to snatch some peaceful enjoyment.

OCTOBER 10, 1894, was another red letter day for Lake Forest. This was the day of the Temperance March. The question of temperance first appeared in the Chicago area when New England Puritanism met the Irish and German liberalism in the rough and ready days of the Illinois-Michigan Canal building period. The June 11, 1845, issue of the Waukegan *Porcupine* complained that "It is a fact too notorious to be concealed that our town contains seven places where liquor is sold, yet we have not even one church." On October 9 of the same year, a meeting was called at the Methodist Church in Libertyville to organize the promoters of temperance. The temperance question aroused great interest among the people of the Chicago area until the slavery issue became all absorbing. In 1880 temperance once more became a burning issue and the growth of the W.C.T.U. during the 1890's was phenomenal. In its wake many other organizations sprang up with the same general purpose, culminating in the all powerful Anti-Saloon League twenty years later.

The leaders of the 1894 Temperance March were the presidents of Lake Forest University, Northwestern University, the University of Chicago, and the Roman Catholic Societies. They had proposed a parade in Chicago which was to be composed of volunteers, all students. The March hoped to include 2,000 students, and wished to protest the 7,000 saloons of Chicago and their influence on City Hall.

About $200 was collected in Lake Forest, to pay for transportation of the students and the Fort Sheridan Band. The donors included Sam Blackler, E. Buckingham, Ambrose Cramer, Calvin Durand, Henry C. Durand, John H. Dwight, Mrs. F. E. Goodhart, John H. Hamline, J. S. Hannah, D. R. Holt, William H. Hubbard, Dr. James G. K. McClure, Cyrus H. McCormick, Arthur Reid and his sisters, I. P. Rumsey, Mrs. Byron L. Smith, Ezra J. Warner, C. J. Weaver, C. G. Wenban, and L. W. Yaggy.

Upon arrival in Chicago the Band formed and led the parade. Lake Forest students followed, led by Israel P. Rumsey. The Roman Catholic Societies followed, about two hundred boys in all. But the Methodists from Evanston never appeared, nor the Baptists from the Midway. The parade marched across Kinzie Street, then known as Saloon Row. Men rushed out of the saloons and tried to force the paraders to drink, spilling beer on many. The parade ended on State Street at the old Central Music Hall, where Marshall Field's now stands. A continuous session was held afternoon and evening. John R. Mott of Y.M.C.A. fame was the master of ceremonies. Toward evening rowdyism got out of hand, and police came in from all sides to maintain order. Still later, several thousands congregated around State Street and in the Hall to watch the spectacle.

X

UTILITIES

1895–1900

On June 25, 1894, Waukegan received a charter for a small steam railroad which was to operate within that city. By the following year when service began, the line was extended northward to Kenosha, and by 1899 south to Highland Park. The Lake Forest City Council approved the franchise to the Bluff City Electric Street Railway Company, as it was then called, on September 15, 1897. The Council received $10,000 for granting this franchise. Originally three cars were operated, very small by modern standards, attaining speeds up to ten miles per hour. Eventually, when the line was electrified, it operated as the Chicago and North Shore Line. Around the turn of the century, there was no overpass across Illinois Road: the train came down to the level of the street, then up on the other side. A freight house was located near Illinois Road. The viaduct for the line was erected in 1898. By 1919 the name was changed to the Chicago, North Shore and Milwaukee Railway and operated between the Chicago Loop and Milwaukee, Wisconsin, and boasted of some 130 cars.

In 1895, when a City ordinance granted E. F. Chapin, J. B. Durand and M. L. Scudder "the right to erect and maintain a telephone system in the City of Lake Forest, for 15 years," John Chapman arrived from Chicago representing the Chicago Telephone Company. He installed the first telephones in Lake Forest. The first telephones were difficult to sell as no one wanted one if there was no one to talk to. This condition was soon remedied and Chapman lived in a little room in the back of Hogue's Drug Store (later French's) and here he became the first night operator in Lake Forest. A young lady, name forgotten, took over the switchboard during the daytime. By the end of the first year 25 telephones were installed in Lake Forest and the same number in Highland Park and in Glencoe. Due to the winding streets and ravines in Lake Forest, the erection of poles and stringing of wires was especially difficult. Chapman became a resident in Lake Forest, remaining until his death in 1960.

When Hogue, the pharmacist, became the manager in 1896, a direct line to Chicago was established so that remarkably quick service was possible. That year the number of telephones doubled, requiring a total of 77 miles of wire and 507 poles. In 1899 George T. Gibbons became the manager of the Company in Lake Forest. He handled a special project of providing additional equipment to serve the National Golf Tournament at the Onwentsia Club in July of that year. At the time the total subscribers had increased to 113. In 1961 there were 5,531 telephone poles and about 6,000 subscribers.

In 1896 the population of Lake Forest was 1,980, including 894 males and 1,086 females. There were 705 boys and girls under 21, 565 under 16, and 269 under six.

Among the population during the 1890's were two town characters known to everybody. One was James Gordon, the first Lake Forest police officer in the modern sense. He operated on foot and sometimes on a bicycle. He was appointed in 1895. Another popular citizen was The Rev. Washington Adams Nichols, an Amherst graduate and a retired Congregationalist minister. He came to Lake Forest because of its high literary and moral tone and conducted a boarding grade school in the 1860's. Many remember him in a front pew in the Presbyterian Church when he tapped his cane saying "Amen, Amen!" whenever he thought the minister had preached long enough. He lived in a house on the grounds of the present Library where he conducted studies in Isaiah before a group composed of Mrs. Z. Humphrey, Mrs. Norman B.

Judd, Mrs. Walter Larned, Mrs. C. B. Farwell and others. When they were not eager to continue after a year's study, Rev. Nichols was disappointed and said: "What will I say to Isaiah when I see him in heaven?" When he passed away at the age of 93, it was said of him that he had done as much for building up Lake Forest as any man of his day.

The business men of the period included Charles C. Pratt who operated a laundry, which was later continued by Fred Held. It was in this Bank Lane laundry building, that the first issues of *The Lake Forester* were printed, on the second floor. G. L. Smith was the barber. F. C. Calvert and Son were florists. Mrs. Robinson and Moffert operated a restaurant. H. L. Hogue and Dr. G. G. French were pharmacists. Karl M. Rasmussen was a shoe dealer. Dr. J. C. Giltner was a dentist. Ruben and Goldberg had a confectionery store. R. C. Wirth was a butcher. F. N. Pratt sold insurance, rentals and real estate. M. Fitzgerald sold cigars and tobacco. F. C. Richards & Son sold dry goods, groceries, crockery, flour, boots, shoes, caps, hay, straw, and feed. Fred Weis was a tailor. James Anderson operated a general store, selling lumber, building materials, dry goods, groceries, hats, caps, boots, shoes, furnishing goods, and hardware. Dr. C. H. Francis was a medical doctor. John O'Leary took care of plumbing and heating. P. Coughlin, J. Grady and A. McVay were blacksmiths. T. Eastwood sold cigars and confections. C. G. Wenban conducted a livery, as did George Fitzgerald. William J. O'Neill did the tinning, furnace work and roofing. C. T. Gunn conducted a cash grocery. Joseph Barnet sold wood and coal. Charles R. Mills was a harness manufacturer and bicycle dealer. Frank Wondrak repaired wagons and carriages.

The 1896 Mayor was Edward P. Gorton. The Aldermen were Prof. Walter R. Bridgeman, Calvin Durand, David Fales, T. S. Fauntleroy, L. H. W. Speidel, and C. G. Wenban. This Council established the North School for primary grades at the north end of present Sheridan Road on the east side. Children in this area had to walk much too far to reach the West School which they had been attending. The land was purchased from Andreas Anderson. The North School was later sold and became the recreation hall of Thorpe Academy in the late 1920's.

On March 24, 1896, the City Council passed another resolution on the perennial subject of sand and gravel along the beach. It stated:

No person shall take, remove, carry away, any sand, gravel, clay, or other material, from any part of the beach, between the bluffs and the water's edge of Lake Michigan, in the City of Lake Forest, except at that part of the beach opposite Forest Park. Under penalty of $25.00, nor more than $100 for each offense.

One of the outstanding Academy boys of those days was Siegfried E. Gruenstein, who first came to Lake Forest in 1891, when he was 14 years old, and became the organist of the First Presbyterian Church when he could barely reach the foot pedals. He served as organist and Director of Music for forty-eight years. Besides having a great love of music, "Sig" as the boys called him, had an editorial mind and a printer's devil's sense of humor. In 1894 he and Johnathan Jackson published *The Commencement Bulletin*, a daily which claimed to be the first school daily in America. The only printer in those days was a Mr. Coon of Waukegan. The paper was published again during commencement week the following year. This publication was a companion of the college magazine which was a weekly affair. The latter gave news of the College, Academy, and Ferry Hall, but there was need for a publication for the townspeople of Lake Forest.

In 1896, a meeting was held in the Brewster House, later called Deerpath Inn, which stood opposite the present Library. Prof. Walter R. Bridgeman of the College faculty had conceived the idea of a newspaper as a supplement to the college publication, which soon developed into the town's weekly periodical. Prof. Bridgeman asked for suggestions. Miss Ellen Holt proposed the name *The Lake Forester*. S. S. Speer began the publication of *The Lake Forester* on July 16, 1896. In the meantime Siegfried Gruenstein had induced D. W. Hartman to come to Lake Forest to print the College *Stentor* for 1896. Julian Matthews helped Mr. Hartman set up his printing press and the two publications went into production. *The Lake Forester* has had many editors and managers since its beginning. Mr. Gruenstein went on to become a journalist on the staffs of several newspapers and later founded and edited *The Diapason*, the only nationally known and accredited journal for organists.

HOBART CHATFIELD-TAYLOR, Senator C. B. Farwell's son-in-law, brought added distinction to Lake Forest by publishing fourteen books, several on foreign subjects. In 1892–1894 he was an Honorary Consul of Spain in Chicago. He served as Secretary of the Inaugural reception of the Columbian Exposition.

In 1896 he organized the Onwentsia Club. Its humble beginnings date from 1893 when he erected a seven hole golf course on the bluff along the lake in Lake Park. The first holes were tomato cans. In November of the following year, with increased interest in the game, the Lake Forest Golf Club was organized. Hobart Chatfield-Taylor was elected President. Charles F. Smith was one of the moving spirits. Robert Foulis, a Scotsman and a professional golfer, was secured, and a nine hole course was laid out on the Leander McCormick farm on Green Bay Road including 175 acres. The course had no bunkers but contained a very unpopular water hole within sight of the first club house which had previously served as a sheep pen and a chicken coop. Sheep grazed nearby. The Chicago and Northwestern tracks ran along the second hole. President Chatfield-Taylor promoted the Indian name Onwentsia, signifying a meeting place for braves and their squaws. The club members voted in favor of this change.

In 1896 the Henry Ives Cobb home and farm were secured, including two hundred acres; the home becoming the first suitable club house. Grass tennis courts were now installed. The first annual Fourth of July fireworks on the Onwentsia grounds took place in 1896. There was music all evening. In 1897 a yearbook containing the rules of the club was published which included the rule: "No golf games shall be played or practised on the Club grounds on Sunday." Another rule forbade the playing of any games of chance in the clubhouse. The annual dues at this time were $35.00. The United States Golf Association Amateur Golf championship was played at Onwentsia in 1899. H. M. Harriman was the winner.

Onwentsia Polo originated in 1896. It was played on Ferry Field at the north end of town near Sheridan Road. The originators were W. Vernon Booth, Charles G. King, William W. Rathbone and George A. Seaverns, Jr. These were soon joined by Frederick McLaughlin, Edward Hasler, Robert and Medill McCormick and Clive Runnells. Gus Malmquist brought the first polo ponies to Lake Forest. Before World War I, Frederick Mc-Laughlin was considered the outstanding player in the Mid-west, an 8 goal man. General George S. Patton, of World War II fame, played polo on the Fort Riley team about 1910 in Lake Forest. Polo was revived after World War I by Lawrence Armour, John Borden, Charles Glore and Earle Reynolds. An International Polo Tournament was held at the Onwentsia Club in July 1931. East-West Tournaments were held in August 1933 and July 1934.

SEVERAL beautiful homes were built in Lake Forest during the 1890's. The Henry Ives Cobb house, built in 1890, was the first to utilize a view westward from Green Bay Road with beautiful vistas and gorgeous "Italian" sunsets. Soon the Onwentsia Club members enjoyed the house and grounds. In a few years the entire western border of Green Bay Road was lined with homes some of which were actually outside of the Lake Forest city limits until by 1912 it was all included in Lake Forest from the northern extremity of the city to Westleigh Road on the south.

The Presbyterian parsonage was not noted for beauty of architecture as it was a large frame building and looked more like a country hotel. However, it was a very busy home in Lake Forest used for entertaining frequently. It was located in the area just west of the present Market Square. This property was bought by James Anderson, Sr., when the property next to the Church was acquired by the Presbyterians for a new parsonage, and the original site has since provided the space for the present Post Office, Marshall Field & Company, and the Recreation Center.

Levi Yaggy built his home on Mayflower Road in 1890, just south of the Rosemary corner. Mr. Yaggy visited Switzerland in the summer of 1891 where he saw a beautiful maze made with bushes. He secured the plans and upon his return to Lake Forest erected one in his garden, much to the entertainment of the youth of Lake Forest.

Granger Farwell built a handsome colonial home on the corner of Sheridan and Rosemary, in 1892. The general design and plan was copied from *Westover*, the ancestral home of the Byrd family since 1691, on the James River, in Virginia. Robert G. McGann built a large frame summer house on Lake Road and Jessie L. Moss built "Meadowcroft" on the corner of Mayflower and Maple, both in 1892. Carter H. Fitzhugh built "Insley" on Mayflower in 1893. William Henry Smith built "Lost Rock," an excellent copy of a Virginia Colonial on Green Bay Road, north of the Onwentsia Club. The property contains the largest glacier boulder in Lake County. This house was finished in 1894. T. S. Fauntleroy built "Parkhurst" on Woodland and Sheridan Roads, in 1894. This house was soon and for long occupied by the E. A. Russell family. Mr. and Mrs. David B. Jones opened "Pembroke Hall" on Green Bay Road, just west of St. Mary's Church, in 1895.

Byron L. Smith built "Briar Hall" on the lake, in 1894. He had been among the many who had rented houses during the summer, from 1885 on. Mr. Smith had an agreement with young Harry Durand, who with his pair of shetland ponies picked him up and took him regularly to the 8:00 o'clock train for a fee. Mr. Smith, a large man, filled up the whole back seat in the pony cart. He was also known as the greatest practical joker in town.

Mr. Smith was a great friend of the Arnolds of Boston, whose father, James Arnold of New Bedford, Massachusetts, had set aside a large sum of money with which the Arnold Arboretum (of Harvard University) was established, in Boston, in 1872. The Arboretum occupied 265 acres of rolling country and contained 6000 varieties of trees, bushes and vines from four continents. When "Briar Hall" was finished, many varieties were shipped from the Arnold Arboretum and were planted on the Smith property in Lake Forest. Some of these flourished in Lake Forest; others were more successful in Boston. The beautiful trees of the 1961 Smith property include: Arbor vitae; aromatic sumac; European and single leaf ash; birch; Brewer spruce; Chinese lilac; cucumber tree; cut leaf Linden; double-flowering horse chestnut; English elm; European elder; European linden; false cypress; hickory; Norway, pink velvet, schwedler and sweet gum maple; mockorange group; mulberry, red cedar; slippery elm; yellow horse chestnut; and many others. Several of these species found their way to other parts of Lake Forest as Mr. Smith had more saplings than he could use on his own property.

Cyrus H. McCormick, (Jr.), built "Walden" in 1896, in the area in the south-east corner of Lake Forest. The architect was Stanford White who had designed the Madison Square Garden, the Madison Square Presbyterian Church, the Herald Square

building, the Washington Arch and the Century Club, all in New
York. He renovated the White House in Washington, D.C., in
1902. "Walden" was on generous proportions, but unpretentious.
It was in the English Cottage style of architecture with tile especially made to look as though it was moss covered shingles. The
several chimneys were tapestry brick. Lawns and a semi-circular
pergola led to gardens and service houses on Westleigh Road.
There were dairy cow barns on Ringwood, where also seasoned
firewood was carefully classified and stored.

The house and grounds were most charming in a natural way;
the pergola was planted with wild flowers. There were attractive
vistas in all directions; westward to the ravines lined with oak,
maple and pine, eastward to the shores of the lake and out to the
endless horizon; or one could stand on "the point" from which one
could get a sweep of the Lake Michigan shore line northward and
south. This "Look-out" over the lake resembled one in Ravello,
Italy. The estate contained a half dozen steel-concrete private
bridges crossing ravines, ivy covered. There were thirty miles of
private roads, bridle paths, and other paths which Lake Forest
residents were permitted to use and to enjoy, surrounded with
myriads of wild flowers, artfully planted, so that nature received
all the credit and human skill and good taste were not immediately
apparent.

J. V. Farwell, Jr., built "Ardleigh," just to the north of
"Walden," in the same year. Ambrose Cramer built "Rathmore,"
just north of "Ardleigh." Edward F. Carry built "Broad Lea" on
Green Bay Road. The following year, 1897, Charles S. Frost, the
architect, built two homes on Westminster, just east of Sheridan
Road, one being his own "Eastover." Howard Van Doren Shaw,
another celebrated architect, built "Ragdale" on Green Bay Road.
Alfred Granger designed and built his home on the corner of
Westminster and Sheridan and called it "Woodleigh." The Alfred
L. Bakers built "Little Orchard" in 1898, on Mayflower Road, on
the bluff.

The house most appreciated by the students in this period was
"The Lilacs," the home of Mr. and Mrs. Simon Somerville Reid
who lived across the street from the College campus. A spacious
lawn swept three sides of the grounds, which contained many
lilac bushes. During the spring blossoming season, the whole area

was fragrant with blossoms. Mrs. Reid frequently entertained faculty and students, promoting a friendly spirit among the various groups in town.

ELECTRICITY was brought to Lake Forest by the Highland Park Electric Light Company, to light the residences of Cyrus H. McCormick, J. V. Farwell, Jr., Frank Farwell, and J. A. Miller. First tested on July 15, 1896, it was hoped that soon other residences and the beautiful streets would all be lighted by electricity. Two years later a few electric street lights were installed, which were turned off on moonlit nights. Between 1:00 a.m. and 4:00 a.m. all electric power was turned off for purposes of conservation.

Lake Forest was dotted with primitive refrigeration in the form of ice houses. The Farwell Pond furnished two or three crops of ice each winter. Another source was a much larger pond in Lake Bluff. If families did not own an ice house, they had a reliable ice box. The ice man, in his leather jacket, made his rounds two or three times weekly, while his horses waited meekly in front of each house and the ice wagon stood dripping. Milkmen delivered their wares, but as yet there were no milk bottles or any container furnished by the milk company. The customer supplied a pitcher and the milkman measured the milk with a tin dipper. Butter was delivered in stone crocks. Dr. Clifford Barnes and Barat College owned the last cows east of the railroad track. With the death of Dr. Barnes, in 1944, came the end of the tradition of private milk supplies for each family.

For lighting the larger homesteads, a rather elaborate system was required. A 100-gallon tank was sunk at a distance from the house. This tank held the gasoline which was forced by an ingenious method into the basement of the residence where it was forced again through a primitive carburetor, which created an inflammable gas, which in turn was fed into a drum. From this drum it was conveyed by pipes throughout the house. The pipes terminated in wall fixtures with burners, and the gas was often carried by tubes into the kitchen and there used as fuel. The fixtures were later equipped with the famous old Welsbach Mantles which gave off the last word in illumination, before the turn of the century. The gasoline was delivered in oak barrels of 60 gallons.

The Academy After the Civil War

Samuel Fisher Miller,
Engineer, Surveyor,
Postmaster,
Academy Principal

Sylvester Lind,
Mayor four times

The New Deer Path School, 1955, Partially Landscaped

"The Eight O'Clock" Train,
1909

The First Northwestern Train,
1855

Henry Durand Family,
1890

Simon Reid Residence on Sheridan Road, 1900

1913 Football Team

School Boys, 1880:
Harry Durand,
Preston McClanahan,
Scott Durand

1889 Football Team, Victors Over Northwestern and Chicago

Lake Forest Day Promote
Robert Oliver
  (Legion)
Dr. T. S. Proxmire
  (Originator)
Mrs. M. C. Lackie
  (Woman's Club)

Peter Page,
Pioneer Lake Forest
Promoter

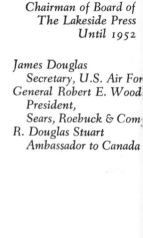

Thomas E. Donnelley,
President and Later
Chairman of Board of
The Lakeside Press
Until 1952

James Douglas
  Secretary, U.S. Air For
General Robert E. Wood
  President,
  Sears, Roebuck & Com
R. Douglas Stuart
  Ambassador to Canada

ALMOST EVERYONE worked in the Church and taught Sunday School in those days. There were lavish luncheons, dinners and receptions. The Art Institute Club was an important social and cultural outlet throughout the nineties. Its basic purpose was the study of art. Walter C. Larned started the group, and Prof. John J. Halsey was a leader and director for many years. The club met in various homes every two weeks where a lecture was given, attended by nearly all the leading citizens of Lake Forest and the professors of the University. The club had originated at the suggestion of Mrs. Z. M. Humphrey. Quite a library was collected and several prominent lecturers appeared before the Institute after the building of the Durand Art Institute.

Sunday evening services at the African Methodist Church were an attraction. Boys had to get permission to attend these meetings. The singing of the colored people and the receiving of the offering were interesting. Two officers of the Church took seats at the end of the table in front of the pulpit. Each person arose, went to the front and laid his offering on the table. The Academy boys came last. They made quite a show as they marched up in a body to deposit their offerings. "Guv" Marshall, the former janitor of the original Academy building, was an officer of this church and was noted for his most sincere prayers, which he delivered aloud, leading the others. Many white people attended services and Sunday School at the African Methodist Church because it was in their own neighborhood and they appreciated the simplicity and sincerity of the little congregation. This was the only Colored church in Lake Forest until the organization of the First Baptist Church, around the turn of the century.

In the 1890's occurred several debuts in Lake Forest, following the city pattern. At one party of three parts, three young ladies were presented. Miss Frances Larned, "tall and fair, of graceful carriage and a graciousness of manner that has an indefinable magnetism"; Miss Florence Dwight, "who is rather of a brunette type"; and Miss Marion Hall, "who is a little above the medium height, is bright and piquant, and has wonderfully expressive brown eyes." Miss Larned had graduated from Dobbs Ferry, Miss Dwight from Ogontz and had spent the past winter in Europe, Miss Hall from the Rye School outside of New York City. Each was introduced at afternoon tea, extending into a party in the evening for all the young people. Sixty young men and women were invited, many coming from Chicago on a special train. They were driven by carriage from the station to the three homes, then to dinner parties, and then to Mrs. Larned's dance. After the round of parties, they were driven to the station for the trip back to Chicago.

Miss Isabel Scribner, the daughter of Mr. Charles Scribner, the New York publisher, and later Mrs. Carter Fitz-Hugh, made her debut at the home of her sister, Mrs. Walter C. Larned at "Blair Lodge." The house was beautifully decorated with Christmas greens as four foot logs burned away in the fireplace as a welcome to the many guests. Johnny Hand's orchestra furnished the music for the evening's dancing. A unique feature of the entertainment was a "gypsy tent" in which fortunes were told. Miss Scribner wore a "white costume somewhat after the Greek fashion, without sleeves, and gracefully draped in classic folds." Miss Scribner, a tall graceful blonde, had made her home with the Larneds since the death of her mother.

The Journal (Chicago) published an interview with a Lake Forest resident on the subject of Lake Forest women. He said:

> Yes, those ladies there you ask about are from Lake Forest. Never mind their names; they are not anxious to appear in print. Lake Forest ladies all dress well; they are all smart and all good-looking. When you see them together you may not see much difference in them. But put them alongside of a Philadelphia or Boston or Baltimore woman and you will see the difference. They have got better blood than the Philadelphia women, they know more than the Boston women, and they are better looking than the Baltimore women.
>
> I know these women like a book, and their equals in all that makes up a real woman don't live on earth. I'm not talking of what makes a show in society, tho' even when it comes to that you will never be ashamed of them, but they are women that take possession of your home when you are in trouble; that fill your heart till it almost breaks —with kindness. You will find them where there is sickness and death and poverty. Why, some of them leave a streak of sunshine wherever they go. They hunt up sick and outcast and friendless. If I should tell of the kind acts of some of them you would think I was crazy. And all the while they don't seem to think they are doing anything. There is a more enduring pen than yours, sir, writing their record, and some day that record will be read.

The homey type of entertainment, patriotic and melancholy, was popular amusement for all Lake Foresters, as all seem to have taken part. One such extended evening in April, 1889, is described, when fifty youths under the direction of Charles S. Holt, with the accomplished accompanist, Miss Kate B. Skinner, rendered stirring patriotic choruses with spirit and precision. This chorus was composed of Academy and College students and Lake Forest citizens. Dr. George F. Root, the veteran composer, sang "The Battle Cry of Freedom." William L. Tomlins sang with splendid effect, "The Battle Hymn of the Republic." Mrs. Abbie F. Ferry sang an exceedingly popular number, "Drafted into the Army" and then "Jimmie has gone to live in a tent." Miss Jennie Durand sang beautifully, "The Swanee River," with a pretty harp accompaniment of Miss Lucy Rumsey. Miss Durand also sang the "Star Spangled Banner" as the audience waved flags which had been previously distributed. Miss Louise Learned sang "Tenting on the Old Camp Ground," with a trumpet prelude by Lloyd M. Bergen. Miss S. Rhea sang "When this Cruel War is Over," accompanied by Miss F. Rhea on the guitar. Readings included "Wake Nicodemus" by W. C. Larned; "Babylon is Fallen," by George H. Steele; "When Johnny Comes Marching Home," by W. D. McMillan. They were all rendered by Messrs. Benedict and Danforth. Messrs. Steele, Armour, Smith and Stroh touchingly sang the familiar quartet, "Just before the Battle, Mother." Mr. Calvin Durand spoke a few well chosen patriotic words. Mr. Holt's Academy and College chorus then ended the program, as they sang with enthusiasm "Tramp, Tramp, Tramp"; "The Battle Cry of Freedom," "Tenting in the Old Camp Ground," "Marching Through Georgia," and "The Battle Hymn of the Republic." "The audience dispersed with a greater love for country, more appreciation of its cost and value, and with their patriotic impulses aroused and strengthened."

The schools introduced a grand affair which was called "The Promenáde." It was held in the new Gym and all the young people in town were invited. It was a gala affair. The boys attended in their best regalia and filled out their programs. Couples then formed in line and marched around the Gym floor. It was a long procession, severely kept in line by a monitor. It would have been an evil thing for anyone to depart from the line of march, till the music ended. Dancing in couples was thought of as cavorting, with certain implications as to its degenerative effects on the morals of the participants. In 1895 a dancing teacher in Waukegan held classes, which many Lake Forest boys attended and dancing in the more modern sense was gradually introduced.

ALICE HOME HOSPITAL was erected on the College campus in 1898. It was intended to serve everybody, including the College, Academy, Ferry Hall and the town. Students boarded here for as little as $1.00 per day until 1930. Dr. Alfred C. Haven, the only medical man in town at this time, a friend of all, beloved by all, was the president of the board of health and had pointed out the need for a hospital in Lake Forest. The Henry C. Durands furnished $12,000 for the building, naming it as a memorial to Mrs. Durand's sister, Alice Burdsal Burhans. It was built in English half-timber country cottage architecture. Mr. and Mrs. Cyrus McCormick financed the operating room. Rooms were endowed by Mr. D. R. Holt, Mrs. Franklin P. Smith and Mrs. Walter C. Larned. There were many contributions toward the equipment including those of Mr. John V. Farwell, Mr. Louis F. Swift, Mr. Byron L. Smith, Mrs. Albert M. Day, Mrs. Bessie Swift Fernald, Mrs. Alfred L. Baker, Mrs. Calvin Durand, The Lake Forest Horse Show Association, the Lake Forest Presbyterian Church and the City of Lake Forest. Mr. T. S. Fauntleroy donated an ambulance, horse drawn, of course. All these gifts were the results of Dr. James G. K. McClure's requests for them.

This building and equipment, intended for a population of about 2,000, served its purposes adequately until the growth of the city necessitated the building of the present much larger, better equipped, and more expensive Lake Forest Hospital, finished in 1941.

There was need for an expansion of the public school system with new grade school and public high school facilities. On April 2, 1897, a petition was signed by Mayor E. F. Gorton and five aldermen of Lake Forest for a Township High School Board of five members, who would in turn decide the location of the Township High School. At the Council meeting of that date it was said that "a High School in Lake Forest must come. If we do not get the Township High School we must take the entire burden of a City High School." Land was purchased for the erection of the South School in 1898 from John and Joanna Johnson. The old Mitchell Hall on College Road, the original Dickinson Seminary building of 1860 was moved to the property at the corner of Sheridan and Maplewood Roads. In this location a grade school and an interim high school were operated.

The City Hall was built in 1898. It contained the Lake Forest Fire Department, administrative offices, police department, and the Lake Forest Public Library. The tower contained a bell to announce all fires and it continued to do so until Armistice Day, 1918, when it was rung so hard and so continuously that it became disengaged from its hinges and broke. The building cost $10,234 of which $10,000 was franchise money received from the North Shore Electric Railroad Company.

To decorate the City Council room, the Council voted to spend "not over $175 for (photographic) portraits of each of the Mayors, prior to 1895, to be properly framed and placed on the Council Chamber in the City Hall." This tradition has been continued to the present, so that during this centennial year the portraits of all Lake Forest mayors may be seen in the Council chamber.

Five hundred people turned out for the dedication ceremonies on the evening of June 24. Mayor Edward F. Gorton presided and spoke. He said: "Improvements were forced upon us" and advocated lectures in the Library on "landscape gardening, nature study, and birds and animals." Prof. John J. Halsey, a part time President of Lake Forest College, hoped that the library would "take the place of the club room and saloon, by giving young people a place to enjoy themselves." Little did he know that soon the Librarian's report would complain that too many youngsters came to the Library, not to read, but to meet one another and have a good time. Rev. Edward O'Reilly, pastor of the Church of St. Mary's spoke on "The First American (Public) Library," founded by Benjamin Franklin. Dr. J. G. K. McClure spoke on "The Library and the People." There were solos and duets interspersed in the program.

The original Lake Forest Public Library board consisted of Calvin Durand, Charles S. Frost, Mayor E. F. Gorton, Prof. J. J. Halsey, D. W. Hartman, David B. Jones, John Kemp, Rev. Edward O'Reilly, and R. G. Watson. George H. Holt was Secretary-

Treasurer and David Fales was a member of the executive committee.

The Library, on the second floor of City Hall, was a busy place. The City Council met here. It had been meeting in the Anderson Hall for which the Council had paid $75 per month rent. For a few years high school classes were conducted during week days until 3:00 p.m., except Sundays. On Sundays the Episcopal Mission held services here. Miss Marie A. Skinner, a graduate of Lake Forest College, was the first Librarian. She began with 1,149 books and a yearly levy of $1,200. The original library rules specified that only one book could be borrowed at a time. It could be kept for two weeks. Fines were 2¢ per day for overdue books, and $5.00 to $100.00 for wilful destruction.

Two public servants passed away at the turn of the century. Council resolutions spoke of Charles C. Pratt, his "frankness, thoughtfulness, kindness, integrity, courage and devotion to duty." It described Luther Rossiter as having "most sterling and manly qualities with an unusually loveable and sweet character. The community has lost a citizen who as a member of the City Council, rendered it faithful and efficient service."

On April 19, 1898, eight days after President McKinley's war message, a long train took 500 men of the 4th Infantry Regiment from Fort Sheridan to Tampa, Florida. The regiment went on to Cuba, then to the Philippines, under Colonel Herman Hall. Several cavalry units left the Fort under Major Robert P. Wainright for the same destinations. Major Wainright lost his life in the Philippines. The Spanish-American war had little effect on Lake Forest compared with the wars of the 20th Century.

XI

THE SUMMER RESIDENTS

1900–1910

In 1900 the population of the United States stood at 75,994,575. The Lake Forest population was 2,215 with 400 students in the Academy, Ferry Hall and the College, making a total of 2,615. Even this total did not represent the true picture, for, from the outset, the population of Lake Forest would swell every summer when families rented houses for a few months or stayed in the Deerpath Inn, or Onwentsia Club. At the turn of the century and for the next twenty years this growing summer colony built permanent homes which were occupied only during the warm weather. Some did not even have heating systems. A few families stayed into the late fall and returned early in the spring, causing problems in the school programs of their children. They attended summer worship and soon found themselves supporting two churches, making close the ties between the Chicago and Lake Forest congregations. The summer group was partial to golf and tennis, but the horse was still king.

Many families which came to Lake Forest only for the summer often entertained Chicago notables of literary and artistic prominence. In the Aldis "compound" Eugene Field, Eunice Tietjens, Albert Bloch, Harriet Monroe, Edgar Lee Masters, spent quiet weekends, sometimes taking part in creative drama written by Mrs. Aldis. Young people enjoyed their own dramatic productions on the Howard Van Doren Shaw place which boasted a natural outdoor stage. Sometimes the scene shifted to the stables where the villain jumped on a real horse, clutched the fainting heroine and was pursued by the hero on horseback out of sight into the pasture.

The high point of each summer was the Lake Forest Horse Show held on the Onwentsia Club grounds and for years devoted to the project of raising money for the Alice Home Hospital and the Contagious Hospital. Vines covered the arbors over boxes on the north side of the ring; bleachers and standing room along the rail were open to all. Among the many accomplished performers were Ida May Swift (Countess Minoto), riding side-saddle, and Helen Morton (Mrs. William Swift) handling a tandem of six horses. The Samuel Chase daughters, Polly, Libby and Janet, were experienced jumpers. But the most anticipated event was the procession of flower-covered pony carts. Little boys and girls had ponies and carts to match their size, the smallest child with the tiniest Shetland gaining the greatest applause. Among the prettiest were those of Lolita Armour, Mary Baker, and the Dorr Bradley girls (later Mrs. Fred Fisher and Mrs. Benjamin Carpenter), Edith Cummings (later Mrs. Munson), and Muriel McCormick.

Weekly polo matches attracted many spectators, and later on, international steeplechases thrilled the grandstands. Dudley Rutter was a frequent umpire. These were often dangerous sports as attested by the plaque in the vestibule of the First Presbyterian Church in memory of Nathan Butler Swift, placed there by his polo associates. He died in 1903 as a result of being struck on the head during a polo match at the Onwentsia Club.

The Onwentsia Hunt Club was started in 1900 by a fine horseman, Vernon Booth of Chicago. Arthur D. Paley was huntsman. He wore a red cap and scarlet coat and blew a horn. Arthur Aldis was the first Master of the Hounds. The hunt was discontinued in 1908, then revived by Joseph T. Ryerson as Master, followed by Austin Niblack and Prentice Porter. Under the last two it was known as the most difficult drag hunt in the country and became very formal. The jumps got increasingly difficult, causing amusing incidents and serious accidents.

A near tragedy of a different sort occurred on February 12, 1900, when two college boys, Guy Caron and George Mallory, together with five Academy boys, went to the beach on a bitter cold Sunday afternoon at two o'clock. They found the lake frozen solid as far as the eye could see. They walked out on the ice about three miles, then turned to come home, only to find that the ice was fast receding from the shore. One of the Academy boys, William H. Bailey, jumped off in time and ran to the Academy to inform Headmaster A. G. Welch. Soon a large crowd of Lake Forest people gathered at the beach wondering what to do next. Prof. Welch went to Waukegan with a group of boys, hired a tugboat and began to search down the coast. Fog, then darkness, hampered operations. Life boats arrived from Highland Park and Evanston. Crowds built beacon fires and kept them going all night long.

About 7:30 Sunday evening, the Academy boys were rescued by L. O. Riper, Milton H. Baker and Fred Perryman of Highland Park, and brought into the Fort Sheridan pier. The search continued for the two college boys. At four o'clock Monday morning, three men from Rogers Park found and saved these two boys, still floating on the ice. A happy crowd met the Monday noon train at Lake Forest, as the two youths returned to school. It was a miracle that none of the boys had frozen to death. Prof. Welch was soon stricken with appendicitis and died after an operation, his condition perhaps complicated by tension and exposure.

Not long after this, a happier incident occurred when an English traveller by the name of Winston Churchill made a tour of American cities, including Chicago. Here he was entertained by a small group of young lawyers who showed Churchill all the points of interest in our great city. After supper at the University Club, the group exchanged views on world affairs until three o'clock in the morning. One of these lawyers was Bertrand Walker, Harvard 1891, one of the charter members of the Onwentsia Club. He remembers Churchill saying: "I don't know what the future holds, but I do hope I can be of some service to my country."

In the winter of 1902–1903 a severe epidemic of scarlet fever broke out in Lake Forest. The whole city was quarantined including all public gathering places. All schools were closed. The boarding schools were confined to their own campuses. There were no church services. One girl died at Ferry Hall and the school was moved to Winona Lake, Indiana, for the remainder of the winter and spring, returning to Lake Forest in time for commencement. This was an especially trying winter for all of Lake Forest. In March 1903 when very few new cases were reported, the O'Neill and Eastwood billiard room petitioned to be permitted to open since they had sustained severe losses of revenue. There was no record that this was allowed immediately.

AT THE TURN of the century several changes occurred, in the appearance of Lake Forest. Many fences began to frame properties. The wide and open spaces of the previous decades had ceased to be. Bushes were planted as herbaceous borders, or hedgerows, to insure greater privacy for property owners. A new railroad station was erected, designed by Charles S. Frost, which is the present structure in 1961, the gift of the citizens of Lake Forest. The old station, the third since the founding of Lake Forest, was moved across the street from the present Police Station and for two decades served as the West Side Sunday School for the Presbyterian Church, and for Sunday evening services. It was razed in 1960. The original station had become the kitchen of the Sylvester Lind house and was burned with it in 1905. The second station became a dwelling house on Western Avenue. The present station is therefore the fourth in over a hundred years.

The new station became the meeting place of many families who came with their carriages pleasurably awaiting the arrival of the evening train, at the same time visiting each other. Lady passengers wore large feathered or flowered hats, and long flowing ruffled skirts. The youngsters came along to watch the procession of carriages. Horses were hitched along the board walk on the west side of Western Avenue, opposite the station. Charlie Grimes drove one of the two Onwentsia Club "busses," horse drawn passenger coaches, meeting trains and carrying passengers to the Club. Grimes was a special target of children who waylaid him when he had no passengers and he generously gave them rides in his yellow bus.

Arthur Farwell, one of the J. V. Farwell boys, became the talk of the town by bringing the first automobile, a black Winton, to Lake Forest. To begin with, the contraption was a source of amazement; but soon opposition built up, as horses bucked, shied, and became unmanageable since the new vehicle chortled and roared with the deafening sounds of a threshing machine.

One quaint newspaper article decried the horseless carriage, in these words: "Clear the way. The automobile is coming. Proud horses prancing ahead of victorias and landaus, horses of lower social degree that trot along between express-wagon shafts, and weary mules with attached dump carts, all scent trouble when they hear the cry. It heralds the coming of the common foe, and they dash wildly into the side streets or other places distant from the path of the automobile. Mothers take the children under their arms and rush frantically into the nearest house. Dogs go yelping through back alleys and cats seek the uppermost branches of the trees. The street is deserted and quiet hovers over the village."

The writer had a sense of humor but the picture was not far from the truth, as many citizens were making frantic calls to complain about the new vehicle. Mayor Gorton joined in the crusade. He said: "A few evenings ago when I was driving home, I saw groceries and merchandise strewed along the street for several blocks. Finally I came upon a grocer's delivery wagon, broken and battered, reclining against a large tree. I was told Grocer Richards' son was seriously injured in the runaway, which was caused by the horse taking fright at Mr. Farwell's automobile. The 'mobile makes a noise like a thrashing machine. The ladies of Lake Forest have been afraid to go out driving unless they learned from the Farwell mansion the highways the automobile was likely to traverse. They organized a crusade against it and the council passed an ordinance regulating the operation of self-propelling machines, which I at once signed. This ordinance is going to be enforced if I have to arrest the operator every hour in the day."

The ordinance passed on July 2, 1900, stated in Section 1: Operating of any automobile in such a manner as to endanger life or property . . . to frighten horses or other animals . . . is declared a nuisance and is hereby forbidden. Section 2 set the penalty at $5.00. Section 3 set a speed limit of 5 m.p.h. Section 4 stated that no vehicle shall be left standing unattended. Section 5 required that: "Someone shall precede the same on foot in such street, avenue, highway or public place, at a distance of 300 feet ahead of any such vehicle . . . shall warn all people of the approach of any such vehicle."

Mr. Farwell saw the Mayor after this ordinance and explained that he had bought the auto for his own amusement and that he intended to continue to use it. He thought that if people did not like his machine, they should educate their horses to become accustomed to it, and thus remove the cause of the whole problem.

Another flurry of resentment broke out after an automobile accident which involved the Hibbard family. On July 13, 1903, Carter H. FitzHugh, Calvin Durand, David Fales, and W. A. Morgan signed a letter to Mayor Herman F. Gade: "We venture the suggestion that the Council should take action at once with reference to the speed and conditions under which automobiles may be used in Lake Forest. The chances of an accident from an automobile in the hands of an intelligent and careful person, are not likely to be great. There are a large number of users of automobiles who are neither intelligent nor careful." They suggested that the Council place large signs at the northern, southern and western entrances to the city of Lake Forest. This was done. The signs read: "City of Lake Forest. Automobiles limited to 8 miles per hour and four miles per hour in turning corners within corporate limits. Under penalty of not less than $20.00."

Gradually adventurous spirits accepted the automobile; at the same time caution was maintained. Mrs. Arthur Farwell asked Mrs. Calvin Durand if she wished a ride home after a meeting of the Coterie. Mrs. Durand replied: "Yes, thank you, but let me call home first and make sure that our driveways will be clear of horses when we arrive."

Not all accidents of the period, however, were caused by the automobile. In 1901 *The Lake Forester* reported: "Mr. George Frisbie's team ran away near the Academy Wednesday morning. The wagon was broken up somewhat, several cases of eggs were mixed up promiscuously, and one horse slightly injured. Mr. Frisbie escaped unharmed." A year later, Grace Tuttle, a young girl who was often given a ride in the Anderson delivery wagon, got into it at her house. When the driver seemed to have delayed too long, she picked up the reins and the horse started out. Seeing a whip in front of her she applied it to the beast not knowing that he was not accustomed to being whipped. The horse charged ahead but was barely brought under control when Alex Robertson ran in pursuit and catching the back end of the wagon, climbed into the driver's seat in time to save both the horse and the child.

Walker Sales, a Negro, was added to the Police force in 1900. With James Gordon on duty during the day, and Sales, during the night, there were now two policemen in Lake Forest. Gordon served until 1907, Sales until 1919. In 1907 Albert Hopman joined the force and continued until 1928. William Fletcher joined the force in 1910.

By the turn of the century the Onwentsia Club had become a center of attraction for summer residents. At the end of the golf and tennis season, the doors of this club were closed. A group of permanent residents felt the need of a club, which might provide winter sports and social outlets for entire families. As a result the Winter Club was formed by Frederick C. Aldrich and Edward M. Samuel. Charter members included Bland Ballard, George Cobb, Scott Durand, Granger Farwell, T. S. Fauntleroy, Alfred H. Granger (a son-in-law of Marvin Hughitt), Herman Gade (the Norwegian Consul who married a Chicago girl, Alice King, and served twice as Lake Forest Mayor), Johnathan Jackson, Mark Morton, Edmund A. Russell, and Sidney R. Taber.

Land was leased at the present location on North Sheridan Road and a skating rink was laid out and a warming shed built the following year. Soon tobogganing became a favorite sport when an impressive slide was built in 1903. It went eastward along the north end of the club property, arched over Sheridan Road and debouched into the area across the street to be brought to a halt by the rising ground in the field which is now part of the present Middleton J. Blackwell property. Cars on Sheridan Road drove under it. This was considered the most daring sport afforded anywhere, until an even more precipitous one was erected on the Onwentsia grounds in the 1920's, which lasted only a short time for reasons of safety. Mary Peddle broke her leg from a fall at the Winter Club and Mima di Manzionley had a similar fate at Onwentsia.

Winter Club skating carnivals were held from 1904 onward, also costume parties, and bowling; later a baseball field, swimming pool, tennis and finally squash courts were built. The present club-house was erected, about as it now stands, in the autumn of 1903. All of this has been especially suitable for youngsters under fifteen. Professional supervision and instruction have been provided. The

Club also supplied the athletic programs of the Alcott (Bell) School.

ONE OF the town characters of this period was Charlie Gray of livery stable fame. He taught many youngsters to ride horseback. When a prospective rider explained apologetically that he was a beginner and wanted a gentle horse, he was given "Ice Wagon." When a customer boasted that he was an excellent and experienced horseman, he was given "Spitfire." In each instance it was the same horse. Charlie's helper, Otis Smith, was also held in affection during his long service at the Community Grocery Store.

GREENHOUSES AND FLORISTS have been traditionally of high calibre in Lake Forest. Anderman and Calvert were forerunners on Illinois Road of the present-day Jahnke, Konradt and Grace McGill. But no one who ever visited the Hild's Greenhouse on the corner of Illinois and Sheridan Roads will ever forget Eddie and George Hild, who were probably the first local collectors of clippings, being newspaper cut-outs of Lake Forest socialites. They delivered their flowers and plants by horse and buggy even after other businesses were using trucks. Children were delighted to ride along. The old Hild house and the last privy in Lake Forest were removed only a few years ago. The house was never adorned with plumbing. The old barn still stands.

Lake Forest was now growing at a faster tempo and changes were becoming the rule. Even the Presbyterian Church was affected. A handful of Protestant Episcopalian families had been happily worshipping in the Presbyterian Church; but with growing numbers the hope of an independent church arose. Several families rented carriages which took them to the Trinity Episcopal Church of Highland Park. To cause coachmen and even horses to work on the Sabbath was considered less than good judgment by many.

The first Episcopal service in Lake Forest had been held in the old schoolhouse off Western Avenue as early as August, 1872. These services were conducted by several of the ablest Episcopalian divines in the Chicago area. In 1898 a new series of services began in Blackler Hall, at the corner of Deer Path and Western, on Palm Sunday. There were 52 worshippers present. Dr. Peter

Wolcott, rector of Highland Park Trinity Church, conducted this and other early services. Meetings were then transferred to the City Hall until 1902, then to the "Brewster House," afterwards called the "Deerpath Inn," opposite the Lake Forest Public Library of 1961. These series of meetings eventually led to the organization and construction of the present Church of the Holy Spirit.

The cornerstone of the Church edifice was laid in 1902, and the building was ready for the first service at Whitsuntide, in May of the same year. Alfred Granger was the architect and the Rev. Owen J. Davies, was the first rector. The early Episcopalian families included the Appletons, Bricknells, Burridges, Calverts, Dwights, Gortons, Goulds, Hibbards, Huntoons, Tabers, Sterlings, and Viponds.

The tradition of fellowship with the Presbyterian Church has continued to the present and was well illustrated in 1937, when a new parish house was named "St. Anne's," after Lake Forest's Presbyterian "Saint," Miss Annie Brown, whose home it had been. Combined services have been held quite regularly on Thanksgiving and Christmas days. In 1926 the Church of the Holy Spirit installed a set of chimes, the gift of Mrs. Russell Lord, in memory of her husband.

THE Woman's Club of Lake Forest was organized in November, 1902, at the home of Mrs. Charles T. Gunn. Dr. Elva A. Wright, a practising Lake Forest physician served as president during the first seven years. In 1904 the Club united with the Illinois Federation of Women's Clubs.

The earliest members and officers included: Mrs. John Griffith (2nd Vice President), Mrs. Charles T. Gunn, Miss Margaret J. Gunn (Secretary), Mrs. Orpha Jones, Mrs. Alan Murrie, Mrs. E. A. Nordling, Dr. M. Olive Read (Vice President), Mrs. M. Volkman (Treasurer), and Mrs. Curtis Wenban.

The Club has sponsored cultural projects including music, art and history. Lectures were delivered before the Club by Prof. J. J. Halsey, John T. McCutcheon, Dr. Theodore Proxmire and others. In serving the community, the Club inaugurated Lake Forest Day, introduced Tuberculosis testing in the schools, granted scholarships, and brought the first visiting nurse, Miss

Gertrude Barker, to the school system. During two world wars the Club contributed to several Red Cross activities, orphans, and veterans' needs. It also helped staff the local defense cottage during World War II.

BEFORE the turn of the century, Lake Forest streets were lighted with kerosene lamps on wooden posts. Boys on horseback lit and extinguished them. A few electric lights had been introduced before this, but in 1902, the North Shore Gas Company brought illuminating and fuel gas to the city. Soon gas lights illuminated the streets. These were called Baltimore Lights, and a lamp-lighter lit them every evening and turned them off in the morning. There was considerable opposition to this improvement, and the objection was voiced that the village had become too metropolitan and soon the gas would kill both trees and shrubbery.

Youngsters felt that the older generation's opposition was an invitation to target practice. Several city gas lights were broken, but Puritanical parents believed in the "spare the rod, spoil the child" principle. Arthur Tuttle, one of these light extinguishers, was severely punished. Opposition to the gas lights ceased when no casualties were observed among trees and bushes. Although many of these lights have been removed from the Lake Forest scene, the city of St. Augustine, Florida, has just secured duplicates of these, purchased at great expense from Philadelphia, and placed them on their water front, in keeping with the tradition of being the oldest city in the United States.

In 1902, with the formation of the North Shore Electric Company, electric power was increased in Lake Forest. The executives of this company were Samuel Insull, John P. Walsh and Frank J. Baker.

Another improvement was effected at this time by the removal of the Lake Forest Hotel (The Old Hotel) from Triangle Park to its present location on Wisconsin Avenue, opposite the American Legion home. For a year Samuel Dent lived in the rear section of the hotel after the front part had been removed. This hotel had outgrown its usefulness and remained in a dilapidated condition. In 1894 Dr. J. G. K. McClure raised a sum of money from sixteen citizens for the purchase and removal of the hotel. The donors were C. Buckingham, E. Buckingham, Calvin Durand, H. C.

Durand, J. H. Dwight, David Fales, Senator C. B. Farwell, John S. Hannah, D. R. Holt, David B. Jones, Thomas D. Jones, Cyrus H. McCormick, Abram Poole, M. L. Reid, Byron L. Smith and Ezra J. Warner. The property was transferred to the City of Lake Forest in 1924 after the payment of $10,000 to Lake Forest University, the heirs of the Lake Forest Association.

In August 1903, the new telephone building was finished at 235 East Deer Path, affording an efficient exchange until the introduction of the dial system in 1960, when the new and modern plant was erected a block west of the former exchange. Another addition was the three story Anderson block at the corner of Deer Path and Western, which became the largest business house in 1904. It housed the new and expanded Anderson Store, one of the earliest business houses in Lake Forest, and also provided offices and other stores.

THE Convent of the Sacred Heart, later called Barat College, was transferred to Lake Forest in 1904 from Chicago, where it had existed since 1858. The name of the liberal arts women's college was derived from the Burgundian-peasant girl, Madeleine Sophie Barat, who showed an unusual aptitude for scholarship including languages, mathematics, sciences and literature. In 1800 she had established the French Society of Sacred Heart in Paris, to provide a well-rounded education for young women. Purity, truth, and service have been the basic ideals of the school and college from their inception.

In 1898, a small Public High School was operated in the old South School at Sheridan and Maplewood, and then at the City Hall. In 1904 the Lake Forest boys and girls were sent to the Deerfield Township High School, which had been organized in 1890, in Highland Park. During the school year 1904–1905 thirty-two Lake Forest boys and girls attended this high school. It cost the Lake Forest taxpayers $35 per pupil that year. The following school year the tuition per pupil increased to $56 and a total of $2,576 was paid. With the improved railroad facilities, it became desirable to continue this plan for all who preferred a public high school education. A plan to have these students attend the local private schools was considered until it was discovered that it was illegal for the city to pay tuition to a private school. In 1906 Dr.

John J. Halsey of Lake Forest College became the President of the Board of Education. The following year a Lake Forest group sponsored a movement for an act of the State Legislature in Springfield which provided the consolidation of that part of Shields Township which was in Lake Forest with the Deerfield Township High School District, forming the new Deerfield-Shields Township High School District. This was a happy solution until new problems were faced in the 1920's and 1930's.

The Gorton School had been erected in 1894. It was designed by James Gamble Rogers, who also designed the Sterling Library of Yale University. Mrs. Rogers was the former Annie Day of Lake Forest whose family's home was on the lake at the east end of Illinois Road. The land for the Gorton School had been purchased from Colonel W. S. Johnston. This school had been called the Central School. In 1905 it was renamed The Gorton School, in honor of the beloved Lake Forest Mayor, Edward P. Gorton. The Gorton School housed the upper grades. In 1907, Howard Van Doren Shaw enlarged this school. There were now four grade schools in Lake Forest—Central, North, South and West. The total number of grade school pupils numbered 450 in 1905. There were 27 faculty members in the entire public grade school system.

In April 1904 the Water Company raised the rates to its consumers. A year later the City Council made an investigation, following complaints from many citizens and passed an ordinance in January, 1905, fixing the rate for private consumers at 25¢ per 1,000 gallons and a minimum rate of $4.00 per year. The Water Company claimed this "Unjust, unreasonable and insufficient to give reasonable compensation to its stockholders. The ordinance is invalid." After three years of litigation the appellate court in *Water Company vs. City of Lake Forest* said: "The evidence shows that the rates *are* reasonable and give a fair and reasonable return to the stockholders." The dispute continued until the city purchased the private Water Company in 1921.

In the fall of 1905 a group of Lake Forest young men formed a club to foster organized athletics. They called it the Young Men's Club. The original sponsors included Dr. W. H. Wray Boyle, pastor of the First Presbyterian Church, Mrs. Alfred Granger, and Mrs. Simon Reid. The first members included Carl and Walter

Krafft, James Griffis, William Dickinson, William Kemp, Otto Schaffer, Harry French, Carl Voght, Jr., William Marshall, and Lindel Darby the first president.

A constitution was written stating the aims of the club: "To furnish healthy social intercourse among the members; to promote good fellowship between them and furnish them entertainments; to develop athletics; to further and support all movements and enterprises calculated to benefit Lake Forest; and to own and manage a club house for the foregoing purposes and do all things suitable to carry out the above." The slogan for the club was: "No class, no creed."

The first athletic director was G. C. Bradstreet of the College athletic department. All kinds of team athletics were sponsored, especially football, basketball and baseball. The club operated under the direction of a group of older men who were designated "The Cabinet." Much of the early prosperity of the group is credited to Dr. T. S. Proxmire who had just moved to Lake Forest. The club promoted lectures, song recitals, concerts, and other entertainments at the Durand Art Institute.

In 1907 with the purpose of encouraging the purchasing of homes, the Young Men's Club sponsored a Young Men's Subdivision and bought several acres of land from the original William Atteridge farm. Seven acres were laid aside and became West Park. The rest was sold to members at modest prices and generous terms. A permanent building to house the club was finished in the winter of 1915–1916, in conjunction with the creation of Market Square, the building behind the 1961 Marshall Field Store, which to this day serves the original purposes of the club, although the Young Men's Club no longer exists. Its facilities now house the City's Recreation Department.

Another Lake Forest organization was begun on July 19, 1905, "The Horticultural Society of Lake Forest." Its purpose was "to encourage and promote the study and practice of horticulture, floriculture and arboriculture and general gardening. To hold exhibits of flowers, vegetables, fruits, shrubs, trees and other products of the soil at seasonable times and places; to supply its members with reliable information pertaining to gardening and kindred subjects."

During a meeting in September 1905, Horace H. Martin presided and the following sponsors were present: Mrs. Scott Durand, Dr. G. G. French, Walter Larned, Mr. and Mrs. Cyrus H. Mc-Cormick, Byron L. Smith, and Mr. and Mrs. James Viles.

In 1912 when a number of new members were received from other parts of the North Shore area, the name of the Society was changed to "The North Shore Horticultural Society." The Society cooperated with the Garden Club and received many prizes in Lake Forest, Chicago and elsewhere for floats in Fourth of July parades, and for various exhibits of flowers, fruits, and garden displays.

Membership began with thirteen charter members. In 1945 seventy-six were listed. The 1960 membership was 221, extending from Chicago to Kenosha. Meetings have been held in the Durand Art Institute and in the American Legion home. Summer shows have been held in the Gorton School, and fall shows in the Durand Art Institute. The Society has sponsored trips to famous gardens and greenhouses and made contributions of money for Farwell Field of Lake Forest College, West Park, and the Deer Path Golf Club.

Lake Forest owes a debt of gratitude to the organization which has had such a great share in the beautifying of the city. The interest it has generated may be even more valuable than the hard work and the scientific knowledge promoted by the Society. Karl Geppert worked at the 1893 World's Fair. Emil Bollinger was the first President of the Society.

A partial list of past and present artists of nature, gardeners and the families for which they worked, include: Alexander Allen (Laflin), John Anderson (Woods), Otto Anderson (E. L. Ryerson), Emil Bollinger (Byron L. Smith), Eric Benson (McBirney), Alex Binnie (Viles), John Brown (Gwethlyn Jones), Ralph Clauson (Brewster), Thomas Dobbin (Norris), Andrew Eide (Sample), Ernest Gernenz (Lawrence Armour), Karl Geppert (Chatfield-Taylor), Nels Hanson (Clow), Chris Jensen (McLaughlin), Robert E. Kuehne (A. Watson Armour, A. B. Dick), George Kuppenhoefer (Swift), Kay Lindemman (Coleman), Knut Lofen, Carl Lundeen (Barnes), Harry Lynch (Cowles), Andrew Martenson, John Newbore (McElwee), Axel Nielsen (Cudahy), William Oke (Warner), Elbert Parshall (Ryerson), Hjalmar E. Peterson (Hamill), Albert Rippon (Mrs. Stanley

Keith), Gottlieb Schaefer (Clayton Mark), Frank Schreiber (Calvin Durand), Walter E. Steinhaus (J. O. Armour), John Tiplady (Dick), Marc Twinney (J. O. Armour), Camiel J. Vander Bennet (F. P. Smith), Robert Vipond (C. B. Farwell), Henry Wallace (Hamill), Fritz Zarte (Runnels), Andrew Zavaodka (J. O. Armour).

Lake Forest College received an important building in 1906, the Calvin Durand Commons. Previously men students had dined in cooperative clubs or with private families. It was now possible for two hundred to eat at once in a building erected in the English collegiate gothic style, lined with oak panelling. It followed the design of the Trinity Dining Hall in Cambridge, England, and was erected in brick and stone, in the center of the campus. Charles Frost was the architect. That same year Mrs. Timothy Blackstone gave two attractive red brick men's dormitories, Blackstone and Harlan Hall. Frost and Granger were the architects.

During the summer of 1906, the entire student body, faculty and their families, of the McCormick Theological Seminary, in Chicago, including Dr. James G. K. McClure, the president and former pastor of the Presbyterian Church of Lake Forest, made an excursion to Lake Forest as guests of the Cyrus McCormick's at "Walden." They were driven around Lake Forest and through the "Walden" ravines, before they were entertained at dinner. This was typical of what has continued for many years when large groups from the city come out to be entertained by various citizens or institutions of Lake Forest. Private gardens, school campuses, and city parks offered a welcome change.

The First National Bank of Lake Forest opened its doors on October 31, 1907, during a mild recession. The first head of the organization was the Chicagoan, Frank W. Read, who came from the Central Trust Company of Illinois. David H. Jackson was the first president of the board of directors. The original bank building was located where the Deerpath Theatre now stands. In 1915 the First National Bank united with the older State Bank of Lake Forest, which had stood on the northwest corner of Deer Path and Western, and moved to this new location.

In 1916 when the Market Square project was completed, the bank again moved, occupying the west end of the square. At this time the narrow street in front of the new building running north and south was named Bank Lane, having been called "The Alley." The bank has grown with the city, surviving the 1919 depression and the bank moratorium of 1933. A new Georgian building of brick and stone was built in 1931, on the corner of Deer Path and Bank Lane. The deposits have grown from $40,835 to $35,095,717 in 1960.

In early July, 1907, there was heavy storm damage following wind and rain. Charles C. Pratt of the Street department reported that the retaining wall near Blair Lodge and the tiles of the street drain were washed out. The bridge near the College Gymnasium was threatened by a bad slide of the bank. Trees were almost down, causing additional strain on the bank. South of Julian F. Rumsey's on Washington Avenue, water had washed away the earth, exposing sanitary sewer pipes. On Rosemary, east of the Dow's, two sewer catch basins were washed out. At the long bridge just south of Alfred L. Baker's on Mayflower Road a slide of the bank had washed away much soil, endangering the bridge. The need to protect the sewer plant from lake storms was indicated. Mr. Pratt thought that some of this damage was due to "much temporizing in the original construction, light work and cheap construction."

XII

COSMOPOLITANISM

1908–1916

THE FIRST Lake Forest Day was held on Wednesday, July 15, 1908, on the Lake Forest College campus. It was suggested by Dr. Theodore S. Proxmire, and promoted by the Woman's Club. It had the community purpose of raising money for a contagious hospital to be constructed at South Park, a homey, country affair, with local talent well in the foreground. Admission cost 25¢, as did a carriage ride to Lake Bluff, the carriages being supplied by local residents. Vegetable, flower and baby shows were held, and Orson Smith appears to have won a sort of "Mr. Lake Forest" contest. The town band played; the musicians included Dr. T. S. Proxmire, Frank Wenban, George Wenban, Carl Krafft and others. People sat around on the campus in family groups, eating lunch. Several games were going on at once. Everybody knew everybody.

The climax of excitement was reached with a balloon ascension, followed by a parachute jump. The single, intrepid parachute jumper, a brave colored man, whose identity ought to have been preserved, landed on the Thomas E. Donnelley place on Green Bay Road. The only features to survive the first Lake Forest Day were prize competitions and dancing. Floats were introduced in 1911. The contagious hospital was insured through a gift of Mrs. Cyrus McCormick.

In 1908 Dr. Clifford W. Barnes of Lake Forest, former president of the oldest college in Illinois, Illinois College in Jacksonville, founded the Sunday Evening Club in Chicago, a unique religious institution, often imitated in cities over the country.

Mr. Barnes was among the first social workers at the famous Hull House on Chicago's Halsted Street. In 1898–1899, Mr. and Mrs. Barnes were in Paris in behalf of the Student Christian Movement. They ministered to English-speaking students in the Latin Quarter who were often destitute. They set about the task of remedying this situation when it suddenly occurred to them that they were faced with a deeper problem. Their efforts were then directed toward a non-denominational student group which met on Sunday evenings to hear the finest speakers of the day, including the American Ambassador to Paris. Opera singers and others high in the musical profession volunteered to furnish sacred music. The program was so successful that Dr. Barnes started the same type of program in Chicago's Orchestra Hall in 1908. He received the backing of Chicago business men, who made the program a continued success. Among the recent backers are found many familiar Lake Forest family names. The businesses listed include Armour & Company, Butler Brothers, Hibbard Spencer Bartlett & Company, Carson Pirie Scott & Company, Marshall Field & Company, The Pure Oil Company, The Quaker Oats Company, Joseph T. Ryerson & Son, Swift & Company, and Wilson & Company.

The Sunday Evening Club has heard the leaders of Christian thought including Lord James Bryce, Dr. Henry Van Dyke, Reinhold Niebuhr, Cordell Hull, Harry Emerson Fosdick, Henry Pitney Van Dusen, John R. Mott, and Robert E. Speer, to name only a few. Its choir has nearly a hundred voices, singing each Sunday the finest sacred music. The meetings bring together a congregation from all walks of life and from many nations, with a special invitation to students.

In 1915, the Chicago Community Trust was established with Dr. Barnes as chairman. Beginning with some ten millions of dollars in the fund, it has grown steadily, becoming the largest fund of its type in the United States. During the difficult years in the 1930's it was a sustaining help to many educational and medical institutions in the Chicago area.

The death of Dr. Barnes in 1944 was a loss to the community of one of its most devoted and dedicated friends.

JUST NORTH OF "Clark's ravine," at the eastern end of Woodland Road and south of the Cemetery, homes were built along the bluff for two decades. Across from the Charles Durand's lived a Colonel MacClanahan with his wife, Rose Hill MacClanahan, a sister of Mrs. Durand and their daughter, Bess. The home of Mrs. Donald R. McLennan now occupies this property. The Colonel, a Tennessean, six foot five inches tall, had been a Judge Advocate General on the staff of Braxton Bragg and had fought under General Robert E. Lee during the Civil War. Upon his death, soon after settling in Lake Forest, his widow and daughter made their home with the Charles Durands. Next door lived the W. R. Stirling family.

In the summer of 1908 Anna Bess MacClanahan was invited by the Stirlings to accompany them to Europe. On the return trip on the *Mauritania* she met Wilfred T. Grenfell, the English doctor whose work among the Eskimos in Labrador was already well known. Her subsequent marriage to him in Chicago on November 18, 1909, has always been a source of pride to Lake Foresters who were honored to be associated with him in that way. In his autobiography, Dr. Grenfell refers to his visit to his wife's "beautiful country home among the trees on the bluff of Lake Michigan (as) one long dream," though he did not enjoy having to ride horseback, his lady's favorite pastime.

THE ORIGINAL PLAT OF July 1857 brought the lot lines along the lake to the crest of the bluff. The entire Lake Forest beach and Forest Park were not platted in lots. As a result, the beach area was used indiscriminately by the public for picnics, bathing, and fishing. Teamsters had continued to haul away sand and gravel in spite of City Ordinances to the contrary. An injunction had therefore been issued on June 5, 1882, forbidding anyone to "dig, remove, or carry away, or cause same to be done, any soil, sod, stone, earth, sand or gravel from any street, alley, or public grounds in this City." This injunction was pressed by the property owners along the lake who claimed that their property was being undermined by wind and wave as a result of these excavations.

In 1894, the Trustees of Lake Forest University deeded to the owners of adjoining lots the abutting strip of beach, but in 1908 the City of Lake Forest claimed the entire beach area, based on the original plat. Abram Poole contended that his property included the beach area, based on the 1894 gift of Lake Forest University. Kenneth R. Smoot, City Attorney, and David Fales argued for the City of Lake Forest before the Illinois Supreme Court. Henry N. Tuttle supported Poole's contention. Both Fales and Tuttle had served as city aldermen.

In *Abram Poole vs. City of Lake Forest,* February 19, 1909 (Illinois Reports, Vol. 238, p. 305), Justice Vickers gave the following opinion:

There are no words on the (original) map indicating what the beach strip north of the north line of Forest Park and south of the south line of the said Park was intended to be used for. . . . When (Abram Poole) first purchased (his) property, he supposed that lots 30 and 31 extended to the water's edge . . . The mere leaving of a blank upon the plat without any designation of its purpose can not be held sufficient proof of an intention of the owner to dedicate the premises represented by such blank or undesignated space to public use . . . To establish a dedication it should clearly appear that the owner intended to give the land to the public. It is not enough to show that it is not intended for private use. The particular use for which the land was intended must plainly appear.

The City of Lake Forest never expended any money or labor in the construction or maintenance of the premises, either as a street or park. The evidence simply shows that the owner of these premises, whose residence was on the bluff above, acquiesced in the use of this beach by the public so long as such use did not interfere with their own rights . . . The owner obtained an injunction against teamsters and stopped them from hauling sand across these premises . . . The law does not demand forfeiture of title simply because the owner of property does not cause it to be listed for taxation.

Where a party is in actual possession of a part of a tract or a piece of land claiming to be the owner of all of it, the paper title under which he claims is evidence of the extent of his possession. . . . We think the evidence sufficiently shows that the appellees were in the actual possession of all of the premises. The evidence shows that such acts of ownership were exercised over this property as might reasonably be expected in view of the nature and situation of the premises. This is all that the law requires in this regard.

Little did it occur to those involved in the litigation that as time went on, the owners of the beach area would be subjected to a great expense to arrest the erosion caused by storms, and would be taxed for this additional property. The case was especially significant because it became the precedent for all suburbs of the state which adjoin Lake Michigan. In Lake Forest the effects of the case have been tempered by the generosity of the property owners who have not objected to the use of their beaches by the general public.

In 1904 the world's largest naval training station had its inception five miles north of Lake Forest when the Federal Government was considering locating a station on the Great Lakes. There was a movement toward interesting the great Middle West in the United States Navy, since the naval burden of the Spanish-American war had been borne by the coastal areas only. To help the government to decide in favor of the Chicago area, the Merchant's Club of that city, which later merged with the Commercial Club, raised an initial $93,000 for the purpose of buying land. When the moneys reached a total of $175,000 fifty-two acres of the Joseph Downey farm were purchased on the edge of the shore north of Lake Bluff. The property was offered to the government for $1, "a gift of Chicago's foremost citizens." Lake County Congressman, George Edmund Foss, pressed for authorization of the Station. This was achieved on April 27, 1904, accompanied by $250,000 in federal funds for buildings and development. Congressman Foss was soon called "The Father of Great Lakes" and Foss Park containing athletic fields and a rifle range were named after him.

Seven years later the station was completed with 39 buildings and a capacity for 1,500 enlisted men. On July 2, 1911, a whistle was heard by a group of several hundred interested Chicago and North Shore people which inaugurated the formal opening of the Great Lakes Naval Training Station. After the whistle, a gun was fired and the band struck up the Star Spangled Banner. The flag then was slowly raised aloft, until it reached the pinnacle exactly at high noon. Admiral Albert T. Ross took official command of the Station and made a brief speech.

The Station was dedicated by President William Howard Taft on October 28, 1911. At that time the first class of recruits was graduated. The President made a ten minute speech, and true to his Yale background, dedicated "the station to our country, our God and our flag." A large crowd from the Chicago area was present. Lake Forest Academy Headmaster William Mather Lewis was there with the entire student body. The first recruit to graduate was Joseph Wallace Gregg. At the time of dedication the cost of the Station had reached $3,000,000.

The first inmates of the Great Lakes Brig were two eleven-year-olds, Stuart French of Lake Forest and his friend, Harry L. Bixby. These boys, together with their families, had been visiting the Station before its formal opening. When they misbehaved, they were warned of the consequences by Admiral Ross who was showing them around. When they continued in their mischief, several large sailors were summoned and committed the boys to the Brig. The gates crashed behind them, for a twenty-minute incarceration. Ten years later H. L. Bixby graduated from the Naval Academy and eventually became a Captain.

Rear Admiral Albert Ross, that grand old man, became a familiar figure as a Lake Forest resident, a loyal Presbyterian and a great social favorite. He was followed by Captain William A. Moffett, who also lived in Lake Forest during his tour of duty at Great Lakes which covered 1914 through World War I. During that war 125,000 men were trained at Great Lakes. During World War II over a million bluejackets passed through the Station. Today (1961) there are a thousand buildings in the Station, in 1,567 acres, housing over 20,000 trainees.

LAKE FOREST was the smallest town to organize a branch of the Young Women's Christian Association. It had its beginnings in Mrs. Arthur Aldis' Red Bird Cottage. It served the needs of women and girls and provided many community services for thirty-nine years, 1911–1950. In 1950 the Y.W.C.A. became inactive, but retained a Board and membership in order to hold title to its property and to be a nucleus for future activities. It began with a budget of $2,700 but spent as much as $17,000 during its year of greatest activity.

The Y.W.C.A. program included religious services, gymnastics, baby clinics, swimming instruction, Americanization, dancing, camps, lectures, projects of world-wide interest, clubs, and a welfare program. During two world wars it conducted programs for service men and their families. It is now providing scholarships for college students.

In 1912 a large reception was given at the home of Mr. and Mrs. Louis E. Laflin in honor of Booker T. Washington, the Negro educator and author. There were many invited guests including the Julius Rosenwalds of Winnetka, chairman of the board of Sears Roebuck, in whose private railroad car the Laflins later visited Tuskeegee College, in Alabama.

Evangelist Billy Sunday preached several times at the Academy and at the First Presbyterian Church, over a period of fifteen years. His two sons attended the Academy, and the J. V. Farwell family were good friends and promoters of the Sundays. Capacity crowds turned out to hear the former baseball star, many coming from miles away. His description of his conversion during a baseball game was related in detail, each year, and "got better every time he told it." Several young Lake Foresters recall this sermon as a highlight of the period. Charles C. Buell remembered the sermon to report it forty years later as follows:

This is the testimony of an errant sinner. Boys, I was playing center field (1886) on the old Chicago team (Chicago White Stockings of the National League, the forerunner of the Chicago Cubs). The race for the championship was very close, and on a Saturday night late in the season, it became apparent that the big game to be played on the next day, Sunday, would decide the championship.

That night I got very drunk, and was picked up in a drunken stupor, out of the gutter at Van Buren and State streets, by the Salvation Army. They cleaned me up, sobered me up, and converted me to Christianity.

Feeling much the worse for wear and my transgressions, I went out to the old West Side Ball Park, for the championship contest. Clarkson and Flint were our battery for the crucial game. Clarkson's speed was blinding, and going into the ninth inning everything was in our favor. We were protecting a two-run lead, then as often happens, we had several bad breaks and the stage was set: the bases were full, two out, and the mighty Delehanty coming to bat. Clarkson blazed the first two past him, and as he wound up for the third time, I started back. With the crack of the bat I looked over my shoulder and saw disaster winging its way in my direction. I ran harder and harder and prayed: "O God, O God, O God, if you ever helped a converted sinner, help me catch this ball." Way out in the deepest part of center field I made the most spectacular catch of my career. I have been a Christian ever since.

Tim Brady came into the dressing room after the game, and said: "Sunday, here is a thousand dollars. Your catch saved me fifteen thousand which I had bet on the Chicago team." Many have asked me since if I took the thousand dollars. Boys, I *did!*

The Great Charlie Flint caught the mighty Clarkson without chest protector, leg pads, or mask. He was a great competitor but liquor was his undoing. He travelled the primrose path into drunken oblivion. His wife divorced him and later married a well-known Chicago banker. Years later his car, driven by a chauffeur, ran down a drunkard. At the morgue it was discovered that the body was that of the famous Flint. I preached the funeral service over Charlie Flint, attended by high and low, business men and harlots, bankers and bartenders, and my mind wandered back over the years, to that great game in which God helped me on my path of reformation.

Remember boys, remember well, that you should never allow liquor to manage your life. Better yet, never touch it.

ANOTHER CELEBRITY to speak in Lake Forest was Senator J. Hamilton Lewis, U.S. Senator from Illinois, who was the Fourth of July speaker in Triangle Park, in 1912. The chairman of the occasion was Mr. Robert J. Thorne who had recently moved his family to Lake Forest. He introduced the Senator and added: "We have Mrs. Lewis with us also." The people smiled knowing that the only Mrs. Lewis in the audience was Mrs. William Mather Lewis, not at all related to the Senator.

A MEMORIAL SERVICE was held in the Academy Chapel in May 1912, for the mother and sister of Howard Hippacks, an Academy student. They were lost in the *Titanic* disaster on the night of April 14–15 when the ship crashed into an iceberg just south of Newfoundland in an attempt to set a new world speed record for crossing the Atlantic ocean. A total of 1,517 lives were lost.

IN 1910 Mayor C. Frederick Childs introduced the first macadam pavements in Lake Forest. These gradually replaced the hodgepodge of dirt, brick, wood and stone pavements so that by 1920 macadam pavements were the rule. In 1911 he organized the oldest and largest business in America specializing in Government Securities. In 1913 he created the first professional Lake Forest fire department, raising $2,500 by personal solicitation for a hook-and-ladder and hose truck, the first motor driven fire truck in the city. The present fire station was built in 1925.

In 1913, a group of Onwentsia members organized the Old Elm Club, just south of Lake Forest. It was for men only, with golf the sole feature. There were two reasons for a new club at this time. Sunday was the only time these men could play golf since all business men worked six full days each week. Because Onwentsia was crowded and had a rule against Sunday golf, Old Elm seemed to offer a satisfactory solution. The original membership included Colonel R. Harvey McElwee, Alfred Landon Baker, Clyde M. Carr, John V. Farwell, Jr., Stanley Field, Albert A. Sprague and James Viles. The membership was restricted to 150 members to make it pleasurable for all.

There was a furor in 1915 over the subject of Sunday movies. After a long discussion Mayor William Mather Lewis called for a city-wide vote. Four hundred fifty-two wanted Sunday movies, 495 voted against it.

The Lake Forest Improvement Plan for remodeling the business district was formulated, culminating in the Market Square in 1916. This was a pioneer shopping center, planned and executed with an eye to beauty and usefulness, "the first integrated and artfully designed shopping center in this country." It comprised twenty-five stores, 12 offices, 28 apartments, occupying 400 feet by 260 on Western Avenue. The stores which previously occupied the area were an eyesore, and the back lots had created slum conditions. Several buildings were moved to new locations. Others were torn down. The O'Neill Hardware Store erected a new and much larger building, in 1916, on Westminster.

Howard Van Doren Shaw who designed Market Square was a graduate of Yale and M.I.T. One of the first citizens of Lake Forest in the first century, he was an outstanding architect, equally skillful in several styles of architecture. He could execute the

Gothic as in the Fourth Presbyterian Church of Chicago, or the Italian as in several homes he designed in Lake Forest. He built the Lakeside Press building in Chicago and the Market Square in Lake Forest. He was also the teacher of several younger men who continued his ideals of utility and good taste. Stanley Anderson and Ralph Milman were among his loyal students.

The Market Square was designed with "rows" or arcades in the eastern corners. Two Tyrolean towers and an Italian Renaissance central building, across the west side, were all coordinated in cultivated taste and enduring beauty, making it one of the most attractive business centers in the country. Ground was broken in September 1915 and many of the stores were opened in 1916. The completed project cost $750,000.

The square contains a fountain at the east end, dedicated to Howard Van Doren Shaw, and a flag pole at the west end, dedicated in 1917 to the "Men of Lake Forest who gave themselves for the safety of their country and the world." The grass plot in the center is surrounded with elms and flowering bushes. The original trustees, who made Market Square a reality, were Arthur T. Aldis, D. Mark Cummings, John V. Farwell, Jr., David B. Jones and Cyrus H. McCormick. The unit makes a fine impression on anyone arriving at the Lake Forest station for the first time, and every time.

In 1912 one hundred motor cars were listed in Lake Forest. The number increased rapidly in the next four years. These were in all sizes and descriptions with Fords predominating. Almost within a year the horse and carriage disappeared from the Lake Forest scene. Other automobile makes included Buicks, Chandlers, Duryeas, Hupmobiles, Overlands, Stanley Steamers, Stevens, Stoddard-Daytons, Stutzes, Wintons and others which took care of the necessary transportation or for sport. The hunter and the mount were still found in several stables which provided hunting, polo, or riding for pleasure.

There was one kind of car which seemed to agree with the Lake Forest temperament and scene—the electric. Many families favored these for their quietness and controlled speed. There was one Sheridan Road resident who learned to start and steer her electric before she learned to stop it. She could do nothing but circle her house until the battery ran out. Another young lady met a mounted soldier from Fort Sheridan as she drove her electric across the Sheridan Road bridge at Deer Path. His horse went completely wild and backed into the front wheel of her vehicle. In the end, one front wheel hung over the buffer of the bridge, barely missing a thirty foot drop into the bottom of the ravine. The horse had to be destroyed. Early electric owners included the Allings, Casselberrys, Colvins, Holts, Laflins, McLennans, Shaws, Trowbridges, Viles and Warners.

As the gas engines were improved, the electrics were gradually retired. A few reappeared on the Lake Forest streets during the gas shortages of World War II.

With more and more cars and a steadily growing city, more macadam roads were built and new streets came into being. New street names appeared and some older streets were renamed to correspond with the several attractive names already in use. Here and there a city ordinance changed a name. In 1897 one significant ordinance changed University Avenue to Sheridan Road. In 1915 the Mayor's wife, Mrs. Leverett Thompson, nee Alice Poole, took the initiative and changed nearly all Avenues to Roads. She renamed several streets. Elm Street became Elm Tree Road, Deer Path east of Sheridan was straightened and the old extension became a part of Westminster, Linden was renamed College Road, Poplar became the western end of Rosemary, Myrtle became Ringwood, part of Winona became Hawthorne Lane, Huron became a part of Elm Tree Road, and Winona disappeared, becoming a part of Barberry Lane, while Strawberry Lane became Hawthorne Place.

There were many objections to these changes. One incensed resident remarked: "To think that she presumed to do this when she had lived in Lake Forest only twenty-two years." On October 21, 1927, the Council approved by ordinance 29 additional changes in street names without serious objection from anyone. It is interesting to note that the present McKinley Road has been called by three other names during the past one hundred years— Railroad Avenue, Depot Avenue and Waukegan Road.

THE Garden Club of Lake Forest was organized in 1912 by several Lake Forest women including Mrs. Finley Barrel, Mrs. Tiffany

Blake, Mrs. Samuel Chase, Mrs. J. Andrew King, Mrs. Cyrus McCormick, Mrs. Arthur Meeker, and Mrs. John T. Pirie.

In 1913, Gifford Pinchot, chief forester in President Theodore Roosevelt's administration, and his pretty red-headed wife were guests at Walden, to consult with Mr. and Mrs. Cyrus McCormick on matters of the national conservation program which had begun during the first Roosevelt administration, and then neglected. The new President, Woodrow Wilson, a long-time friend of the Mc-Cormick family, was able to reactivate the conservation program as a result of conferences and studies made at Walden during this visit. Mrs. Pinchot became one of the founders of the Garden Club of America in 1913, and the Lake Forest Garden Club served as one of the pilot organizations of the country-wide movement. The first horticultural exhibit in Lake Forest was held at Walden as were many succeeding exhibits.

ANOTHER unusual event of the period involved two local boys, about ten years old, Jack Durand and Arnold Sprague, who boarded a Northwestern engine at Lake Forest, while the engineer was absent in a restaurant, and drove it to Lake Bluff without mishap.

A less dramatic but continuing activity involved the study of bird-lore in our midst. John Ferry had made a famous collection of birds, nests and eggs which had been installed in glass cases in the rotunda of the Durand Art Institute. Henry Tuttle, Mrs. Jesse B. Moss and Mrs. Sara A. Hubbard were early students of bird life in Lake Forest. Ellen Drummond Farwell (Mrs. J. V. Farwell, Jr.) left us a legacy of her bird observations from 1907 to her death in 1919, collected in a book published by her husband, entitled "Bird Observations Near Chicago." From the windows of her home "Ardleigh," high on the bluff above Lake Michigan, she spotted many of the species appearing on her lists. She was instrumental in organizing the Audubon Society of Illinois.

A second "Ellen," Mrs. Hermon Dunlap Smith, Associate in the Division of Birds of the Chicago Natural History Museum, fifty years later, is continuing to watch the birds from the windows at "Ardleigh," and has compiled a booklet for the use of bird enthusiasts in the Chicago area called *Chicagoland Birds—Where and When to Find Them.*

Marion Clow, a few miles north on the same bluff, is also a well-known bird expert reporting regularly to the National Audubon Society's migration studies. She remembers seeing two black-billed magpies on the lawn of her family home in 1918. She comments that as wooded areas and cow pastures have disappeared, such species as the great horned owl, the orchard oriole and even the bluebird are rarely seen in the suburb, while others such as the cardinal and the starling are more plentiful than at the turn of the century. For the most part, however, the statistics have remained fairly constant throughout the years, including some 180 species, comprising migrants such as warblers, residents such as the chickadee, and breeding birds such as the goldfinch.

The increase of shrubbery and newly planted trees have added to the permanent shelter provided by the wild growth in the ravines. In recent years with increased interest in birds, more and more people have been engaged in feeding them during the winter months. Few people know that the cardinals might never have been so plentiful had they not been imported by John T. Pirie from Florida in 1915. He brought a pair from which only the male survived the first winter. Pirie then secured a female from the Lincoln Park Zoo, put her in a cage on one of the bird feeders. When the male was seen near the cage several times, he released the female. They returned to the feeder together; and so are thought to be the ancestors of our many cardinals in Lake Forest.

For the visitor to Lake Forest, the beautiful homes have been the most impressive sights. After the turn of the century there were many additions and new trends. More and more citizens discovered the advantages of building to the west. Green Bay Road became known as "The Ridge." These westward facing residents claimed the superiority of their "Italian sunsets" above the sunrises over Lake Michigan. It was possible to have long vistas and to capitalize on the nearness to the Onwentsia Club, and the bridle paths, as well as to avoid city taxes as some did. Several of these homes had secret panels and secret staircases, some even had theatres in which plays were produced. In the fall, pheasants landed in their backyards to give these homes a touch of the north woods.

In 1900 still another trend began when Miss Helen Culver bought a neglected farm and built "Rookwoods," on Telegraph Road (now Waukegan Road). She was one of the first to appreciate the advantages of the "Second Skokie." Miss Culver was the well known philanthropist who gave her Chicago home to Jane Addams who in turn developed the pioneer settlement-house, Hull House, named after Miss Culver's cousin, Charles J. Hull. Miss Culver's brief residence in Lake Forest was a source of pride to the city, as she had served as a nurse behind the battle lines during the Civil War. She had been in charge of a hospital at Murfreesboro with 40 beds. She and two other women kept the beds sanitary, the wounded clean and comfortable, prepared their food, administered their medicines and wrote letters for them. She and her staff followed the armies to be on hand at Chickamauga and Chattanooga. After the war she returned to Chicago and became the first woman to be commissioned a notary public in Illinois. In Lake Forest she was known by many as "the old lady who rode a bicycle all over town." She died in 1925.

Many unusual homes were built after the turn of the century. The area near the lake was still a popular place to build. Mark Skinner Willing employed Henry Dangler to build his home at 45 North Stonegate Lane, but never lived in the house. The Charles I. Danglers bought the house in 1908 and later sold it to the Charles H. Morses who added an art gallery and named the place "Fairmore." Next door to the Willing house, the James A. Miller family erected a large frame structure, at the easternmost end of Illinois Road; but they too lived in their new home only a very short time. This house was soon bought by the Albert M. Day family. It has been the home of the James Douglas family for the past fifteen years. D. Mark Cummings had erected "Ioka," meaning "beautiful place," in an Indian dialect, at the north end of Lake Road, in 1903. Just south on Lake Road the Colvin sisters built "Halcyon Lodge" in 1910. Donald R. McLennan built "Sturnowzy," an Italian house on Lake Road at the edge of the bluff in 1912. Louis E. Laflin had designed and built "Ellslloyd" on Hawthorne Place in 1907. Albert A. Sprague built a classical colonial home, "Woodlands," on the corner of Elm Tree Road and Hawthorne Place. This house was for long owned and occupied by the Byron S. Harveys. Solomon A. Smith built "Mari-

Sol-Ed-Cai Lodge" on Elm Tree Road in 1916. The Clayton Marks built an Italian villa, designed by Howard Van Doren Shaw, on Lake Road overlooking the lake, in 1914. Bernard Eckhart erected "Pinewold" in 1908 on Lake Road. John T. Pirie had built a traditional colonial home on Rosemary, across from Ferry Hall, in 1903. This house was later famous for an addition which contained an "African Room," an excellent museum of "Big game" tropies, rifles, and other equipment collected on African safaris. In 1915 the Charles H. Schweppes built "Mayflower Place," just south of Ferry Hall, on the grounds of the historic "New Hotel," an English country house of the Tudor type, with spacious rooms and a panelled library looking out through lovely vistas of gardens to the lake. One long vista led to the knoll-top fountain, copied from one in the Villa d'Este in Italy. The French gardens, with clipped hedges, were reminiscent of Versailles. A rock garden and a swimming pool completed the picture.

Mr. and Mrs. Walter Kirk built "Vallombrosa" in 1914, on Illinois Road, overlooking Mayflower Road. Edwin H. Clark was the architect and the model was a villa near Florence, Italy. Solid concrete throughout, simplicity was its enduring charm. Italian workmen executed interesting details. This house is now occupied by Dr. and Mrs. Philip Shambaugh. Clyde M. Carr built "Wyldwoode" near the intersection of Mayflower and Illinois Road in 1916. Architect Harris T. Lindeberg, who designed the present Onwentsia Club-house later on, came to public notice in building the Carr house. He also erected the Cotswold English gem on Stone Gate Road, in 1926, on the site of a frog pond, for the Lowell Chapins. Since 1929 this house has been known as the Mrs. Francis Beidler house.

Edward A. Ryerson built "Havenwood" on Ringwood Road in 1914, an early Renaissance masterpiece reminiscent of the Pitti Palace in Florence, Italy, with a garden and statues and ornaments bearing religious and poetic sentiments, the unit reflecting the best of the Italian Renaissance. This property is now properly a monastery of the Franciscan Fathers. The Harold McCormick's "Villa Turicum" was erected in 1912, just south of "Walden" and north of Fort Sheridan. This too was an Italian villa, containing 44 rooms, and a great number of old world garden statues. Charles A. Platt was the architect and designed the gardens with vistas and panoramas. It covered 300 acres and was said to be the finest example in America of the Italian treatment in landscape design.

The name, McCormick, had appeared in Lake Forest maps in 1890. It indicated properties in various districts. In 1896 Cyrus H. McCormick, (Jr.), and his brother Harold soon after, had developed estates on the lake, north and south of Westleigh Road—"Walden" and "Villa Turicum." Along with these two families who came for the summer months only, Mrs. Cyrus H. McCormick, (Sr.), widow of the famed inventor of the reaper who died in 1884, also had a Lake Forest home.

Mrs. Cyrus H. McCormick, (Sr.), was noted for her support of the McCormick Theological Seminary in Chicago which was her husband's life-long enterprise. She worked with prominent women of Chicago and Lake Forest to found the Women's Presbyterian Board of Missions of the Northwest in 1870. Mrs. Robert W. Patterson, Mrs. John V. Farwell, Mrs. George H. Laflin, Mrs. William Blair, were among the first officers. Mrs. McCormick served as vice-president or honorary vice-president for 34 years. The women met in "Room 48" in the McCormick block at Dearborn and Randolph, which was given rent-free by the McCormick family. They said of Nettie Fowler McCormick that her "interest in the spreading of Christianity over the world was as natural to her as breathing." Her special interest was Christian education. Her unusual business acumen was a boon to her husband's business and to the several religious organizations over the world which she promoted.

In 1916 "Madame" Nettie Fowler McCormick moved to her "House-in-the-woods" in Lake Forest, built for her by her daughter, Mrs. Emmons Blaine, bounded by Ringwood, Sheridan, Illinois and Mayflower Roads. Here she lived a quiet, secluded life until her death in 1922 at the age of 87. She kept close to her family, welcoming the younger members and newcomers into the circle, and keeping abreast of their activities. She kept up a voluminous correspondence and received a stream of visitors representing her far-flung interests. During her lifetime she entertained Dr. James McCosh, President of Princeton University; Woodrow Wilson, also President of Princeton University and later of the United States; Dwight L. Moody, the famed evangelist; John R. Mott, whom she supported throughout her life, helping him organize the Student Volunteer Movement; Samuel A. Moffett, pioneer missionary to Korea; Dr. Henry Winter Luce, missionary to China and father of Henry Luce of *Time Magazine* fame; Sam Higginbottom, farmer-missionary to India. Though friendly to all, Mrs. McCormick was never attracted to Chicago or Lake Forest society as such. A typical reaction at first to her daughter's choice of fiancé was that he was "too worldly, a club-man." In politics and religion she and her husband made an effort to maintain moderation.

Two large homes were built on Sheridan Road in this period. The Edward A. Ryersons built their first home in 1907, the work of Howard Van Doren Shaw. When the Reuben H. Donnelleys purchased this property, they called it "Thornehurst." It contained beautiful planting and Italian gardens. Clifford W. Barnes erected "Glen Rown" in 1909, across from the college campus. This house has become the host of great-name visitors from all over the world.

Several homes were built on Green Bay Road. Louis F. Swift had built "Westleigh" over a period of years, finishing it in 1900. This was a combination of farm and country home. It stood just south of the Onwentsia Club and west of Green Bay Road, on 37 acres, on which there were originally only 17 trees, while eastward across Green Bay Road on what is now known as the Bertram J. Cahn place, still stands the last foothold of the original forest. Mr. Swift brought full grown trees from Libertyville, pulled by six-horse teams. He employed a Japanese landscape architect to lay out "water gardens" including a rustic tea house, moon bridges, and a Torii gate.

The Walter S. Brewsters had built "Covin Tree" on a part of the Atteridge Farm in 1907. Thomas E. Donnelley built "Clinola" in 1910. Edward S. Moore built "West Highlands" in 1912, on the highest spot on Green Bay Road. This farm was a historic site near Lake Forest during Indian and pioneer transportation periods. In old documents this farm is referred to as "Signal Hill" or "Oak Hill" or "Cemetery Knoll." It was first developed by William H. Hubbard. Arthur Heun built "West Highlands" for the Moores in the Italian style. The Charles Edward Browns built "Desbro House," opposite the Onwentsia Club, in 1916. The William V. Kelleys built "Stonebridge House" at the north end of

Green Bay Road, in 1916, a home which in the 1930's became the "Stonebridge Priory" of the Servite Fathers.

In 1902 two large homes had been constructed on west Deer Path. George A. McKinlock built "Brown Gables" in the open prairie at the intersection of Waukegan Road and Deer Path. The A. B. Dicks built a French Renaissance home with gardens and an extensive farm. The Dick property is now occupied by the Lake Forest Hospital, a part of the Deerpath Golf course, the Lutheran Church, the Lake Forest Club, and miscellaneous home sites. The Joseph M. Cudahys built a Louis XVI house, "Innistail," across from the Dicks, in 1915. Nearby on Waukegan Road, the Arthur Meekers built "Arcady," dairy farm and summer home, in 1906. Arthur Heun was the architect. Six hundred cows and a variety of wild and domestic animals were pastured on 100 acres. The Charles D. Nortons remodelled one of the oldest houses in Lake Forest, part of the Sylvester Lind house, at the corner of Deer Path and Washington. They called it "Roadside," finished in 1905.

Many others erected beautiful homes in Lake Forest at this time. The most pretentious of all was the J. Ogden Armour house with its entrance on Waukegan Road, finished in 1908. The property comprised one thousand acres including land which had been a farm belonging to Patrick Melody. Mrs. Armour called the whole property "Mellody Farms." The area before the turn of the century had also comprised what was called "the second slough"—a small edition of the Louisiana bayous, where earth and water mixed in an undisciplined swamp, and where the Lake Forest young men of 1858 onward had found a paradise for their hunting expeditions.

Mr. Armour had the area of the slough drained so that five ponds, later combined into two, were created and stocked with bass and perch. A large enough mound was built to afford the site for a fireproof steel-concrete home in the Italian villa architecture, designed by Arthur Heun, who also designed the Fuji Lake Hotel on the slopes of Mount Fujiyama, Japan. Morton R. Mavor was the contractor. Two feet of black dirt were imported to cover the entire area surrounding the immediate grounds and buildings. A pretentious gate on Waukegan Road, flanked by two apartments, led to a large concrete and steel bridge over the tracks of the Milwaukee railroad. The driveway from the gate to the house was nearly two miles. Double rows of trees were planted on either side, along ten miles of driveway on the property. West of the bridge a large herd of deer was kept behind tall fences. A dozen beautiful horses lived in a large fireproof stable, with the name of each horse inscribed over its box stall. Orchards and an orangerie, similar to that of Voltaire at the Potsdam court of Frederick the Great, supplied fruits, while greenhouses furnished exotic plants and flowers. Antique vases and statuary from old gardens of Europe, also a beautiful Italian well-head, decorated the house, the formal gardens and the front of the main house. Imported marbles were in evidence inside and out.

The main building was 180 x 500 feet, containing a bowling alley in the basement. The first floor contained a dining room with marble walls, a breakfast room, an enclosed porch, a library panelled in Circassian walnut, and off this a little green panelled Georgian room which Mrs. Armour bought in London. The ground floor also contained an elaborate music room where a pipe organ was concealed in the panelling. The second story contained complete suites for each member of the family of three and for their guests. Mr. Armour's two offices, one above the other, connected by a concealed staircase, have been a source of admiration to visitors since. The plumbing and hardware were of very special manufacture. Gold and silver were frequently used in door knobs and electric fixtures. There was silk panelling and especially chosen furniture brought over from various countries of Europe. The main building had an elaborate communication system: one direct line to the Stock Yards, and fifteen other direct connections with the outside. There were also fourteen phones connecting various rooms and buildings on the entire estate.

Twenty marble fireplaces gave the house a cheerful aspect. The formal gardens contained unusual trees and three large reflecting pools, not to mention the myriads of flowers which bloomed in a continual procession from early spring until late fall. A private electric power plant furnished all the electricity and a private spur of the Milwaukee railroad made it possible to deliver large consignments with the least amount of handling. In 1915 the Armours built a wall just west of the railroad tracks to fence the view of passing box-cars from the house and to minimize the roar of the engines. It cost $65,000. *The Chicago Tribune* called it the "costliest and longest wall in the world."

Occasionally when the Armours entertained, it was done in the grand style. Even small dinners were quite formal. One lady remembers coming out from Chicago, being met at the Armours' private railroad station by uniformed and cockaded grooms, being escorted to a horse-drawn sleigh, and jingling up to the Great House. Huge fires burned in every fireplace, and the air was heavy with the scent of flowers everywhere, in addition to the Christmas decorations.

Another time Ruth St. Denis and her company danced in the formal gardens on a platform built over the central reflecting pool. Mrs. Armour was disappointed in the flowers in the garden at the time, so she and her guests inserted gladioli in the beds to make it look more gala. This may have been the introduction of a new trend followed since during festive occasions requiring garden perfection.

Another guest recalled the wedding and reception of Lolita, the only daughter of the Armours, and John J. Mitchell, Jr. This was in the early twenties and an outstanding social event as all of Lake Forest and Chicago friends of the two families were invited. Arthur Heun, the architect, came to decorate, and he used long-stemmed pink roses everywhere. "Lolita came down the rose embowered stair-case dressed in magnificent white velvet," and walked to the floral background, where the ceremony was performed.

XIII

WAR AND NORMALCY

1917–1919

WHEN THE *Lusitania* was torpedoed off the coast of Ireland on May 7, 1915, one of the 114 Americans to lose her life was Mrs. Catherine E. Willey. She was the mother of Mrs. Robert J. Thorne of Lake Forest, on her way to her Paris home with surgical dressings for the French wounded. The war in Europe suddenly invaded the thinking of United States citizens. The word was now Mobilization.

Many young men were called for serious drilling and training camps. Some reported for duty on the Mexican border. People at home set up maps indicating the battle lines with colored pins. Then came the declaration of war on April 6, 1917, followed by the registration of all men between the ages of 21 and 31.

With Fort Sheridan and Great Lakes as neighbors it was said that Lake Forest was as safe a place as any in the world. These military establishments, which had barely been noticed, suddenly became objects of curiosity and visitations. Weekly reviews were attended by many Lake Foresters. Fort Sheridan speakers included Samuel Insull, Governor Frank Lowden, Ex-President Theodore Roosevelt, and the most popular speaker of all, Judge Kenesaw Mountain Landis. Civilian advisers and workers included Alfred Cowles, James C. Hutchins, Sr., William V. Kelley, George A. McKinlock, Sr., John J. Mitchell and Wallace Winter.

Fort Sheridan graduates and officers of the Training Schools included A. Graham Aldis, Waldo M. Allen, Richard Bentley, John S. Broeksmit, Kent Chandler, Knight C. Cowles, Edward A. Cudahy, Jr., Donald B. Douglas, J. M. Ely, James C. Hutchins, Jr., Henry P. Isham, Clay Judson, Gordon McCormick, Frederick C. McLaughlin, Joseph Patterson, Lawrence Robbins, George Richardson, Albert A. Sprague, Wayne Chatfield-Taylor, Charles H. Wacker, Hempstead Washburne and Farwell Winston.

Parades, band concerts, displays, war bond sales, Y.M.C.A., Red Cross, French Orphans, Belgian Relief, occupied nearly all the citizens. Troop trains were in constant motion through town carrying uniformed men or draftees to or from the two adjacent military establishments. Most of the Lake Forest draftees were taken to Camp Grant, in Rockford. Some served on the Mexican border in 1916. Many were mustered into the 67th Brigade of the Rainbow Division, the first non-professional division to arrive overseas. Others became members of the 86th Division. Volunteers who preferred the Navy were usually sent to Great Lakes. A Home Guard unit was formed in Lake Forest, drilling in the streets or at the Young Men's Club with wooden rifles.

Huge and gay parties (fetes) were given to raise money for various projects. Those who were beyond the draft age volunteered their services, in an advisory capacity or for doing special jobs for which they had had experience before the war. Soldiers and sailors began filling the parks and streets. The town responded with a War Community Y.W.C.A. It took over canteen service, recreation and amusement. It looked after the needs of women engaged in war work. Mr. John D. Rockefeller, Jr., a Red Cross worker in the Chicago area, created a mild sensation by dancing with the young lady who was the official dish-washer of a Lake Forest Y.W.C.A. party for service men. Volunteers went to Great Lakes and Fort Sheridan to serve in the Hostess Houses. Entertainments, dinners and dances were held for large groups, and many Lake Forest homes were opened for the entertainment of strangers who were in uniform. Service men were driven about town and shown the places of special beauty, and entertained at many Sunday dinners: several hundred. Churches went "all out" in organizing for the entertainment of service men who came to Lake Forest. Miss

Helen Culver made a record by knitting the greatest number of scarfs, socks, and other pieces in Lake Forest. Mrs. Arthur Aldis and Mrs. George A. McKinlock headed the Canteen work of the greater Chicago area. Alfred E. Hamill served as Deputy Commissioner for France for the American Red Cross. There were meatless days and gasless Sundays. Everyone joined in singing the war songs and knew the words to "Over There," "It's a long way to Tipperary," and "Keep the Home Fires Burning." This was a highly emotional war, and a musical war.

On May 23, 1918, there was a Red Cross Rally at the Young Men's Club. The gymnasium was crowded to capacity. The band from the Great Lakes Naval Training Station furnished the music. Ezra J. Warner, Jr., was chairman, and several speeches were made. Captain E. J. Beyington, one of the survivors of the Princess Pat regiment, told about his experiences in the trenches and praised the work of the Red Cross. John Griffith presented a lot on Washington Circle to be auctioned off for the Red Cross. Henry Rumsey, as auctioneer, sold it to William O. Lindley for $1,000. He gave it back. Mrs. Reuben Donnelley paid $1,000 for it and promptly gave it back. John T. Pirie then bought it for $800 and returned the property. In all about $5,000 was raised for the Red Cross from this lot alone. Mr. Rumsey then wanted to lead the singing of the "Star Spangled Banner." Captain Uri Grannis offered $10 if he did not sing. Mrs. Charles Schweppe then said she knew that Mr. Rumsey could sing and offered to pay $25 if he would take the platform. Pledges were signed long after the end of the meeting.

Charles S. Dewey of Lake Forest became assistant and special adviser to Captain W. A. Moffett, Commandant of Great Lakes, who himself resided in Lake Forest. On a Saturday, Secretary of the Navy Josephus Daniels was due at a Great Lakes Review. On the night before, Captain Moffett received a telephone call from the war-time Mayor of Lake Bluff saying that the bridge over Sheridan Road was found to be defective and that the Secretary had better take a train from Chicago to Great Lakes, since Sheridan Road through Lake Bluff was the only automobile road to Great Lakes at the time. Captain Moffett assured the Mayor that the bridge would be repaired in time for the Secretary's arrival. A group of engineers with a large crew of naval personnel from

Great Lakes worked all night until a new bridge was built on Sheridan Road in Lake Bluff. At war's end the city fathers of Lake Bluff named the former Sheridan Road in Lake Bluff, Moffett Road, which is its name to this day.

Captain Moffett organized teams of eloquent speakers called "Minute Men," who travelled over the country with Sousa Bands, making speeches to encourage the purchase of war bonds. Several Lake Forest volunteers were so used. One of these was William Mather Lewis, a graduate of Lake Forest College, a former Headmaster of Lake Forest Academy, and a former Mayor of Lake Forest. Mr. Lewis was also instrumental in organizing the Chicago chapter of the Navy League of the United States and became one of its early Presidents.

These several Lake Foresters, working with Captain Moffett, established such a cordial relationship with Great Lakes that the Lake Forest people of all ages became habitual visitors at the Great Lakes Naval Training Center. There were roller-skating parties in the drill hall for young and old, to a spirited Navy band. On Wednesdays and Saturdays crowds sat in the bleachers to watch the parades and to give an outlet to their patriotic feelings. They heard the Sousa bands, the greatest concentration of music in our country. They got glimpses of visiting celebrities: Josephus Daniels, Secretary of the Navy; Admiral W. S. Benson, the first Chief of Naval Operations; Dr. Henry Van Dyke, author and one time Ambassador to Holland; Ex-Presidents Theodore Roosevelt and William Howard Taft; Governor Frank O. Lowden of Illinois; and many others who occupied the reviewing stands as guests of Captain Moffett and his Staff. The "Peacock of the Navy," Micheaux (Monk) Tennant would lead 1,500 picked musicians playing martial music, followed by battalions of four companies (singing squares) with a hollow center, and a band in the middle of each battalion; the men singing as they came past the reviewing stands, spotless in white uniforms. Another stirring sight was the "human flag" in which ten thousand sailors, dressed in red, white or blue, formed a living flag and marched past the reviewing stands.

A recent navy historian records that during the first fifty year's existence of the Great Lakes Naval Training Station, the high water mark of service morale was reached during World War I.

He says the music of John Philip Sousa was greatly responsible for this, also the fine athletic teams which won championships with great regularity. He mentions also the large patriotic demonstrations and visiting celebrities. He fails to credit Captain Moffett with superb leadership, wonderful imagination and an intensely human and personal organization.

In 1917 the flag pole in Market Square was dedicated with troops and a large band from Fort Sheridan taking part, assisted by the Home Guards. The base of the flag-pole contains a quotation from President Woodrow Wilson: "We are glad to fight for the ultimate peace of the world and for the liberation of its people." It was "dedicated to the men of Lake Forest who gave themselves for the safety of their country and the world."

When the end of the war came and the losses were counted, there were sixteen casualties from Lake Forest. Ten had died of disease and six were battle casualties. The honored dead included Guy Bezy, George Alexander McKinlock, Jr., William J. Sandy, Ellsworth W. Stoker, Leroy H. Wheeler, and Lewis Yore. Guy Bezy went into the battle line in August 1914 and was killed 20 days later near Charleroix. There were five sons of the Robert Sandy family in the service, two of whom did not return. Influenza took a heavy toll among both the military and the civilian population.

Colonel Noble B. Judah, a Chicago lawyer, served in the Rainbow Division throughout our participation in France. He became assistant Chief of Staff of this division which suffered 16,000 casualties. He received the Legion of Honor. Stanley Gublin received the Croix-de-Guerre because he took 19 German prisoners single-handed in the Verdun sector. A total of 345 Lake Forest men served in the armed forces.

Lake Forest celebrated Armistice Day, November 11, 1918, by ringing all the church and school bells in town. Children from the Halsey School came to the City Hall to ring the bell. It was rung with such vigor and so continuously that the bell broke, never to ring again to announce fires. It was replaced by a siren two years later. Fearing that this siren might get out of order, the city fathers ordered that it be tested every noon. This testing has continued.

Uniformed men returned to Lake Forest to change into citizens' clothes as soon as possible. Some of these got together to form the George Alexander McKinlock, Jr., Post No. 264 of the American Legion. After several meetings, they received their charter on February 1, 1921. The post was named after a Lake Forest boy, a Harvard graduate, who was reported missing in action in France at the age of 25. The first meetings were held in John Griffith's real estate office. The charter members included Stanley Anderson, Wilbur Chapman, Ellis Griffith, William H. Harding, Stanley Kiddle, Joseph H. Lindenmeyer, Oswald E. Obermiller, Colonel Albert A. Sprague, Chaucer Westbrook, and the first Commander, Montague R. Rassmussen. The present American Legion Home was dedicated in 1935—it had served as the Rassmussen Shoe Store on Western Avenue and had been moved to its present location when the Market Square was erected.

The American Legion has sponsored Lake Forest Day since 1921, and devoted itself to the service of the community. Early in its existence the Legion made a gift to the city of elm trees on Deer Path, dedicated to those who lost their lives in the war. They have sponsored a youth program including athletics, citizenship, national holidays and several Lake Forest charities. Its very special interest has been the Veterans' Hospital at Downey (Great Lakes).

On October 2, 1919, occurred the "Welcome Home Celebration" for all returned service men. The Durand Art Institute was filled to capacity for the dinner; then the entire party moved across the street to the Presbyterian Church where the program took place. War-time Mayor Keene H. Addington made an address of welcome. Major General Leonard Wood delivered the main address of the evening. Mayor Henry Rumsey presented each veteran with a bronze recognition medal, bearing the Seal of Lake Forest on one side and an inscription on the other which read "Presented by the City of Lake Forest in grateful recognition of patriotic services rendered in World War." Montague Rasmussen of the American Legion made an appropriate response in behalf of the veterans.

In May 1919 there was a milk strike, but there was no shortage in Lake Forest as a fleet of private cars drove to the Bowman Dairy in Highland Park and supplied the need until the strike ended. The 1919 version of Lake Forest Day was held on Labor Day and sponsored by the Commercial Association. This was an in-novation as most Lake Forest Days had been sponsored by the Young Men's Club and held on July 4th. 2,400 bottles of pop and 100 gallons of ice cream were consumed. Sports were the main feature. There was a baseball game, then a 100-yard dash, a 50-yard dash for boys and girls, a 50-yard married ladies race, a three-legged race, a mile bicycle race. A trained dog performed. There was a Punch and Judy show. Prizes were given to the oldest couple on the grounds, to the youngest baby, to the most popular boy, to the best woman nail driver. Dinner was served on the grounds at reasonable prices. Everybody enjoyed everything.

When Mayor Henry Rumsey was elected in the spring of 1919 he made the following remarks in his speech of acceptance before the City Council: "Your mayor has ridden around the town in a high two-wheeled cart with a lamplighter when we burned coal-oil in our street lamps on nights which were not moonlit accord-ing to the calendar. He has helped Miss McLoughlin put up and distribute mail in the old post office. He has played baseball with our fire chief, but not recently. He has called on the young ladies at Ferry Hall with our health officer. He has hidden on the side of Green Bay Road watching for automobile speeders. He has run onto red-light island on a Saturday night and demolished the 'Safety First' signal. He has sat at the southwest corner of this table. He has been Chairman of the Garbage committee. He is now on the Cemetery commission. So, do you wonder, that he appreciates the honor which has been conferred upon him by being the unopposed candidate for the position of your Mayor?" Mayor Rumsey served six years.

DURING 1919 Lake Forest lost two of its leading citizens. Prof. John J. Halsey passed away on May 31 and James Anderson on July 11. Dr. Halsey had come to Lake Forest in 1878 as a member of the faculty of Lake Forest College. For fifty years he served as the connecting link between town and gown, between Church and Education, cutting across all groups that developed in the village. He served as Alderman, President of the Board of Educa-tion, member of the first Library Board, President pro tem of Lake Forest College, elder in the Presbyterian Church, a mainstay of the Art Institute Club, eloquent leader, and a promoter of Lake

Forest's civic and cultural interests. The Halsey school was named after him in 1912. His greatest monument remains the "History of Lake County" which represents an enormous amount of work, for he interviewed several thousand people in order to write this original work. His dedication to truth, without petty prejudice, and without trying to prove something, makes the book a source book for local history for many years to come.

James Anderson was born July 11, 1831, in the Parish of New Deer, Aberdeenshire, Scotland. He arrived in Quebec on May 26, 1851, after a six weeks' passage by sail. He came to Chicago on June 4, 1851, from Quebec, by boat nearly all the way. He married May Davis in 1857 and moved to Lake Forest in April 1859. He became a member of the Presbyterian church and served as deacon, trustee, and elder for thirty years. His early work in Lake Forest consisted of opening streets, clearing of roads and lots. In 1865 he went into general merchandising and continued in this business until his last year. He served as Postmaster, City Treasurer, Supervisor of Shields Township for 28 years. He raised a large family. By his friendly and humble spirit he made everybody his friend.

The last Memorial Day in which the G.A.R. took part was in 1920 when the original forty member organization of 1900 had dwindled to only four. The service was sponsored by the City of Lake Forest, the G.A.R., and the newly formed American Legion. Mayor Rumsey presided. Abraham Lincoln's Gettysburg Address, the bible of all patriotic speakers, was read. Major Rathbone of Fort Sheridan made a brief address; then taps was sounded.

XIV

PROHIBITION

1919–1929

GRADUALLY Lake Forest settled down to normal living and civic improvements at war's end. The seemingly insoluble problem was that of the city's water supply. The Lake Forest Water Company had been formed in 1890, supplying many homes with water from Lake Michigan under pressure provided by steam pumps. Many families continued to get their water from private wells. However, as the population increased, automobiles multiplied, as did the hard surfaced roads, rain-water found its way directly and quickly through the sewer system to the lake. The water level within the city sub-soil dropped appreciably, rendering many wells unproductive; and so more city water was needed. The private Water Company was not able to cope with the increased demand and the complaints of many citizens.

Beginning in 1904 litigation and expense had continued in this water controversy. After the election of Mayor Rumsey in April 1919, the new Mayor wished to carry out former Mayor Addington's suggestion that the city should purchase the waterworks and pay for them in certificates issued under the Act of 1913 with 5% interest and constituting a charge against the earnings of the plant alone. He wished to complete this project himself before he stepped out of office, but the cloak fell upon Mayor Rumsey. The plan seemed fair enough; and all stockholders agreed to accept the plan, except George S. Holt, the President of the Company, who wanted $40,000 cash for his share.

The controversy was kept very much alive when on May 6, 1919, due to the failure of electric power, the new electric pumps did not function properly and the water lines spewed heavy sediment. The newspapers exaggerated and wrote humorous articles and headlines. One paper said a new game had been devised in Lake Forest. "It consists of drawing a tub of water for a bath, then drawing it off and seeing who finds the deepest sediment." It reported that John T. Pirie, Jr., drew six inches of water for a bath; couldn't see the bottom of the tub, and gave up the bath idea in disgust. James King, the City Clerk, drew a tubful, drained it off and wrote his initials on the sediment.

The controversy came to a head again in connection with the election of Mayor when on April 12, 1921, the popular vote gave the city authority to buy the Water Company and re-elected Mayor Henry Rumsey (Regular Party) over his opponent, Van Wagenen Alling (Independent Party). The plan which obtained was the payment of $250,000 to the Water Company. It had originally cost $384,823. The Independent Party contended that no one knew the condition of the pipes underground, after thirty years of service, and stressed the idea of *depreciation*. The Regular party stressed the loyalty and generosity of these citizens who had furnished the city with 40,000,000 gallons of water per month for thirty years, and stressed the idea of *replacement*. It was said that it would cost the city twice as much to build a comparable plant by current cost of materials and labor. The clincher may have been the testimony of William E. Clow who claimed that cast iron pipes should last indefinitely. The Water Company was purchased.

In 1919 the City of Lake Forest received a gift of a stone gate for the Cemetery; the donor was Mrs. Finley Barrell, in memory of her twenty-four-year-old son who was drowned.

President Harding's "Normalcy" meant heartache and loss to several prominent Lake Forest residents during the first postwar business depression of 1921. The story of J. Ogden Armour was one of the most distressing. During the war years Mr. Armour had built up his meat packing house of Armour and Company into a billion dollar a year business. He had also substantial interests in the wheat market and in the Milwaukee Railroad, and was known as the second richest man in the world. A mild-mannered, quiet little man, he aspired to become the richest.

During the period of post-war trade adjustments, Mr. Armour became involved in the purchase of more and more grain, to stem the tide of falling prices. As a result he is said to have lost "one million dollars per day during 200 days," losing nearly all his fortune, including his beautiful home, Mellody Farms. Mr. Armour died in 1927, in London, England, at the age of 64 and his body was brought home on the *Berengaria* in August to be buried in Chicago.

The years following the war were difficult times for the police department. Five police officers were on the staff: Aubrey Warren (special), James Gordon, Albert Hopman, F. Berghorn, and James Watt. The increase of the number of automobiles and the increase of accidents greatly extended police responsibility. Mayor Rumsey expressed his ideas on speed limits in 1919: 6 m.p.h. around corners and curves, 10 m.p.h. in the business district, 15 m.p.h. in close residential districts, 20 m.p.h. in open residential districts and 30 m.p.h. on public highways. Sons and daughters of well known families were frequently fined for exceeding these limits, some repeatedly. It did not occur to anyone that automobile engines of those days could not operate smoothly under 15 m.p.h., nor was it possible to patrol all the circuitous thoroughfares of the fair city with four patrolmen even though they were on duty around the clock. Car thefts were continually in the police reports and in the local newspapers. On May 5, 1920, a Police car was stolen from the front of City Hall. This was considered a very humorous incident. After two weeks, when no leads had been reported regarding the theft, the Police Department purchased a new squad car. Then, on June 17, the stolen car was recovered. It had been abandoned in Peru, Indiana.

In 1923 James Sage was killed in line of duty; Clyde M. Spralding had lost his life in 1915. These have been the only casualties of the police department.

Prohibition was necessitated by the food shortages during World War I. After the war, the 18th Amendment of the U.S. Constitution was ratified in January 1919. Many problems arose as a result of this amendment, since some did not wish to obey the new law as they saw no excuse for it on the basis of shortages of grain. In Lake Forest the special headache for the police, resulting from prohibition, were the so-called Booze Robberies. Reports indicated that a syndicate was bringing Canadian whiskey through Valparaiso, Indiana, to the Chicago area. A moonshine still was located at the south end of Lake Forest, which was operating and doing a brisk business. Yeast and raisins became sold out in Lake Forest and impossible to buy. The police were confident that the stolen automobiles were the work of booze smugglers.

A great number of houses were broken into. Apparently nothing was touched except alcoholic beverages. At the C. H. Acherts' only bourbon was taken. The police report showed "booze robberies" every night in a different home between December 11 and 21, 1919. The total loss was estimated over $150,000. On January 23, 1920, nine ex-convicts were arrested. Several others were picked up during the month. Two stills and five distilleries were seized in February. In April 1920, three cases were tried in the Waukegan courts in three weeks. Juries refused to convict anyone stealing liquor even though homes were broken into. They seemed to hold the view that it is against the law to possess liquor, therefore they could not convict anyone for stealing it. No more Lake Forest "booze cases" were brought before the county courts. It went even beyond these particular cases, as there grew in Lake Forest a belief that it was impossible to get a judgment in favor of any Lake Forest citizen or organization. It was felt that all controversies should be settled out of court.

One of the strange prohibition era incidents involved a saintly woman, a life-long resident within the shadow of the Lake Forest Presbyterian Church. Her funeral service was conducted in Lake Forest and she was to be interred in the Forest Home Cemetery in Milwaukee. Her coffin was placed in the hearse and the procession formed behind. On the way north on Green Bay Road the hearse became separated from the rest of the procession and continued north at a somewhat faster rate than the rest. In a half hour the hearse returned with a police escort, to the procession. The police had suspected that the coffin contained liquor and wanted permission from the nearest relative to open it. Their suspicion was based on the fact that the hearse had been exceeding the speed limit and they assumed that the driver himself was under the influence at the time. After opening the coffin the hearse turned north again to the final resting place in Milwaukee. The family chuckled over the incident knowing that the deceased would have enjoyed the joke herself as she had a good sense of humor.

In these days of law-breaking tendencies the Lake Forest Police department was busy with many and diverse infractions of the law. The reports show that people cut trees on properties not their own, many articles were lost without a trace, bad checks, robberies involving money, jewelry, bicycles, and cars; innumerable accidents including a car overrun by the Chicago North Shore line; family quarrels, drunkenness, street lamps damaged in great numbers, assault and battery, hunting and shooting within the city limits, a car damaged by a horse, and several mistaken identity cases in which the "culprit" turned out to be a close friend of the family. Big-time safe crackers broke into the Lake Forest Laundry and did away with $3,100. The robbers were identified through fingerprints, but the money was never recovered. The Frank Farwell house was shelled. Several shells entered the house, one landed on the lawn. It turned out that soldiers at Fort Sheridan had been practicing with a one-pounder gun, but were poor marksmen. There were red faces at the Fort. All of this indicated the need for a much larger police force. This was gradually achieved by 1930, when the department numbered twenty officers.

In 1921–1922 Leon Bix Beiderbeck attended Lake Forest Academy. He showed great talent as a musician, playing jazz arrangements on the campus. He helped form a dance orchestra composed of Academy boys, which played professionally in the Chicago area. He became one of the great trumpeters of all time. As a member of Paul Whiteman's orchestra he was the idol of many budding musicians, including Louis "Satchmo" Armstrong. His reputation is firmly established in European countries as the outstanding exponent of American jazz. Some of his best known compositions are "Davenport Blues," "In a Mist," "Flashes," and "Candlelight."

On November 9, 1923, a significant zoning ordinance was passed which has been a mainstay in regulating the expansion of the city. Five zones were described with detailed regulations for each. The first zone, east of the Northwestern railroad tracks and generally west of a line following Washington Road, required a lot area of 7,500 square feet. The second zone, from Washington Road to the Lake required a lot area of 20,000 square feet. Also a duplex area, a retail business area and commercial districts were described, each to be governed by special regulations.

DURING THE 1920's there was a general prejudice in our school system against married teachers. The Board of Education passed a resolution in 1920: "Resolved that whereas the marriage of a woman teacher is inconsistent with the performance of her duties in jeopardizing that regularity and continuance of service which is essential thereto, now therefore the appointment of a woman teacher shall hereafter terminate upon her marriage." This same rule was also the practice at Ferry Hall. At the Academy, teachers were released at the end of a school year when it was discovered that they were married.

THE 1920's were noted for increased interest in sports and athletics in Lake Forest as well as over the country. George Lott, William Tilden and other national tennis champions appeared frequently at the Onwentsia Club. Charles Garland won the Davis Cup doubles championship at Wimbledon in the early twenties. Later in the decade, as an active member of the Onwentsia Club, he attracted nationally known tennis players to Lake Forest. Edith Cummings of Lake Forest won the U.S.G.A. women's championship in 1923, and the following year took the Women's Western Amateur title. Samuel T. Chase was a Western Golf champion. Robert A. Gardner was a two-time winner (1909, 1915) of the amateur golf championship. In an interesting Onwentsia exhibition in the early 1920's, "Bob" Gardner, "Bobby" Jones, Alexis Sterling, and Edith Cummings performed as hundreds of spectators followed each shot.

Shoreacres Club, just south of Great Lakes Naval Training Station, was opened for play on July 28, 1921. The Club had been incorporated in 1916, "To promote and encourage boating, swimming, tennis and such other sports as may be authorized by the Board of Directors or Governors." The original Governors were Messrs. O. E. Babcock, Hobart Chatfield-Taylor, Stanley Field, Frank Hibbard and E. L. Ryerson. Stanley Field was elected president. Membership was not to exceed 225. The 1916 purchase of land included 89 acres.

The First World War stopped all progress; but estimates were secured in 1919, and construction began in earnest with revised and simplified plans. The property was increased to 150 acres. Seth Raynor was secured to design the Golf course, completed in August 1922. At the time of completion the full membership of 225 was achieved. The total cost exceeded $500,000. Two En-Tout-Cas tennis courts were added in 1923, as they were also at Onwentsia. The Clubhouse, designed by David Adler and located near the edge of the bluff, was finished in 1924. Shoreacres has concentrated on golf and has given up entirely the original dream of water sports as some of these were available next door at the Great Lakes Naval Training Station.

Knollwood Club was started west of Waukegan Road on the site of the Granger Farwell and Dr. Alfred C. Haven farms, in 1924. Knollwood, the name of the Farwell farm, was adopted for the name of the Club. The golf course was designed by Captain J. Allison. Thomas E. Wilson was the first president and Samuel Insull was a moving spirit in the project. The Club sponsored golf, tennis, swimming, and horseback riding with seventy-five miles of riding trails available in all directions.

During the fall, football games at the Academy were popular events. Everybody came early enough to park his car on the fifty yard line, if possible. They watched the game; and, later in the decade, at the same time listened to a college game by the new car radios. There was no admission charge. Some of the best college freshman teams played against the Academy teams coached by Ralph Jones, who left the Academy to become the first coach of the professional Chicago Bears.

One memorable game was played against the Notre Dame Freshmen, who were defeated 22–0. This was on October 15, 1921. The Notre Dame team was known the following year for the famous backfield "The Four Horsemen," so called by Grantland Rice, the New York sports writer. This team included Captain Jim Crowley, left half, Elmer Layden, fullback, Don Miller, right half, and Harry Stuhldreher, the greatest quarterback of all time according to Knute Rockne, the famous Notre Dame coach.

The Academy team composed of Allen, Coleman, Ferguson,

Flues, Frump, Hastings, Howe, Kidd, Lipe, Pattison, Pearce, Perkins, Rohrback, Straight, Welge, and Whitehill put on a great exhibition of blocking, running, and tackling. Notre Dame seemed much less coordinated. The visiting stars were Vergara, guard, and Crowley, half back. Whitehill, Perkins and Coleman scored the touchdowns for the Academy.

Fret, a Notre Dame guard, was given permission to go home. He cut across the 30-yard line with his suitcase which fell apart in the middle of the field and the game had to be stopped till he had gathered up his belongings. Engright, a fullback was also told to go home, since an easy game was anticipated; but when the substitute fullback Rex got hurt, Engright was brought back from the station and entered the game half dressed. To cap the confusion, when the Notre Dame team took the train for Chicago, they suddenly noticed with apprehension that the train was proceeding on the left track. Nothing went right that afternoon for "The Four Horsemen."

The first parcel of land for the Deerpath Municipal Golf Course was received by Mayor Rumsey, from A. B. Dick, in the fall of 1922. It consisted of seventy acres. John Griffith then added 44 lots. Mayor Rumsey and James Gordon then added other properties. Property owners on the western edge of Green Bay Road made additional gifts of land. These donors included Walter S. Brewster, William E. Clow, Thomas E. Donnelley, Owen Jones and Noble Judah. Several acres were bought by the syndicate to round out the golf course property. The only restrictions were that the course would be used for park purposes only and that no trap-shooting would occur on it, and if it ever should cease to function as a park or a public benefit, it should revert to the donors of the property. Mayor Rumsey was interested in the project as a community effort for the benefit of all.

The Deerpath Syndicate comprised contributors of $1,000 or more toward this project. The list included P. D. Armour III, Lester Armour, B. L. Behr, Walter S. Brewster, Edward F. Carry, Joseph M. Cudahy, Alfred T. Carton, Miss Helen Culver, David Dangler, J. V. Farwell, Jr., C. N. Goodwin, Byron H. Harvey, E. A. Hamill, Thomas D. Jones, William V. Kelley, Robert P. Lamont, Clifford M. Leonard, H. H. Martin, Cyrus H. McCormick, George A. McKinlock, Mrs. Edith Rockefeller Mc-

Cormick, Mark Morton, Donald R. McLennan, Henry A. Rumsey, Edmund A. Russell, Charles H. Schweppe (Secretary and Treasurer), Mrs. Charles H. Schweppe, Franklin P. Smith, Mrs. Byron L. Smith, Oliver T. Wilson, and Thomas E. Wilson.

Other gifts were received from G. M. Collins, The American Realty Company, The American Legion, the Horticultural Society, and the Lake Forest Garden Club. Alex Binnie, an expert gardener, donated one green and assumed the responsibility for several others.

The 18-hole course was laid out by Alex Pirie of Old Elm. The first nine holes were opened on August 21, 1926, by Mayor Henry A. Rumsey, who made a short dedicatory speech. The remaining nine holes were finished the following year, when Alex Pirie (Old Elm) and Phil Gandin (Skokie), played against Willie Hunter (Onwentsia) and Austere Claeyssens (Glen Flora) in an exhibition match. The first committee in charge of the course included John Griffith, C. T. Gunn, Carl L. Krafft and Frank W. Read. Resident membership was $18.00 a year. Terry McGovern was the first Deerpath professional, 1937–1941. He was followed by Charles Nordberg, Robert Ledger, Harry Peddle and William Cascarano, the incumbent, who has served since 1951.

A SPECTACULAR FIRE occurred on Sunday May 23, 1924, when the Volney Foster home, on the corner of Washington and Rosemary burned, in part, with damage estimated at $50,000. This was the original Granger Farwell house which had been moved from Sheridan Road to Washington Road in 1915, blocking Rosemary in the process for six months. A great crowd from all over town gathered to help or be entertained. Fire departments from Glencoe and North Chicago arrived. The heat could be felt far beyond the street. Crowds of people salvaged furniture. Mirrors and chairs were thrown out windows, while pillows were gingerly carried down to safety. In the center of the crowd on the lawn was Libby Chase with her pet bear. Contents of the basement were carried out and away by the visiting firemen. The top floor was completely burned out, the second floor was partially destroyed, the first floor was ruined by water.

SEVERAL Lake Forest weddings in the 1920's were lavish and accented with unique features. Sarah Brewster Hodges was whisked off from her father's garden in her bridegroom's private plane. Claire Childs and Lloyd Laflin departed in a shower of rice over their horse-drawn sleigh one snowy afternoon. When Daisiana Smith married John Pirie on a warm October day, in her family's garden, ushers and bridesmaids proceeded from the house down to a terrace and across a bridge over the swimming pool, to a fountain surrounded by an iron filigree arbor covered with purple clusters of grapes. Because the orchestra was stationed far back by the pool and could not see what was going on during the service, one member was stationed along the way to give the signal for the recessional. On his knees, he peered through a mass of legs and missed the proper moment for the recessional to begin. The reception was held under a large tree hung with Spanish moss, transported from Florida for the occasion. Another impressive outdoor wedding was Ellen Thorne Smith's on the lawn of her grandmother's home, Mrs. George R. Thorne. A three-course dinner was served, after the ceremony, at tables under the trees. This was customary at many weddings in the twenties.

THE Prince of Wales (Edward VIII) visited Lake Forest on a beautiful Monday morning, on October 17, 1924. A large crowd of curious had gathered at the station from miles around for a glimpse of the popular World War I figure. He came as a guest of Louis F. Swift, to show the appreciation of the British government for the enormous quantities of meat products sent to the British Empire throughout the war by the Chicago Stock Yards.

At 8:20 the special train came to a screeching halt: a Northwestern locomotive with eight Canadian National coaches. There was cheering and handclapping as the English Prince appeared on the rear platform, where he was greeted by his host. He was accompanied by Brigadier General Cotter and Major Metcalf of the British Army, Captain Allen Lascelles, brother-in-law of Princess Mary, Sir Walter Peacock and Inspector Burt of Scotland Yard, and two Americans, Major Oscar Solbert of the U.S. Army and Mr. Oliver Sawyer of the State Department, representing President Calvin Coolidge.

The Prince got into Louis Swift's limousine looking shy and bored. The rest of the party got into three Buicks driven by George

Wenban, Henry Rose, and Maurice Fitzgerald. There was a brief conducted tour of a few Lake Forest streets. The party stopped in front of Ferry Hall, a special interest of Mr. Swift, where the students had gathered on the porch to greet the Prince. The party lingered long enough to hear the singing of "Prince of Wales, we are true to you," then moved on to the Swift estate on Green Bay Road.

Breakfast was served soon after 8:30 with Countess Minotto, daughter of Louis Swift, as hostess. The Prince seemed worn out with the thought of the day ahead and asked plaintively about the proposed visit to the Chicago Stock Yards: "Will there be much killing?" "Oh yes," was the reply, "A great deal—in your honor!" After breakfast the Prince viewed the Swift property and greenhouses and departed by automobile for his Stock Yards appointment by 10:30.

Peter Kelley, local blacksmith, had a special interest in this royal visit. Several years previously he had served as a guard at the coronation of King George V, and at the christening of the Prince. It should also be mentioned that the Prince's future wife was living in Lake Forest on Oakwood Avenue at the time, the wife of a Great Lakes naval officer.

Another state visit was made on June 25, 1926, when Crown Prince Gustavus Adolphus and Princess Louise of Sweden came to Lake Forest as guests of Mr. and Mrs. Charles H. Schweppe of Mayflower Road. The Princess, the former Lady Louise Mountbatten, was a great granddaughter of Queen Victoria of England, and a daughter of Prince Louis of Battenberg and Princess Victoria of Hesse.

The party arrived at Great Lakes by motor yacht from Chicago and made a tour of the Naval Station. It was a rainy day. They were then entertained at the Onwentsia Club where the Prince played golf. At the Schweppes', a large reception was held in the afternoon.

The gate of the Schweppe grounds was gaily decorated with American and Swedish flags; yellow roses and larkspur carried out the Swedish national colors everywhere. Thousands of electric light bulbs illumined the grounds. The Princess was dressed simply for the occasion. Among those present at dinner that evening were Cyrus Hall McCormick, Edward T. Blair, the John G.

Shedds, the Kersey Coates Reids, the John J. Mitchells, the Samuel Insulls, the Swedish Consul in Chicago, Carol and Mrs. de Dardel, also the Hon. Bostron, Swedish Minister to the United States.

Ruth Page, premiere danseuse of the Chicago Opera Company, danced on a little pavilion close to the terrace balustrade, with lights playing on her and her leading man, the gray lake for a background, and a huge moon, sailing in and through threatening clouds. It was an exquisite sight, and one that the Prince and Princess enjoyed.

A dance pavilion east of the house, overlooking the lake, was covered with a green and white marquee, lending a picturesque effect to the grounds. Over 300 guests attended the dance, for which three orchestras played inside and out.

On the return trip to Chicago the Prince and Princess were entertained by Vice President and Mrs. Charles G. Dawes in their Evanston home. In Chicago a luncheon was held at the home of the Swedish Consul, Carol O. de Dardel, and a reception at the Casino Club given by the Hon. and Mrs. Ira Nelson Morris, followed by a banquet at the Palmer House.

Perhaps the Princess enjoyed most of all the trip to Marshall Field's escorted by Mrs. Schweppe, whose father, John G. Shedd, was president of the firm for many years. Here the Princess admired a Tiffany desk and dressing table, which were soon packed to accompany the Prince and Princess on their return trip to Sweden. The Princess' parting words were: It was "a delightful revelation."

IN THE ANNALS OF Lake Forest education, 1925 was an important year. The Academy, Ferry Hall, and the College had been chartered originally as Lind University, in 1857, then as Lake Forest University, in 1865. For sixty-eight years there had been only one Board of Trustees presiding over whatever institutions were embraced by the University. The finances of these institutions had been pooled, so that the profits from one went to make up the deficits of another. During World War I the College enrollment had naturally suffered, whereas the Academy and Ferry Hall had had prosperous years. The juggling of finances became an emotional instead of a financial problem.

Mr. Clayton Mark, president of the Board of Trustees of Lake Forest University in 1925, acquired the impossible task of legally separating the three institutions, at the same time keeping each organization happy. Each institution was therefore chartered separately with the provision that the College was to receive $200,000 from each of the two other institutions, over a period of twenty years. Mr. Mark thought the plan was a fair decision, and suited to the best interests of all three institutions. The plan and its execution became a source of irritation and strife during the depression years through the 1930's. However, Mr. Mark's plan has proved its wisdom and each institution enjoys its present independence.

On November 13, 1926, Lake Forest College observed the 50th anniversary of the matriculation of the first class of Lake Forest College. Anna Farwell De Koven, a member of the original class arrived from Florence, Italy, and received an honorary degree.

Also in 1926, the League of Women Voters of Lake Forest was started under the aegis of Mrs. Frank Hixon who has continued active as the League has grown in membership and in importance as an integral part of the city. In 1960, the League received the World Understanding award from the Chicago Council on Foreign Relations for its work on foreign policy within its own membership, and within the community as well.

IN THE TWENTIES business houses had to make adjustments and changes. The Post Office now occupied space in Market Square. New businesses and names appeared in the marketplace. Joe O'Neill built a new hardware store on Westminster, since his store had been destroyed to make room for Market Square. The new O'Neill store contained a movie house, The De Luxe Theater, which became a very popular spot. At first Joseph O'Neill managed the theatre and attempted to introduce Sunday movies with "clean, quiet, educating amusement." It was later operated by Vincent Quarta. Here William S. Hart played in "The Silent Man," Billie Burke starred in "The Land of Promise," and "East Lynne" was featured in 1921.

Based on an Illinois statute of 1889, Green Bay Road was declared a "pleasure driveway" in 1925 by a city ordinance, making it illegal to operate burden carrying vehicles on that road.

Following a series of petitions signed by several hundred Lake Forest residents, a special city election was held on May 11, 1926, at the headquarters of the American Legion on Forest Avenue, for the purpose of voting whether to annex the area west of the Skokie to the City of Lake Forest. The area under consideration comprised about ten square miles of territory. 302 votes were cast for annexation, 5 against. This was the largest area ever added to the City of Lake Forest during the first hundred years.

The Deerpath Theatre and other adjoining units were planned in 1926 and finished in 1928 on Deer Path between Western Avenue and Bank Lane. Joseph C. Emma, a friend of the famous movie actor Rudolph Valentino, has been the manager almost continuously. Before coming to Lake Forest, Mr. Emma had directed a successful silent picture in Hollywood, *The Iron Horse*. Mrs. Emma ran a successful dancing school for several years. Their daughter, Rosemary, is a well-known musical comedy and television actress, under the name of Joan Taylor.

Until 1927 the center of Lake Forest was determined by the intersection of Deer Path and the Northwestern Railroad tracks, and street addresses were numbered accordingly. The present numbering system, established in March, 1927, is based nearer the actual center of the expanded City of Lake Forest. The north-south zero line is along south Ridge Road northward through the Deer Path School. The east-west line corresponds with the south line of Shields Township. The center of town is brought to an imaginary point near the Onwentsia Club stables. In October of the same year a city ordinance changed twenty-nine more street names. The greatest achievement was in changing Jessamine Road to Westleigh Road. The Deerpath Golf Club was named in April of that year. At this time the city reported 69 miles of paved streets in Lake Forest.

Also in 1927, Vilasco Chandler, the only living member of the first graduating class of Lake Forest Academy in 1861 attended the June Commencement.

In the 1920's several accidents occurred at the railroad intersection at Deer Path. Drivers and pedestrians were often confused by the left hand drive of the Northwestern; and often when one train went by they did not anticipate another from the opposite direction. After several tragedies, the railroad company was prevailed upon to install a gate-house and a gate-keeper who held a stop sign until the train or trains had passed. In January 1927, Henry F. Williams became the gate-keeper. He was a long-time Lake Forester who had herded cows in the 1880's as a young boy. He served for twenty years as a gate-keeper until automatic electric signals were installed in 1946. The older generations remember him as a jovial conversationalist and friendly protector of children and pet dogs.

Cyrus H. Adams, President of the Onwentsia Club, announced plans for a new clubhouse in May 1927, a $500,000 structure. The architect, Swedish-born Harris T. Lindeberg, finished the building in 1928. The building committee included James O. Heyworth, Albert B. Dick, Jr., William E. Clow, Jr., and Farwell Winston.

Through the many changes and improvements in Lake Forest, it seemed that the unifying spirit fostered by the war effort had dwindled and would have suffered except for a strong program afforded by the Young Women's Christian Association. In the hospitable rooms over the First National Bank and the Public Service Company, now the Marshall Field building, men and women joined with young people at annual dinners when club groups gave presentations of their activities and all listened to some outstanding speaker. Often the Kiwanis Club was present lending their collective voices to community singing.

Another unifying influence was the series of baseball games between the Eight o'clock young Chicago business men and the Market Square team, town boys who held local jobs. Everyone enjoyed these games, especially when former Mayor Henry A. Rumsey, President of the Chicago Board of Trade, was the umpire.

Added to the activities of the country clubs, many Lake Foresters were busy with garden weddings, beach parties, baseball games on the lawn, and for those recently out of college, the annual Barn Dance held at the "Gus" Carpenter's Garage. At these Barn Dances the high point was a surprise entertainment written and directed by Louis E. Laflin, Jr. From a modest beginning of barber-shop singing, the entertainment developed into operettas that were repeated in Chicago at the new Goodman Theatre for the Fortnightly Club. *La Illinoisa* was a take-off of grand opera and the rivalry between Chicago and Ravinia Park, and the *Young Marrieds* was a parody on life in the suburbs.

Opera was in the forefront of Chicago's cultural life during the twenties. One of the most glittering moments was the appearance of Queen Marie of Roumania at a gala performance of *Aida* in the old Chicago Auditorium. For many Lake Forest people, opera was at its best at Ravinia, where great artists from New York's Metropolitan performed shortened versions of the favorite works of Verdi, Gounod, Wagner and others in the open-air pavilion. No one who heard him that night will ever forget the voice of Martinelli soaring out into the darkness as he continued his aria without benefit of lights or orchestral accompaniment, due to a momentary electrical storm.

Those were days when celebrities were lionized in Lake Forest homes. James Stephens, the Irish poet, gave readings one evening at the newly completed home of the Robert P. Lamonts on Ridge Road. Donald Ogden Stuart gave a hilarious lecture at the Louis E. Laflin home on "Having a book," as if it were a baby. The Samuel Insulls opened their Libertyville home to winter skating parties, with nearly all the guests coming from Lake Forest. Samuel Insull, Jr., appeared in Tyrolean costume and boasted of the electrical power created for the new Skokie line, power which could melt any possible glacier, even the north pole, and could prevent a future ice age. There was great confidence in those days and the word impossible became an archaic word in the dictionary.

When Samuel Insull's electric trolley cars to Chicago, known as the Skokie line, was just finished, it carried endless trains packed with pilgrims and delegates to the Eucharistic Congress held at the newly finished St. Mary's on the Lake at nearby Mundelein. Three horse riders, Count Tolstoi, Janet Chase, and Mrs. Lowell Chapin, celebrated the occasion in Crusader style by attending Mass while mounted.

That same summer of 1926 saw the last cavalry horse show at Fort Sheridan, when officers daringly jumped through hoops of fire. At the Onwentsia, polo was still being played and the most dangerous riding of all took place there in October, during the International Steeple Chase. Onwentsia was well established as a mecca for the most daring sports.

THROUGHOUT the twenties the Library had too many books and too many users. Space on the second floor of the City Hall could not cope adequately with the growing demand. Everyone suggested an "angel." Alfred Hamill, then Horace Martin, Presidents of the Library Board, worked hard to improve the facilities and provide efficient service.

The decade of the twenties started with a population of 3,600 and ended with 6,500, nearly doubling in ten years. In the interim, people had suffered a severe reaction after the brief shock of the year and seven months of war. It was hard to realize that Lake Forest was no longer a friendly small town. Diverse interests separated the town into many cliques. Perhaps the city, for the time, had grown too rapidly. Now intricate social relationships with a certain rigidity became apparent to all. Existing institutions no longer cut across all peoples as formerly. New families living in or near Lake Forest had no special interest in the educational institutions, nor did the churches afford them any knowledge of the interests or problems of a cross section of the town. More and more, the private clubs seemed to offer all that many families wanted.

There was still a core of old timers who valued Lake Forest's private institutions. The McCormicks were one of these. Cyrus McCormick said that he was especially proud to serve as a trustee of Ferry Hall and Lake Forest Academy. With the increased enrollment during the war and post-war years in these institutions, additional facilities were indicated. It was deemed that Ferry Hall should receive the next substantial gift; so a gift of Mrs. Cyrus McCormick made two new dormitories possible in 1928. These have remained the distinctive landmarks of the institution.

That year a syndicate of 26 Chicago executives, headed by Samuel Insull, the English born public utilities czar and former secretary to inventor Thomas Alva Edison, bought Mellody Farms, for a reported $2,500,000, to convert it into an Aviation Golf Club. He completed an eighteen hole golf course, and laid out an airport. He expanded the house by the addition of a sizable wing for a locker room. On October 29, 1929, workmen left the half-finished interior of the locker building, never to return to finish the project. The business depression of 1929 had begun.

XV

THE NEW DEAL

1930–1941

By 1930 Al Capone was an international figure. He drove around in an armored car and was accompanied by a bodyguard of eighteen men. Applying the methods of big business to organized lawbreaking, he was said to control the distribution of liquor over the entire country. His and other gangs were involved in rackets. Labor unions were taken over, illicit businesses mushroomed, involving cleaning and dyeing associations, window-washing associations, wholesale florists and others. Even Europeans linked Chicago with gangsterism.

As the rolls of the unemployed increased from one million in 1929 to thirteen million by 1933, there were reports of bankruptcy, losses of fortunes, and suicides. Reports of violence occurred in the daily press, and several families in Lake Forest were under threats of kidnapping. Some families even moved away in order to be able to escape the cloud of threats and fear. Others suffered the constant tortures of having their every move supervised by the police and plainclothesmen. One teen-age boy in Lake Forest could not go out at all until he called the Police Department and was escorted in a squad car with an officer on each side, even to buy a chocolate bar uptown.

Another new phenomenon appeared at this time. Families moved into homes for brief stays; after which pictures and articles in the Chicago newspapers gave accounts of fabulously elaborate weddings and parties. Residents were often amazed to read such accounts, as nobody knew the families existed. This reputation made Lake Forest a special target of lawlessness, pointing to an expanded police department.

In the 1930's Frank Tiffany was Chief of Police. During his regime, the first two-way radio police communication in the country was established, the department was enlarged, and by 1937, eight hour shifts became the rule. Bullet-proof glass was installed in the police headquarters. During the same period, the base of tax assessment dropped from a $60,000,000 figure to $10,000,000, making it difficult to operate the various city departments. The police now underwent more rigid training, involving fingerprinting, photographing, use of arms, first aid, and other services. Some of this training was under the supervision of the Federal Bureau of Investigation.

November 22, 1931, was a rainy night. The William Mitchells of Rosemary Road were having a small party for a few friends when two gunmen appeared at the cottage of "Bill" Matheson, the Mitchell's chauffeur, at 10:30 p.m. The Mathesons, and Arthur Metzger and the night watchman, were corralled by three gunmen, who marched them into the main house where the party was in progress, and a holdup was announced to all assembled.

At first the guests thought it might be a big joke, a special entertainment for the evening, but soon all were on their knees against the wall, as they were ordered. The guests were Mrs. E. A. Cudahy, Jr., Mr. and Mrs. Leslie Wheeler, Mr. and Mrs. McCormick Blair, all of Lake Forest, also Mrs. Louise DeKoven Bowen Phelps of Chicago, and Mr. Ralph J. Hines of Evanston.

In a few minutes four servants were also brought into the living room: the butler, a nurse, the cook and a maid. Amid threats, cash was removed from the men's pockets and placed on the table. Then the women surrendered their jewelry, which was also deposited on the same table. During this collection "Bill" Matheson slipped quietly out the door, unnoticed, as one of the gunmen who was supposed to cover him, became overly interested in the jewelry on the table. Matheson went to Mrs. Mitchell's bedroom and to the telephone. He got Sergeant Frank Whalen on the wire and whispered: "There's a holdup at Mitchell's." The Sergeant couldn't understand the message, but the operator cut in and re-layed it. Matheson crawled under the bed.

The gang leader opened the bedroom door and entered with Mrs. Mitchell to search for the rest of her jewels while a radio patrol car was speeding toward the Mitchell house. The leader searched the room for the missing chauffeur, but was too fat to bend over and peek under the bed where Bill Matheson lay.

Soon there was a knock at the front door, interrupting the search for the chauffeur. The butler was ordered to open the door when Policeman Earl Dunn walked in.

The leader now scooped all the jewels and the money from the table and announced: "Come on, we gotta scram." Dunn fired after them. Policeman Peter Jackson got out of the squad car and joined in the firing. The gunmen fled in all directions into the woods and ravines. The entire north shore, Chicago, Milwaukee area was immediately alerted by police radio. Next day two overcoats found on the Mitchell property yielded all but two of the stolen jewels.

The first capture was made at 4:30 next morning in Highland Park. Later in the day two more of the thieves were captured and identified. Three nights later the fourth was captured. In July 1934, the last and leader of the gang was picked up in a Chicago rooming house. He had escaped to another city, but had made the mistake of returning to Chicago.

Bill Matheson and Earl Dunn became the town heroes.

In 1931 the First National Bank of Lake Forest moved for the third time, to the new building especially built for the Bank, on the corner of Deer Path and Bank Lane. Stanley Anderson was the architect. Two years passed. Franklin D. Roosevelt was inaugurated as President of the United States on March 4, 1933. His official first act, upon assuming office, was to declare a bank holiday, or moratorium, closing all the banks in the country, including the First National Bank of Lake Forest, until they could be examined and the soundness of each could be determined. Fortunately, the First National Bank of Lake Forest had just been examined in February, only a few days before the President's order. Congress then passed a series of banking laws at a special session beginning on March 9.

City Clerk A. Duane Jackman wrote in his diary:

An arm of steel shot out from the White House and closed every
bank in the country except one. A small bank in the remote regions
of Kentucky never heard of the order closing all banks and consequently never closed. People are depending on the government for all
and ceasing to do aught for themselves. A levelling process continues.
The weak and inefficient are exalted, the strong and able are brought
low.

For ten days, the staff of the Lake Forest Bank gathered merely
to: "look at each other," not knowing what else to do. On March
13, the large Chicago banks opened their doors. The next day the
Lake Forest bank received a telegram from Washington author-
izing it to open immediately, UNRESTRICTED, indicating that the
Treasury Department considered this bank thoroughly sound. It
was one of three banks in the Chicago area to receive the word
Unrestricted. Two of the three were operated by Lake Foresters,
the second being the Northern Trust Company of Chicago, with
Solomon A. Smith as President. The Lake Forest Bank opened its
doors on the 15th.

The First National Bank of Lake Forest has grown to be the
largest bank in the county, priding itself on personalized service,
and a clientele which receives monthly statements in all parts of
the world. Great credit is due to Frank W. Read, President at the
time, and an officer for forty years, and to Vice-President Philip L.
Speidel, who have understood the needs of the community and
rendered the necessary services. During World War II banking
services were extended to the Great Lakes Naval Training Center,
where a large volume of business was carried on by five full-time
Lake Forest bank officials. This service has been a continuing one.

THAT Lake Forest had outgrown its Library facilities was obvious
to all after World War I. It continued in the cramped quarters in
the City Hall for another dozen years, when the city received a
generous gift of $250,000 for a municipal library, in 1931. It was
given by Mrs. Charles H. Schweppe and her sister, Mrs. Stanley
Keith, daughters of the late John G. Shedd, President of Marshall
Field & Company, in memory of Mrs. Keith's first husband, Kersey
Coates Reed. The city bought the property on Deer Path just east

of the railroad tracks, and landscaped it beautifully. The building was designed by Edwin H. Clark of Chicago, in a modernized Georgian style with imported Holland brick and Bedford limestone trim. The dome has a lead roof. The murals were painted by the Russian artist, Alexander Remisoff. It received the 1931 architectural award of the Craftsmanship Club of Chicago.

The Library was moved on June 1, 1931, from City Hall to its new home with 37,000 volumes which had been collected under two presidents of the Library Board, Horace Martin and Alfred Hamill. Today it contains nearly 60,000 volumes, and reports an annual circulation of 85,000 volumes. A formal opening occurred on June 7, with 2,000 guests examining the new building. Miss Nell Steele served as Librarian from 1945 to 1962.

THE economic instability of the period was evident in Lake Forest. Some manufacturers put new products on the market to stimulate sales. The sudden influx to Lake Forest of oil burners occurred in 1932 when in February alone forty-six permits for fuel tanks were issued. Everyone was urged to convert from coal and shovel to automatic oil heat. An attempt was made to balance budgets by means of a general reduction in the salaries of city employees and public and private faculties and maintenance forces. Among citizens as a whole, many who were wealthy suddenly had little. A very few who had little, found themselves much better off.

Another public building constructed in this period was the Post Office, begun in 1932. This was the first government-owned Post Office building in Lake Forest. The new structure was in keeping with the Market Square development and cost $60,000. The architects were Ralph Milman and A. S. Morphett. Walter Smith was the first Postmaster in the new building which was completed in 1933. Since that date, Albert G. Lucas and Leroy Moore have been the only other Postmasters. The latter has served since March 1952, weathering probably the greatest changes in Post Office procedure since the origin of the postal service.

The unusual problems confronting this organization have stemmed essentially from the fact that Lake Forest occupies an area of 15.2 square miles with a population of 10,658 as of 1960. It began with 3.25 square miles at the time of the city charter in 1861. The department was strained to the utmost when nine square miles were added to Lake Forest in May, 1926, containing no sidewalks or street lights and without homes built close enough to one another to qualify for foot routes. Today the Lake Forest Post Office delivers mail even outside of the city limits. The result has been a maze of foot and motor routes, the latter an outgrowth of rural delivery.

Prior to 1933, when the Post Office was in the present location of Helander's, three clerks were employed. Today there are ten clerks and four substitutes, eleven regular carriers and five substitutes. The department began with only one employee in July 1859, Samuel Fisher Miller, the Principal of Lake Forest Academy. He was followed by Luther Rossiter in 1861, Joel H. Hulbert in 1865, William M. Loughlin in 1866, Francis N. Pratt in 1869, and Gilbert Rossiter in 1875. When in 1879 the office was made a presidential appointment, Miss Mary McLaughlin became the first appointee. All these early postmasters operated a one-man post office with occasional and often volunteer help. Today there are thirty-two regular employees.

Helicopter service was instituted on October 1, 1946, when Postmaster Lucas decided to receive and dispatch mail by this method. The service has continued. Until around 1950 all out-of-town mail was transported by rail. Today it is carried by truck. Chicago was the clearing house for this service; today it is routed through Desplaines. New York was the point of departure for European mail service; today New Orleans has become equally important. The 1960 gross revenues of the department were $207,-990.75, very substantial, considering that Lake Forest is a residential suburb without industry. Industrial towns such as North Chicago frequently handle five times this volume without having to cope with the distances and other perplexing conditions which obtain here.

SEVERAL important events marked 1933. After leaving Lake Forest and the Great Lakes Naval Training Center, Captain W. A. Moffett was appointed the first Chief of the newly organized Bureau of Aeronautics, and commissioned Rear Admiral. In this capacity Admiral Moffett had the longest term of service of any Chief of this Bureau. On the night of April 3–4, 1933, he was on board the dirigible *Akron* when at 2:30 a.m., the telephone rang at the

Washington home of the Moffetts. It was the Navy Department saying: "The *Akron* has just crashed. Will you notify the Admiral?"

Mrs. Moffett replied: "The Admiral is on the *Akron*."

Admiral Moffett, together with 71 others, lost his life in the greatest air disaster up to that date. The *Akron* went down about 20 miles southeast of Barnegat Inlet Light, 15 miles from shore, off the coast of New Jersey. In reconstructing the log of the *Akron* one writer has pointed out that the course of the *Akron* was "changed nine times during this last flight, and if any one change had been different, the ship might not have met disaster."

IN 1933 the *Century of Progress Exposition* opened in Chicago on May 27 attracting many Lake Foresters and thousands of visitors from all over the country to its Hall of Science, its Belgian and a dozen other villages, its Midway, and its sports arenas, as did the World's Fair in 1893. All types of dining facilities were offered by the finest staffs of the downtown hotels and restaurants. The Columbian Exposition in 1893 covered 666 acres. This Fair covered only 424 acres and extended 3½ miles from 12th to 36th Streets along the lake front.

Though many disliked the angular architecture of the Fair with its flamboyant colors, all were thrilled by the thought that a signal from the distant star Arcturus automatically turned on the lights on the exposition grounds each evening. A Sky Ride between two steel towers, each 628 feet high, gave an excellent view of the whole fair grounds. Other transportation was by rickshaw or motorized wheel chairs. There was a replica of old Fort Dearborn; and Admiral Richard E. Byrd's south pole ship, the *City of New York*, lay at anchor for all to see. Italy's air armada under General Italo Balbo arrived over the Fair on July 15th after a mass flight across the Atlantic.

All types of modern design in architecture were displayed. The Dymaxion house, circular and all glass, could be revolved on a turntable so that any desired room could face the sun. The inside arrangements of rooms was capable of rearrangement so that rooms could be enlarged quickly or made smaller to suit the occasion. The tendency of the architecture displayed was to jar the people of the Mid-West from their static and conventional ideas toward the daring and the practical. There were industrial buildings with complete exhibits in assembly line techniques for various products.

One of the unusual exhibits was the Dymaxion car, which was years ahead of the market in its promoting of the engine at the rear of the car, its doing away with the conventional transmission system, and eliminating the system of muffler, resonator and pipe, as well as the possibility of exhaust fumes inside the car. All this permitted much more room for passengers and made it possible to have movable seats. Its three wheels were less practical than the conventional four. Leland Atwood of the Lake Forest Academy faculty and Buckminster Fuller were the designers of the Dymaxion car.

Entertainment at the Fair included the daring fan and balloon dancing of Sally Rand at one extreme, and the presentation of Shakespearean plays by well-known British professionals at the other. The latter plays were presented in a replica of London's ancient Globe Theatre. *Wings of a Century* was a pageant depicting the progress of transportation from the pioneer to the aviator. It was a thrilling outdoor event, which large crowds watched with the blue waters of Lake Michigan for a backdrop. Chicago's own Helen Tieken was the inspired director. There were also exhibitions of all types of sports, including aquatics and skating. To many, The Chicago Symphony Orchestra's daily outdoor concerts, during the afternoon and evening, were the highlights of the entire Fair. These were led by some of the great conductors of the day: Eric de Lamarter, Frederick Stock, and others.

The Fair was so successful it was revived in 1934, the following year.

ON January 26, 1936, one of the coldest days ever recorded in Lake Forest, 25 below zero, when Lake Michigan was frozen across to Michigan City, fire broke out at the home of Mrs. Abby Farwell Ferry on Lake Road. The fire chief, George Bauman, reported:

The water froze as soon as it hit anything solid. The call came at 8:00 a.m. and we were out until 5:00 p.m. Those were the worst weather conditions for fighting a fire that I have ever experienced. We had to keep the water running constantly to keep the nozzles open. When we finally pulled in, the men had to drag lengths of 50-foot hose. They wouldn't roll in the cold. Our clothes were cakes of ice, frozen stiff. We had to have help to strip them off. Between thawing and scrubbing our clothes and the hose, it was three days before the department was back in step.

They saved the house.

THE YEAR 1936 marked the retirement of two universally loved public servants of Lake Forest—Dr. George Roberts and Superintendent John E. Baggett.

Dr. Roberts was pastor of the Presbyterian Church 1916–1936. He was beloved by children and teen-agers as head of the Presbyterian Sunday School, which was attended by the children of several denominations. He was the leader of the Boy Rangers, antedating the Boy Scouts, and helped organize the Boy Scouts in 1924 as chairman of the committee. As a preacher of rare children's sermons, which grown-ups enjoyed even more, he had no peer. These children's sermons were published in two volumes. He visited every member of his congregation once a year, and enjoyed the hospitality of many and various homes at dinner; but no longer than 9:00 p.m. sharp, when he stood up and took his leave. He was a preacher of concise and practical sermons, a crusader for democracy and a connoisseur of bird life and the Adirondack Mountains.

John E. Baggett was a character out of the past, rooted and grounded in Lake Forest. He was born in Highland Park during the Civil War and taught for sixty years, nearly all in Lake County. He was the Superintendent of the Lake Forest Grade School system for thirty-two years. Experienced in all hardships of the post Civil War era, he was essentially self taught. He began his teaching career with a salary of $24 per month in Iowa. When Lake Forest discovered him, he was at first teacher, then Principal of the North School in Waukegan. Here he had the reputation of being able to handle boys who were exceptionally "tough," and making learning enjoyable to all.

He came to Lake Forest in 1904 bringing with him a wealth of teaching experience, the ability to impart knowledge in an interesting way, to inspire his pupils with ideals of good workmanship, beauty, taste, and noble thought and living. His pupils always had good handwriting and were well acquainted with the finest classical art and music. He filled the Lake Forest School buildings with fine prints of the masterpieces of art, often paying for them with his own money. He was a pioneer in establishing good communications between parents and faculty; parents were asked to conduct cake sales to buy pictures or curtains for the schools. The real purpose was for the faculty to meet parents in a natural way. He brought the first visiting nurse to Lake Forest, Miss Gertrude Barker, who served for 26 years. Though quiet and unobtrusive, everyone in Lake Forest knew and loved Mr. Baggett. He retired in 1936.

PRIOR TO 1900 the great majority of high school students attended the Academy or Ferry Hall. Because of the increase in population after that date, a beginning was made toward the establishment of a high school in Lake Forest. Classes were held in the Old South School, then in the Library of the City Hall. After a few years, high school students began to attend the Deerfield-Shields Township High School in Highland Park. From 1910 to 1935 an increasing number of students attended the Township High School; but after World War I, with another population increase in Lake Forest, the inconvenience of daily travel to Highland Park for so many became more noticeable and the need for a Lake Forest high school became pronounced.

In the middle of the 1920's the site of Lake Forest High School was purchased. Ground was broken; and in 1935 the school was ready for the first fall term. It was erected at the north end of Lake Forest, since the new center of high school population was there, embracing Lake Forest, Lake Bluff and communities just west of the track. The building was designed by Anderson and Tichnor, architects, in Georgian Colonial style, using brick and stone, and giving the appearance of a large mansion.

From 1935 to 1949 Lake Forest High School was still a part of the Deerfield-Shields Township High School, the northern section, District 113. During this period Lake Forest High School averaged 380 pupils as Highland Park increased its enrollment to approximately 1,100. Lake Forest had 18% of the pupils but was paying about 43% of the taxes required. When this was realized, the citizens of Lake Forest and Lake Bluff became concerned over the disproportionately high taxes paid by them, and the possibility that with more rapid population growth in Highland Park the Lake Forest-Lake Bluff taxes would become even more disproportionate.

A citizens' committee prepared a separation petition, which was approved by the Lake County Superintendent of Schools and a new high school district 115 was formed. This was followed by litigation in the Illinois Supreme Court, *People vs. Wood et al,* in which the court ruled, on March 20, 1952, that the separation was valid and that District 115 was fully constituted. Lake Forest now promised to pay $227,000 to Highland Park in three installments. These payments were completed in 1955. This decision enabled Lake Forest-Lake Bluff to have their own school and has saved the residents of the district large sums in tax assessments. The first Lake Forest Board of Education was elected for District 115 on June 30, 1949, including J. Howard Wood, President, Philip Speidel, John C. Trussell, Elmer Vliet, Unity Tomlinson, D. Robert Pierson, and Ethel Jenkins.

In 1959 a new $2,000,000 addition to the High School was completed, providing for a total of 1,200 students. The addition, including two wings and an auditorium, increased the school to a total of 58 rooms, completely furnished, including two gymnasiums, a swimming pool, six science rooms, five industrial arts rooms, two music rooms, two rooms devoted to physical education, two rooms for home economics and others. A cafeteria in the basement is operated during three lunch periods for faculty and students. The Library on the third floor contains over 5,000 books. An electronic communication system connects all the departments. The grounds include two football fields, a running track, and tennis courts. During the first decade there were three football championships in 1937, 1941, and 1944. The track team has won championships in 1938, 1942, and 1945. Coach Edgar Lindenmeyer was the head coach during the first twenty years of the school's operation. Thomas Short is the present coach.

Fifty-eight teachers and administrators preside over 834 students. There are nine in the office personnel, seven in the operation of the cafeteria, and fourteen in the maintenance force of the grounds and buildings. The school enjoys a high scholastic rating among colleges throughout the country. Eighty per cent of the graduates go to college. The first Principal and Superintendent was Dr. Raymond Moore, who served from 1935 until his retirement in 1959. He was succeeded by Dr. Clyde N. Carter.

BY THE END OF World War I it became apparent that Alice Home Hospital, which was built when the population of Lake Forest was 1,750, was no longer adequate. To use the Highland Park Hospital or the Chicago Hospitals was frequently more than inconvenient; therefore plans were discussed for the erection of an independent and publicly supported Lake Forest Hospital. The Hospital Association of Lake Forest was organized in 1918 and incorporated as a non-profit organization, independent of Lake Forest University. The directors at this time were Delevan Smith, Clayton Mark, Dr. Arthur Dean Bevan, John T. Pirie, and Ezra J. Warner, Jr. Partial support for the Hospital came from the Onwentsia Club Annual Horse Show and from municipal tax funds.

In 1941 the 1918 plans were consummated, after a committee of the Association, headed by A. B. Dick, Jr., negotiated with Lake Forest College, and Alice Home was transformed into a college dormitory and the cornerstone for the new Lake Forest Hospital was laid, west of the Skokie, off Deer Path, on twenty-four acres donated by Mrs. A. B. Dick, Sr. A. B. Dick, Jr., raised the money. Mrs. W. Press Hodgkins, daughter of Ezra Warner, Jr., served as President of the Women's Board and organized the Auxiliary. 621 contributions totalled $800,000, ensured the construction of the proposed building. The first patient, Mrs. Scott Durand, received in November, 1942, was a niece of Henry C. Durand, donor of the first hospital.

Dr. Theodore S. Proxmire and Dr. Paul H. Burgert, made significant contributions in organizing the new institution. The first President of the Hospital Board of Directors, A. B. Dick, Jr., worked untiringly, giving substantial contributions himself, including the gift of the surgical suite, to make the institution well organized and at the same time affording personal service. In 1946 the Women's Auxiliary began to operate a series of special services for patients, including hospital shops and three stores in the business section, the Trading Post Gift Shop, the Toy Shop and the

Rummage Shop, to provide additional funds for the Hospital. That same year a nurses' home was erected, thereby increasing the number of available beds for hospital uses. In 1958 the main building was enlarged as a result of a successful $1,463,857 drive. New services and mechanical aids are continually added.

In 1942 the hospital began with 40 beds. There were 1,083 admissions, and a 12 member medical staff. In 1960 there were 101 beds, 3,839 admissions, and a medical staff of sixty. The 1960 President of the Board was Frank A. Priebe, presiding over 26 members. The Women's Board President was Mrs. John C. Christie with 25 members. The Auxiliary embraces 800 members.

The 1960 report mentioned four fully equipped operating rooms, X-ray, Radiology, Pharmacy, air conditioning, and an intercom system. 322,421 pounds of laundry were serviced, 100 pieces of laundry for each baby each day. There were 3,839 adult admissions and 642 infant. 8,461 outpatients and 903 emergency patients were served. The average stay of patients was 7½ days. 250 volunteers and 164 full-time employees staffed the Hospital. There were also 70 part-time employees.

The grounds, buildings and parking facilities are adequate for 1960 Lake Forest. The building is in the late Georgian architecture, with Williamsburg brick, creating a homelike atmosphere throughout. Anderson and Tichnor of Lake Forest were the architects. Other buildings include adequate dormitory space for nurses, service buildings, garage, and quarters for the caretakers. All these facts give little idea of the attractive and cheerful quality of the institution which is a source of pride to Lake Foresters. It has been called the finest small hospital in the United States.

WHILE these public buildings were being constructed in the 1930's with tax moneys and private contributions, many private dwellings were torn down, or in a few instances, were converted into religious, educational or business uses. Owners of certain spacious homes were caught between the sudden and expanding real-estate and income taxes. For a while these homes became a drug on the market, as no one seemed to want to purchase property involving so much of a tax load. Wrecking crews were busy dismantelling a number of beautiful homes which had cost large sums of money to build, many of them architectural gems. This was especially tragic in view of the great need of living space during the following decades.

The thirties were trying times for large and small businesses. Gasoline prices dropped to 12¢ per gallon and eggs were 12¢ per dozen. Debts were difficult to collect with the general sluggishness of business. Reports of bank failures in other parts of the country helped to create a general conservatism. Lake Forest residents, who were Chicago executives, faced the problem of meeting payrolls and keeping their organizations alive, though their businesses did not show enough returns to keep going. The moral problem of providing work and maintaining as high a level of employment as possible was of deep concern to many who continued to take the eight o'clock train to Chicago and the five-ten back home, always hoping for a turn in the tide. Some provided work as a patriotic duty.

On the international scene there were disturbing news reports that an Austrian paper hanger named Adolf Hitler had come into power in Germany and that an Italian tyrant named Mussolini was conducting a war of conquest against Ethiopia. Soon Lake Forest and the country became accustomed to the hardships of the depression period and developed an increased interest in international affairs. Clifton Utley conducted a class in Lake Forest reviewing the fast moving current events. On the radio, he and several other popular commentators carried accounts of disagreements and aggressions which finally grew, step by step, into a European conflict. Czechoslovakia was invaded, then Poland, Norway, the low countries, and France.

A popular newscaster named Allen Scott broadcast that Japan would soon attack the United States or some possession. This was in early November, 1941. On the evening of December 6, he announced that Japan would attack during the next twenty-four hours. The following day, Sunday, December 7, 1941, the actual attack on Pearl Harbor took place.

XVI

WORLD WAR II

1941–1945

WORLD WAR II brought about a noticeable change in Lake Forest by draining the city of its pride and joy—the great percentage of young men and women. Drafts and the calls to service enlisted all except the physically unfit, or those considered indispensable for home front essential activities. 1,200 men and women served in the armed forces from Lake Forest proper, also 800 graduates of Lake Forest College, and 400 Academy graduates. Many of these served in positions of national leadership.

The Hon. Frank Knox, publisher of the *Chicago Daily News*, who had lived in Lake Forest a short while, was now the Secretary of the Navy, having promoted a two-ocean Navy from the time he took office in 1940. Ralph Bard of Lake Road served as assistant Secretary and then as Under Secretary of the Navy during the war.

Lieutenant General William H. Arnold served in the Pacific theatre. As chief of staff of the Fourteenth Corps he took part in the Guadalcanal, New Georgia, and Bougainville campaigns. He took command of the American Infantry Division at Bougainville in November, 1944, and was promoted to Major General one month later. During the time of his command of this division, they were engaged in operations on Leyte, Cebu, Negros, and other islands in the Philippines. He received the first large-scale surrender of Japanese forces in the field when more than 10,000 soldiers surrendered at Cebu Island.

In 1950 General Arnold was assigned as chief of the joint military mission for aid to Turkey, and held this post until 1953. He was then assigned to Austria, on May 1, 1953. He was promoted to Lieutenant General in 1953. He became the commanding General of the Fifth Army, serving 1955–1961. He and his family built their new home in 1961, in "Walden" on the original site of the Cyrus H. McCormick house. He has named it "The General's Bluff."

Captain Thomas G. Cassady, U.S.N., served in the American Field Service, Lafayette Flying Corps and the U.S. Air Force, 1916–1919. World War II found him an assistant U.S. Naval Attache in the Embassy in Vichy, France. In 1943 he was interned in Germany. After his release, following the liberation of France, he became Chief of Secret Intelligence (O.S.S.) for France and Germany.

Admiral Richard L. Conolly, a three-year student at Lake Forest Academy, graduating in 1909, is credited with turning the tide in the southwest Pacific during the war. He directed the landing of Marines at Guadalcanal which stopped the Japanese drive southward. The first Army Air Force planes to bomb Japan took off from the aircraft carriers of Admiral Conolly's fleet. He was the first naval officer to become a full Admiral at the age of fifty-five. Throughout his life Admiral Conolly has been an exponent of the closest possible cooperation between the armed forces of the nation. He has continually expressed his affection for Lake Forest.

Major General Charles Christian Haffner, Jr., "Red" to his intimate friends, served as Captain of Field Artillery in France during World War I. He continued his interest in national defense, taking command of the 124th Field Artillery of the Illinois National Guard in 1931. The new 124th Field Artillery Armory had just been completed, the largest in the country, and Colonel Haffner decided to capitalize on the new plant and to build the best regiment by attracting the highest type of men to the Guard. He built up its efficiency through a series of activities including indoor polo, boxing, football, basketball and track. He developed the "Red Devil" drill battery and the Lancer Troop, which gave great exhibitions of horsemanship at the Armory, during the 1930's. The jumping team, beautifully mounted and coached by Captain Aro, Olympic jumping champion, appeared at horse shows around the country, and defeated several Army teams.

On December 1, 1942, Colonel Haffner was promoted to Major General, and assigned to command the new 103rd Division which he organized, trained and led into combat. He was the only non-professional officer in the war to organize his own division and command it on the battlefield. His was one of the best trained and equipped units to leave for France. It landed in southern France, in October, 1944, as a part of General Patch's Seventh Army, and in its first campaign broke through the Sayles Pass in the Vosges mountains to the Rhine—the first time the Pass had been penetrated in warfare—and then was selected for the drive north into Germany. The 103rd was the first unit of the 7th Army to cross the German border.

The citation for the Distinguished Service Medal awarded General Haffner in May, 1945, states in part: "As Commanding General of the 103rd Infantry Division, General Haffner built the Division into a formidable combat organization . . . In its first field test the 103rd Division made an excellent showing due to the painstaking planning and superior leadership of General Haffner . . . The Division went into combat seven kilometers west of St. Die. Two weeks later it had advanced through the Vosges Mountains to the Rhine plain. French civilians and captured German officers predicted penetration of the Vosges was impossible, but under the leadership of General Haffner this was accomplished in 14 days . . . Throughout his command, General Haffner demonstrated exceptional ability in overcoming great difficulties of weather and terrain . . . His superior handling of his forces manifested itself in a successful offensive drive and contributed materially to the 7th Army's successful record."

General Haffner has been a Lake Forest resident for nearly 35 years, having married Miss Clarissa Donnelley of this city and raised his family of four children. In spite of his heavy duties as President and Chairman of the Board and Chief Executive Officer of R. R. Donnelley & Sons Company, he maintains a continued interest in national defense. One of his pet hobbies is the study of Civil War weapons, especially artillery.

One of the unusual experiences of the war belonged to Corporal Robert T. Isham, Battery B, 693rd Field Artillery Battalion. His unit landed at Utah Beach on July 14, 1944, as a part of General Patton's 3rd Army. After the breakthrough at Avranches, the unit advanced south of Paris toward the German border. Crossing the Marne, the 693rd became a part of General Patch's 7th Army and experienced its heaviest fighting at the Siegfried Line, near the border. The Rhine was crossed near Worms. Continuing east and north to Schonau, they received orders to turn south and take part in the reduction of Nurenburg, the shrine of Naziism. Crossing the headwaters of the Danube, they sped south and east on the superhighway to Salzburg, then to Berchtesgaden, a Hitler headquarters.

Corporal Isham and his comrades were among the first to arrive at the Fuhrer's home and to find it practically destroyed. Most of the section above ground was all but levelled. The big room which has been pictured so many times was completely gutted by fire, but the big window still framed a magnificent view of the Alps. However, 50 yards underground was a luxurious suite of rooms completely untouched. Some of these were under guard, but the rest seemed fair game.

Entering the unguarded portion, Corporal Isham found two silver serving dishes marked with the German crest and the initials "A. H." (Adolf Hitler), various pieces of flat silver, silver pitchers, silver coasters, two German medals, an arm band, napkins, towels, table cloth, a Berchtesgaden telephone directory, Christmas and New Year's greeting cards, and a roll of toilet paper. The silver and many other pieces were initialed. These items were shipped to Corporal Isham's family and have been repeatedly exhibited in Chicago and Lake Forest.

Corporal Isham was awarded the Bronze Star Medal "For meritorious service in action in eastern France, from October 1, 1944, to March 1, 1945. As the non-commissioned officer in charge of an Artillery Forward Observer's Party, during this period, Corporal Isham has performed his duties in a highly commendable manner. He has consistently displayed great initiative, courage and ingenuity in assisting the officer in charge of the party. Corporal Isham's devotion to duty and coolness under fire merit great praise."

Vice Admiral Francis Paxton Old, who took up his Green Bay Road residence soon after the war, served throughout the war in all theatres. He is known as "Pop" by many Lake Foresters. He served in the North Atlantic Patrol with Norwegians, Poles, Canadians and British. He took part in the assault and occupation of Sicily. Salerno was his most harrowing experience. One guided missile exploded 100 yards from where he stood on the bridge of his ship. He was Chief-of-Staff of the attack force at Anzio, 25 miles south of Rome, when the 5th Army was landed behind the German Army, in a swift surprise attack. Not a single man was lost in the landings, though hell broke loose five days later. He then took part in the assault and landings in southern France which were coordinated with the invasion of northern France. This has been called "the most perfect amphibious operation of the war." After the fall of Berlin, Admiral Old commanded the USS *Indiana*, one of the largest battleships of the U.S. Navy, in the Okinawa campaign in the Pacific. For 67 consecutive days he was on the bridge, during this campaign, getting what sleep he could without going below. The *Indiana* was the 3rd ship in the first fleet to bombard the homeland of Japan. She was present in Tokyo Bay as part of the covering force during the Japanese surrender in 1945.

Admiral Old's decorations include the Legion of Merit, the Distinguished Service Medal, the Legion of Honor, all from the United States; the Croix de Guerre, with palm, from France; the Distinguished Service Order signed by his Majesty King George VI of Great Britain, and Bau Dai, a most colorful decoration, which no one in Lake Forest seems able to read, for his services to China as advisor to Generalissimo Chiang Kai-Shek.

The Distinguished Service Medal citation says: "Captain Old capably assisted in the actual assault and in the critical phase of the operations incident to the maintenance of the invasion forces at Salerno and their advance inland, despite strong enemy opposition." The citation on Anzio calls him a "Brilliant administrator, exercising expert professional skill and sound judgment. He rendered invaluable assistance to the Force Commander in the development of organizational and tactical plans for the amphibious assault. He coordinated the plans with other services and Allied units, despite repeated hostile aerial attacks." The

D.S.O. citation mentions that: "During the invasion of the South of France, Captain Old displayed exceptional zeal and ability. His professional skill materially contributed to the operations culminating in the successful assault while his gallantry and inspired leadership in action was outstanding." His citation involving the Pacific reads: "Captain Old directed accurate anti-aircraft fire to aid in the destruction of numerous enemy planes. He fought his ship aggressively to inflict considerable damage on enemy industrial installations, contributing materially to the success of our forces in the Pacific, upholding the highest traditions of the U.S. Naval service."

From March, 1949, to June, 1951, he was attached to the Philippine Navy, which awarded him the Philippine Legion of Honor with this citation: "Outstanding service to the people and government of the Philippines in general and to the Philippine Navy in particular. He took the sincerest interest in and showed profoundest friendship for the Filipino people. By his personal example and consummate tact he promoted and maintained the closest cooperation and the most cordial relationships."

Colonel Jeffery F. R. Seitz was at Pearl Harbor when the Japanese surprise visit was made on December 7, 1941. His family arrived in Lake Forest soon after the beginning of the war, the young Seitzs attending Lake Forest schools until well after the conclusion of the war. If there is such a thing as home for the family of a career officer, Lake Forest would be that place. Colonel Seitz became attached to the First Division, 26th Infantry Regiment, and his career in Europe is nearly the story of the war in Europe. He took part in the North African campaigns, the Sicilian, then in the first attack on Omaha beach. He took part in the battles of Aachen, Hurtgen Forest, the Belgian Bulge, and waited for days at the river Elbe for the arrival of the Russians. "Jeff" Seitz came home a Brigadier General, one of the most decorated officers in the United States Army.

Lieutenant Colonel Marshall C. Strenger, "Marsh" to all his friends, a member of the pioneer Pratt family of Lake Forest, flew 72 missions with the 12th Air Force.

His most difficult assignment was at Anzio when the squadron under his command flew two missions on January 19, 1944, and two on the 20th, against German troop concentrations. Heavy casualties were sustained by the Army Air Force, from enemy flak and fighter opposition. For three weeks after this mission, his squadron was assigned as Air Force Observer for the 3rd Division. Other actions included bombing of targets in Albania, Austria, the Brenner Pass, Bulgaria, Corsica, Greece, Italy, Sardinia, Southern France, and Yugoslavia. His squadron was the first to bomb Sophia, Bulgaria.

The most publicized mission, which he considers routine, was his 43rd mission on his birthday, February 15, 1944, when his squadron of 24 B-25's took off on a two hour mission from its base in Foggia. It flew north and east of the Abbey di Monte Cassino, then turned west under a high cloud cover. The American ground troops were pulled back as the entire 12th and 15th Air Force came on target, the pivot of the German Army. There was some flak, but it was not very accurate. After some difficulty in identifying the target, bombs were released very near our own troops in the early afternoon. His squadron suffered no losses.

Lt. Colonel Strenger's decorations include the Silver Star, the Distinguished Flying Cross with Oak Leaf Cluster, an Air Medal with 7 clusters, an Air Force Citation, Four battle stars, and two distinguished unit badges, as well as the Croix de Guerre. These are usually displayed by his 9 year old son.

Neither time nor space will permit a complete review of the service records of all our native leadership, nor the remarkable experiences of our officers and enlisted men and women who served beyond the call of duty. Many served in special capacities. John L. Clarkson was the chief Navy procurement officer in Chicago. Robert Newberry McCreary was the Army procurement officer in Milwaukee. Donald Phelps Welles served as the head procurement officer in Detroit and Washington. Edison Dick served in the same capacity in St. Louis.

There were many happy and accidental reunions in far off places, some of which ought to be mentioned. Major Gordon L. Kelley and Lieutenant E. A. Archer, USNR, met at Guadalcanal in 1943. They had not seen each other in three years. The Mac-Millan brothers, three in all, met in New Guinea, for the first time in three years. Frank D'Hulst and Malcolm Gyllenberg met on board ship, in Iceland, in 1941, and a year later D'Hulst met Eric Glasel at Pearl Harbor.

World War II, 1941–1945

LAKE FOREST had a look of grim determination, during the war years. Everything was so much bigger and better organized than during World War I. Year after year Victory Loan campaigns were over subscribed, way out of proportion to the Lake Forest population. Knight C. Cowles was chairman of one of these drives. Great Lakes could hardly be comprehended with the feverish activity going on there, thousands being graduated each week. Contrary to World War I, civilians were not permitted within the gates. The station housed as many as 125,000 at one time. Commander Randolph G. Owsley of Lake Forest, as head of the 31st Regiment, trained a total of 42,500 men during his two years of duty at Great Lakes. Basic training for some was as little as three weeks, for others as long as twelve weeks. The 31st Regiment became a model unit and was used for the making of a professional movie, *The Navy Way*, for the promotion of Navy recruiting. Many Lake Forest women served as hostesses, in volunteer and professional services on the base. Flower collections from Lake Forest gardens and greenhouses decorated various public buildings. Several Christmas parties were given for service personnel by Lake Forest women.

Fort Sheridan was likewise a mobilization and separation center, with thousands arriving and departing, and hardly any time for more than formal contacts with our citizens. There was no Officer's Training Camp (as during World War I), through which Lake Foresters might develop a personal interest in the activities of the post. Many women did join the Fort Sheridan Volunteers, promoting several parties.

All cities, situated near military and naval bases, established a chapter of the U.S.O. for the comfort and entertainment of the service men. In Lake Forest a Service Men's Center was established on McKinley Avenue, doing the same things as the U.S.O in a home-like setting with large sums of money expended and hundreds of volunteers serving. Mrs. McKinley Gray was in charge of this operation. The Red Cross conducted an effective blood-donor service, produced several hundred thousand surgical dressings, knitted articles and army kits. Mrs. Charles De Long, who had served overseas during World War I, and Mrs. Russell Lord were efficient executives in Red Cross activities. The Red Cross also conducted classes in first aid.

Thousands of service men flooded the North Shore area seeking a place to live during their training at Great Lakes and Fort Sheridan. Mayor Charles F. Clarke quickly organized The Office of Civilian Defense, as a clearing house for quarters for Officers of the Great Lakes Naval Training Center, with offices at 286 E. Deer Path. The complications were great, as Lake Forest is a town of homes, having very few apartments and boarding houses. Lake Foresters made a thrilling response. Zoning was forgotten; people gave up rooms and wings of their houses; they converted servant's quarters, gardener's cottages and garage apartments into family units.

Mrs. Frank P. Hixon was chairman of the Women's Division of the O.C.D. Mrs. George Chappell, Jr. and Mrs. Howard Linn were co-chairmen of the Housing Committee. Mrs. Chappell's office force turned into a veritable real estate office. Mrs. Howard Linn found houses and apartments which necessarily had to be prepared for occupancy. She took care of papering, painting, cleaning and furnishing these abodes. The Mechem, Rumsey, Chatfield-Taylor, R. H. McElwee, James E. Baum, Swift, Taylor Strawn (the old J. V. Farwell house), and Hopkins houses were among those larger homes which were prepared for this use. The Contagious Hospital at South Park was made presentable for the same purpose. Ensign Joseph Barr assisted as advisor in establishing fair rentals suitable to Navy personnel.

A furniture depot was established, collecting gifts and loans. Furniture was repaired and stored ready to go where it was most needed. The home of Mr. and Mrs. James Hopkins was one of the first to be occupied, serving as a model for many others. The Henry Rumsey home, whose furnishings were chosen and assembled by Mrs. James Ward Thorne, served several families at one time. The Baum home, the last one to be opened, received twenty-three WAVES.

The O.C.D. became the collecting agency for salvaging metals, paper, rags, rubber and grease. Two car loads of paper collections per week were not unusual. In one shipment 12,000 pounds of clothing were collected for people in the war devastated areas. Bins in Market Square held these collections.

Among the most active workers in these projects were Miss Jane Morton, chairman of Officer's housing committee in 1945, Mrs.

Milton Morse, Mrs. Alan Donald, Mrs. J. Beach Clow, Mrs. William P. Martin, Jr., Mrs. William Osborne, Miss Ann Carpenter, Mrs. Sewell Gardner and Mrs. Robert Buckley. These and many others spread the Lake Forest reputation for efficiency and friendly cooperation from coast to coast.

In addition, there was an informal group which provided extensive parties for the entertainment of service men. It is said to have begun early in the war when a naval officer from Great Lakes telephoned Dr. Herbert W. Prince, Rector of the Church of the Holy Spirit, and explained the need. Dr. Prince consulted Mrs. Edward L. Hasler, and soon parties were given for large groups of officers and enlisted men. Miss Gwethlyn Jones, Mrs. William Roy Carney, Mrs. Albert Farwell and many others opened their homes and rendered invaluable services.

Miss Jones was at first reluctant to take part; but her attractive home became the mecca of many officers and their wives. One night, in preparing a large dinner party, she studied the Bluejacket's Manual, and, securing small flags, spelled out the names of all her guests according to signal code, instead of writing them on place-cards. When the officers arrived at the table, not one of them was able to read his own name, and Miss Jones had to seat them by reading their names.

Mrs. Albert Farwell became famous for her "Navy Waffle Parties." Throughout the war once a week, convalescent boys from the Naval Hospital at Great Lakes came to her house for a day's outing. A Navy bus would arrive and 25 or 30 boys would jump out, all smiling and eager for the holiday. They came under the auspices of the Red Cross. A total of four thousand boys were so entertained. Some of these boys had not been off the hospital grounds for months, and they considered this a great privilege. They came from all over the United States, and from every walk of life. Most of them had seen service abroad.

Mrs. Farwell's friends and workers from the Red Cross Recreational Center were very helpful in making these parties a success. All played games, and made and consumed waffles by the thousands. Mrs. Farwell wrote the following account:

> The first group we had were orthopedic cases. They were a jolly lot. In spite of crutches and braces many of them hobbled down to the beach where they basked in the sun, some even went swimming.

Our house was an old-fashioned red brick house, situated on the bluff overlooking Lake Michigan. A good sized lawn space in front, bordered by large elms, lent itself to croquet, baseball, horse-shoe pitching, and many other out-of-door games. Wooded ravines were at the back of the house, and a walk through the woods led to the garden. The rooms of the house were large with high ceilings; a spacious hall led to the sun porch, where there was a ping-pong table. Throughout the house were old pieces of furniture, some of which had been handed down from three and four generations in the family. The fact that it was a home, was what appealed to these boys. One boy said he had not been inside a home in two years.

When the bus arrived, Betsy, our German Shepherd dog would rush for the front door, continue jumping until it was opened, then rush out to the bus and into it. It was a fine welcome for the boys. As the boys filed out they would first throng to the edge of the bluff to look at the lake. It was always a beautiful sight on a clear day. The boys from the East could not understand why one could not see across the lake to the Michigan shore, and wanted to know why there was no tide.

Those who were interested were taken to the gardens, where we visited the beehives. One boy carried an eight pound chunk of honey-comb into the dining-room, dripping all the way. Every boy wanted honey to take back with him. We scraped together every kind of receptacle we could find: jars, cracker cans, tin cans, and others. That night Ward 28 had a honey feast at the hospital.

Next stop was the herb garden. Here they were introduced to the mint bed, many varieties. They tasted the peppermint, they sniffed the orange mints, the spearmints, the curly mints, the pineapple mints. Then we passed on to the costmary, the plant that is used to flavor ale. This had a special interest for them. Each boy took a sprig of rosemary to send to his best girl. The fragrant herbs had the greatest appeal. They could not understand why one geranium plant smelled of apples, another of lemons, another of peppermint, and so on. One boy, who had been an unsuccessful suitor, went through the garden and selected rose geranium, sweet marjoram and lemon verbena as being the most irresistible fragrances, and sent them to his girl. A few weeks later the boy returned with the remark: "Remember them weeds you gave me? Well, they sure did the trick. I can't keep her away from me now."

We passed on to the vegetable garden in which the farm boys were in their element. Some went for broccoli, others for melons and peanuts. The novelties were of special interest, the red spinach imported from England, the strawberry corn and the Welsh onions. Each boy was given seed of whatever he wanted. I often wonder if red spinach is not growing from Atlantic to Pacific which originated in my garden. When it began to get cool we came into the house. At such times household objects became a source of great interest. One boy was interested in the oriental rugs. Another liked old furniture. The Grandfather Clock in the hall had an appeal to all. They stroked it to feel the carving and listened for its strike. The date 1643, carved at the base, was discovered by one of the boys, the first we ever knew of it. Unfortunately after research we concluded that the date was fake. One boy looking at the portrait of grandfather Farwell said: "Is that the old guy who made all the dough?"

At about 2:30 we started making waffles, four irons going at once, one in the dining room, one in the pantry and two in the kitchen. We all felt most at home in the kitchen. A Marine and a sailor had a contest as to who could eat the greatest number of waffles. They would eat a batch, then run around the house so that they would have room for more. They finally stopped at 32. One youngster had a struggle, he retorted: "When I was in the Marianas I had teeth but no decent food. Now I have decent food but no teeth!" An Italian boy found a guitar, under the piano, and with one foot on the kitchen chair, serenaded us in the kitchen. Song after song rang out in the most beautiful tenor. Many a Metropolitan opera audience would have been thrilled to hear him. One ex-policeman was made so happy with the visit that he said: "Lady, if you ever come to Oshkosh I'll let you go through every red light in town." The Library was a busy and quiet place. All types of books were delved into, *Sad Sack* being the most popular.

Each boy wrote his name and address in the guest book—they called it "The Log." We had a boy from every state in the union, two from Shanghai, one from Liverpool and one from New Zealand. It was fun for them to read through the guest book, for often they found friends from their own home towns who had been here. At about four-thirty the big Navy bus returned. There was a call: 'All hands on deck,' and in they piled. With a waving of hands, calls of good-bye, and happy laughter, off they went.

LAKE FOREST, together with the rest of the country, coped with the complicated rationing system involving meat, sugar, gasoline and other commodities. Victory gardens were common. There was hardship at home, connected with shortages and restrictions, but all were borne philosophically. D-day, landings, break-throughs, Belgian Bulge, were eagerly followed by the home front. Soon the

Allies were racing for the Elbe, from the west, and toward Berlin, from the east. On May 7, 1945, General Jodl signed an unconditional surrender, at Allied Headquarters in Rheims, and the war in Europe was over.

In the Pacific, the tide had turned with the invasion of Guadalcanal, when the enemy gradually fought a massive retreat, giving up islands and other possessions until it withdrew into its homeland. Then came the first atomic bomb on Hiroshima, on August 6, followed by the second bomb on Nagasaki on August 9. The Pacific Fleet entered Tokyo Bay on August 27. On September 2, 1945, the Japanese foreign minister signed the surrender documents on the deck of the *Missouri*. The Pacific war was over.

There were no demonstrations or rejoicings to mark the end of hostilities as at the end of World War I in Lake Forest. Forty Lake Foresters had lost their lives in the far flung battle line. Many Lake Forest boys were now released from German and Japanese prison camps including Charles Cascarano, Henry Dangler, Myron Dare, Jack Hemingway, Alexander MacArthur, Cyrus Manierre, William R. Manierre, and Vincent Yore.

Major Cyrus E. Manierre dropped into France with the O.S.S., in 1943. He worked with the Maquis, the French Underground, and was captured in 1944 by the Mili and turned over to the Gestapo. After several weeks, he was tried by the German People's Court and condemned to death. Fortunately, at this time an important uprising of the Maquis occurred, the military files were destroyed, and the Gestapo fled. The prisoners were then turned over to the regular German Army. Cy was now sent to a P.O.W. Camp, Stalag Luft 3, a large center in which final interrogations were made. It was in a mess hall of hundreds of men, in this camp, that he recognized his younger brother, Lieut. William R. Manierre. Brother Bill as a co-pilot on a Liberator had been shot down during his 36th mission and landed on top of a German army barrack.

The two brothers had at first been assigned to different prison camps, but the commanding officer reassigned them together to Stalag Luft 1, on the Baltic. The officer in this latter camp permitted them to send a short-wave message to their mother, Mrs. Edith Harrison Manierre of Lake Forest. They gave their rank and serial numbers and added that they were to be together for the duration of the war. Forty of these messages were intercepted and relayed to their mother by ham radio operators.

V.E. Day was on May 7, 1945, yet, the Russians, though they were our allies, did not permit any messages to be sent from this camp until May 26, 1945. On that date, the prisoners were marched to planes and flown to France, then to England, and on to the United States.

XVII

YOUTH PROGRAMS

1946–1961

DURING the last half of World War II, as parents became more and more involved in the war effort, the problem of juvenile delinquency suddenly reached major proportions for the police department and the city government. Unoccupied homes of families who were in Washington or wherever duty called, were broken into, cars were stolen, vandalism and general undisciplined behaviour became a problem never before encountered to such an extent nor among children of such earnest and respectable parents.

Mayor Charles F. Clarke was frequently called to the Police Department, at all times of day and night, to interview groups of delinquents apprehended in misdemeanors often of a serious nature. Heads of various schools cooperated with the Mayor and the Police to determine punishments, to provide payment for damages incurred, and to give fatherly counsel and direction.

When the war ended, Mayor Clarke wished to do something even more constructive for the youth of the city. He called a dinner meeting, at the Onwentsia Club, including 150 leading citizens representing many organizations in the city. He explained to them the youth problem, which occupied the city government, and expressed his hopes for an organized plan to provide for supervised activities for boys and girls during the times of day and week when they were free from school discipline.

A citizens' committee was formed, and the problem and possible solutions were explored. The committee came up with two salient ideas: that a building should be secured, primarily for recreation for the youth of Lake Forest, dedicated as a war memorial to the dead of World War II. It was hoped that the project would permit the continuance of the Young Men's Club program, the Y.W.C.A. program, and permit a broadened scope for all youth activities concentrated in one Community Center.

The reaction of a dozen organizations in Lake Forest was immediately favorable. School children wrote essays praising the idea. There was every indication that people wanted to conform with the basic ideas expressed. The American Legion, the Churches, the schools, and *The Lake Forester,* joined in this common interest. Many suggestions were received. A lake front harbor, to promote youth activities, was suggested, also a city airport, to encourage flying among the young people, as a timely hobby or career. Those interested in art, recommended facilities for their special interest in the proposed Center.

Caroll H. Sudler was appointed chairman of a committee to explore all the possibilities as to location of grounds, buildings, and their proposed uses. The architect, John Lord King, was asked to draw up plans for a Community Center. It was to contain a gymnasium, locker rooms, showers, canteen, kitchens, and meeting rooms for large and small, civic, educational and cultural organizations. The building was to be run by a staff of five, and upkeep was to be provided by taxation. The services were to be available to *all* Lake Foresters. It was to be located in West Park.

When the blueprints were finished and bids were received, it became apparent that the proposed building would cost $350,000, a great deal more than the committee had anticipated. At this point, the committee cast about to find an existing building which might be capable of conversion to the desired uses, yet costing sub stantially less.

The Bevan estate, on Green Bay Road, was considered in 1947. This beautiful home had been built originally for Noble Brandon Judah, a Chicago lawyer and one time Ambassador to Cuba. The building had been finished in the early twenties, being four years in construction. It had cost $1½ million. The French Norman house contained thirty-one rooms, transplanted piece by piece, from show places of former years in France. No metal nails were used in construction. The gates were brought from Cuba on a special ship. The cobblestone courtyard was brought from France and set over six feet of reinforced concrete. It contained two wells to insure water in case the city supply failed. The location, so convenient for a Community Center, was between West Park and the Deerpath Golf Club. There were outdoor, and one indoor swimming pools, also other pools which might be used by children for wading. Together with thirty acres of land, the house had been left by Dr. Bevan, the second occupant, to the Presbyterian Hospital of Chicago. Now that this property was available to the Committee, at a favorable price, the West Park project was gradually abandoned in its favor.

The first step toward the realization of the Community Center came on April 8, 1947, when a Lake Forest vote of 425 to 242 undergirded the committee's plans by allotting approximately $30,000 of tax money, per year, for the running expenses of the institution, when and if completed. This referendum was the first major step in the program.

In July 1947, the Bevan estate was still in full view, when a group headed by John L. King, assisted by Stanley Anderson and Ralph Milman, began to make studies of the Fred Koch estate, originally built by Wallace Winter, in the late twenties. This property stood on the corner of Deer Path and Green Bay Road, the original Swanton farm dating from 1837. The Koch property contained seven acres, and was offered for approximately $100,000 to the Community Center. The group reported that this property would serve the purposes "admirably." It went on to say: "There is virtually no space within the estate that cannot be fitted into a practical community program; the large drawing room, seating approximately 90 persons, the library, and a combination of two upstairs bedrooms, would provide excellent meeting rooms; the dining room, loggia and drawing room would give adequate space for young people to dance, and a portion of these rooms could be utilized as a canteen for the youngsters; cloak room facilities, office and lodging quarters for the Center's staff are available; the garage could be converted into a manual training room. The construction is of a serviceable type, suitable for a public building. Meeting rooms could be self supporting." The construction of a gymnasium and swimming pool were recommended. As a result of these reports and recommendations the Koch property was purchased.

In October 1947 a fund drive was organized with Samuel J. Sorenson as chairman and collecting agency. The goal was set at $250,000. In four months 800 gifts and pledges, totalling $147,-000 were received.

Early in 1948, several letters and a paid advertisement in *The Lake Forester* challenged the whole Community Center idea, claiming a 10% tax increase, instead of 10% of the mill tax. William E. Clow, Jr., who headed the opposition, wrote an extended criticism which said in effect: "We don't *need* a Community Center." Several adjoining property owners objected to a public building in a private residential area.

In February 1948, former Mayor Clarke announced a poll to take place at City Hall so that the voters could decide whether or not they wanted a Community Center. On the 24th of that month 878 votes were cast *for* the Center, 1,064 were cast *against* it. This was the largest municipal vote recorded in Lake Forest history. After the election, the Koch estate was sold, at some sacrifice, and all who had donated or pledged money were told that they could retract. Some $50,000 remained in the bank.

Actually the Community Center idea was a part of a recurring Lake Forest effort to attain a civic unity, friendliness, and co-operation. The City began with a Lake Forest Association with the stated purpose of promoting a University. All supporting members were dedicated to this cause. People came as residents from everywhere, but the newcomers were soon indoctrinated in the basic ideals of the community, because the town was small and communication was easy. Until the turn of the century there was one protestant church, one catholic church, and one school system. Soon afterwards the Young Men's Club was opened and dedicated to the idea of unity between the old and the new, the Commuter and the non-Commuter, the town and the gown. World War I brought a wave of secularization and a spread of diverse interests which needed coordination. Mayor Henry Rumsey, in the twenties, thought in terms of athletics, a Golf Club and continuous contact among all citizens, to promote a basic unity among all Lake Foresters. In 1930, when the Library building was finished, it was plain to see that it was dedicated "that all may come." World War II brought even greater problems: the emergence of a far greater youth population, which would be facing the community for many years. General world uncertainties made it more imperative that an attempt be made toward an intelligent and planned solution. Ex-Mayor Clarke and Mayor Edward K. Welles could clearly see both the old and the new problems. But the population increase in Lake Forest, immediately after the war, did not permit sufficient time to explain the problem to the voting public or to insure the successful promotion of an idea which was old and tried, but at the same time forward-looking and constructive.

It must be added, however, that as families gradually turned to normal living after the war, juvenile delinquency has been less of a problem. Most of the services required of a Community Center are now being supplied indirectly by the schools, churches and the municipal recreation program. The higher standards of our schools have been especially helpful.

THE Noble Judah house, turned down as a Community Center, was destined to come before the careful scrutiny of another group, this time the Board of Trustees of Lake Forest Academy, when in 1947 a new location, a fourth, was being sought for the school. The sequence began on Sunday evening May 12, 1946, when the usual evening Chapel services were held in Reid Hall. The speaker was the popular Dr. Burtis R. MacHatton, an Academy and College football star of the 1880's. He preached on "What to do with your life." The service ended promptly at 8 o'clock, and everyone retired to the evening study hour. "Pete" Smith rang the bell from the first floor of Reid Hall, to announce the beginning of the study period. At 8:20 Mr. George Blackwell left his chemistry room, walked by the Chapel doors and noticed that the place was dark.

At 8:40 Mr. Bert Grove saw smoke shooting out of the Chapel, as he walked east from the Infirmary on Washington Road. He ran to inform Mr. Fox and others in East House. The Academy fire marshal, Mr. Blair Kinsman, joined these two, and, together with three students: Graham, Minty and Fox, attempted to fight the fire with extinguishers, until they were forced to retire due to the smoke. In the meantime, the fire was reported to the fire department.

The fire trucks arrived at 8:45. Hot ashes were now falling in the yards of the houses on Washington Road. By 9:10 the Chapel itself was burned out and the flames reached in both directions to consume the whole second floor of the building. Fire departments arrived from Highland Park, Great Lakes and Fort Sheridan, but to no avail. The water pipes had not been tested for a long time, so that the small trickle of water obtainable did not have sufficient force to break the windows on the first floor. Soon the bell tower collapsed, and the Memorial bell crashed to the basement with a clang. The crowds, eager to help, were controlled by Jack Pontius and his Student Council boys, until the Military Police arrived from Fort Sheridan to take charge. The fire was under control by 1:00 a.m.

Headmaster E. Francis Bowditch was on a business trip in Boston, during the fire. His little daughter bemoaned the loss of "the nice room with Jesus' picture in it." Dr. MacHatton blamed the holocaust on his hot sermon. The real cause may have been an electric hot box in the area of the chapel platform.

The following Tuesday a wrecking crew levelled the walls. Classes continued without interruption in the gymnasium and dormitories. Damage was total, estimated at $175,000. This is said to have been a major Lake Forest fire of this first hundred year period, comparable to the 1882 fire which consumed most of the business district of the city and the fire which consumed the New Hotel in 1877.

A year later, on April 12, 1947, after careful considerations of various suggestions, the Trustees, following a suggestion of former Headmaster John Wayne Richards, bought the former J. Ogden Armour residence, Mellody Farm, and moved the Academy, lock stock and barrel, to this location. The property was bought from the Frank J. Lewis Foundation. Headmaster Richards had said in the thirties that the Academy had no great future, unless it could secure a much larger piece of property for its purposes. He had said more specifically that Mellody Farm was the only logical area in Lake Forest to house the Academy.

The Academy trustees had discussed purchasing the Noble B. Judah 30-acre property which was more attractively priced and afforded better communication facilities, but was not large enough for purposes of the needed expansion. When Mr. Lewis had bought from The Continental Illinois National Bank of Chicago the Mellody Farm, containing some 1,000 acres, he had originally intended to promote a new religious institution, but the city fathers had interfered with his plans, through an ordinance which prevented any additional tax-free institutions from coming into Lake Forest. At this point, Mr. Lewis was willing to sell a large part of the property, about 600 acres, for approximately the price he had paid for the whole. The Rochdale Community Homes, Inc., made an offer purported to be in excess of $400,000, intending to build a co-operative housing community unit. At that point several hundred Lake Forest citizens donated over $100,000 to the Academy so that the latter could purchase Mellody Farm.

The Academy turned over its Sheridan Road campus to Lake Forest College in place of a claimed $110,000 remaining indebtedness, incurred by the 1925 dissolution of Lake Forest University into three separate institutions: Lake Forest Academy, Ferry Hall, and Lake Forest College. This transfer was a great boon to the College, increasing its acreage from 60 to 90 acres, and providing dormitory space and other housing during the heavy college enrollment of the post-war era, and affording better room for future expansion.

The transference of the school to its fourth home in the new location occurred on Sunday April 4, 1948. Twelve hundred people gathered for the occasion. James F. Oates, Jr., was the master of ceremonies. Dr. Burtis R. MacHatton, an Academy and College graduate, gave the invocation. Headmaster E. Francis Bowditch, Peter Zischke of the Student Council, Stuart R. French of the Alumni Association, and President of the Trustees John F. Fennelly all spoke.

During the first fifteen years on the new campus, the Academy sold 400 acres of land, keeping nearly 200. It has gradually erected a well-rounded school plant for a modern boys' preparatory school, including dormitory space, gymnasium, swimming pool and athletic fields.

THE OUTSTANDING EVENT of the next decade was the Korean war, which started on June 25, 1950. The North Korean Communist armies invaded South Korea without warning. One of the bright spots of that grim "police action" in which many Lake Foresters took part, was an interview by Julian Bentley of WBBM radio station at the front lines with a representative United States soldier. The man chosen was James A. Casselberry of Lake Forest. Many fellow townsmen were thrilled to hear the broadcast on December 20, 1951.

IN VIEW OF THE 1950 census indicating an increase of 619 persons in ten years, and a much greater anticipated increase to follow, the need for more public schools became apparent. A smaller percentage of the new population was interested in private school education, and these schools in turn were unable to expand sufficiently to satisfy even the existing demand.

The Board of Education of School district 67 purchased 31.35 acres of property from Miss Gwethlyn Jones, east of the Skokie and south of Deer Path, for $70,000, "to be used by the purchaser exclusively for the purposes of education and recreation and no other." The contract was signed for this property on January 22, 1951.

Studies were made and general requirements of safety, durability, economy and beauty were stated. Plans were drawn up with architects, administration, and Board of Education cooperating, for the erection of a new school for the upper grades. Ralph Milman and Childs & Smith, Associated Architects, were secured. Their combined work stressed functional interiors and contemporary design, blending the outward appearance into the surrounding landscape. Openness, privacy, efficiency, light and warmth became the theme of each part and of the whole. There was a creative use of galleries and arches. A notable innovation was the glassed-in central courtyard. The exterior was of high quality face brick, trimmed with Bedford stone. The building was intended for public as well as educational use.

Bids were received, and John Griffith and Son Construction Company was secured as general contractors. Franz Lipp, who was hired as the landscape architect, planted the school grounds. The school was completed and occupied in the fall of 1954. It received the Citation of Merit for excellence in architecture from the American Institute of Architects.

The Deer Path School contained 16 classrooms for 400 pupils, also an art room, a science room, a dramatics room, a music room, a library, a cafeteria, two gymnasiums, and office space. The auditorium contained 481 seats. The equipment for this and the next three units was secured by Orville B. Peterson, Assistant to the Superintendent of Schools. The grounds afforded ample parking facilities and room for outdoor athletics. The total cost of this school was $1,385,000. The use of the building and property as a Community Center was explored. The flagpole was a gift of the Lake Forest Post of the American Legion.

While the Deer Path School was being erected, the Halsey School, which had been built in 1895, enlarged and named after Prof. John J. Halsey in 1912, was transferred to the City of Lake Forest. It was torn down in 1955, and the entire school area was made into a city parking lot.

At the dedication of the Deer Path School on January 16, 1955, Frederick F. Quinlan was Superintendent of Schools. McPherson Holt, a grandson of pioneer D. R. Holt was the President of the Board of Education, and Dr. John C. Pearson became the first Principal.

THE 1953 Lake Forest Day featured "Civilian Defense." This was one of the most elaborate ever held. A fleet of jets from the Glenview Naval Air Station flew over the parade and one of the most interesting displays was a mobile telephone switchboard unit which would serve the civil defense units in the Chicago area in an emergency.

In 1956 George S. Landfield conducted a one man crusade for a dog ordinance to prevent the roaming of dogs. *The Lake Forester* carried several articles pro and con. Great interest was aroused and a hearing was held in City Hall on August 6, 1956, before a packed audience. Several eloquent speeches were made on both sides. The need for an ordinance was due to the increase of the dog population to over a thousand (1259 in 1960) and to several incidents in which people were attacked by packs running aimlessly. No ordinance resulted, but the responsibility of dog owners was driven home to be mindful of the welfare and feelings of neighbors. Older residents began to be conscious of the shrinking of space with population growth.

IN QUICK SUCCESSION three more grade schools were built, in different parts of the growing city, so that the most populous areas would have the least transportation problems. Sheridan School, at the north end of Lake Forest, on Sheridan Road, and just across the street from the location of the old North School, was completed and dedicated in 1957. Everett School, in West Lake Forest, was dedicated in 1958. The Cherokee School at the south end of Green Bay Road should be ready for occupancy by September 1962.

When the construction of additions to the High School and new grade schools was proposed by the respective Boards of Education, a criticism was offered to the effect that Lake Forest would draw more than its share of newcomers; and thus the character of the city would be changed. On the contrary, the newcomers have followed the original pattern set at the time of the city charter, coming to avail themselves of the educational and cultural advantages of Lake Forest.

XVIII

FROM CASTLE TO RANCH HOUSE

1946–1961

SOMETIMES Chicago area newspapers, for the sake of humor or glamor, have created a false image of Lake Forest. An article in the *Evanston Review* made this remark: "The economic interpretation of the north shore's history has several versions, but here's the way we understand it: When a Chicago business or professional man earns enough to buy two suits of underwear, he moves to Evanston. When he can afford two cars, he moves to Winnetka or Glencoe. When he can afford two wives and/or a yacht, he moves farthest north to Lake Forest." Those who do not know the spirit and history of our city, might assume from this that all Lake Forest citizens are enormously wealthy, all have yachts and many cars, and all practise an unbridled and irresponsible matrimonial liberty. This image is often projected by descriptions of parties and weddings which made headlines, because of national or international overtones, and receive special treatment. Many types of businesses like to promote the idea of financial superiority by applying to Lake Forest such words as: "unique," "exclusive," "prestige community," "village of millionaires," and the like.

The peculiar quality of Lake Forest lies in its dedication to education, and in its exclusion of any industry. Even a private laboratory, for industrial experiments, has been deemed contrary to the

254

Ordinances of the city. At the same time, several retail businesses have had a long and distinguished service record of fifty years or more. Among these, mention should be made of the James Anderson Company, civil engineers; Fitzgerald's Plumbing; French's Drug Store and its descendants Wenban & Griffis and Martin's Drug Store; John Griffith, real estate; Krafft's Drug Store; Henry T. Strenger, Plumbing; Wells & Copithorne and its antecedent, Harder's. O'Neill's Hardware, of course, has had a continuous existence for nearly a century, being operated by members of the same family.

The business of education has been and remains the basic occupation of a great per cent of our population. The combined educational system of Lake Forest during the centennial year involves a total of 7,188 people. The figure may be a surprise to many. Granting that some of the students attending Lake Forest schools are not permanent residents and may not be counted among the estimated population of 11,000 of the city; at the same time, more than half of the city's residents are connected with one of our thirteen schools, in some capacity. The following figures were reported on November 1, 1961:

	Students	Faculty	Staff	Dependents
Public Grade Schools	1,536	92	36	275
Lake Forest College	1,156	88	150	255
Lake Forest High School	834	58	28	93
School of St. Mary	556	25	4	8
Barat College	400	49	25	43
Lake Forest Day School	390	18	10	44
Academy of the Sacred Heart:				
Woodlands	351	28	17	20
Lake Forest Academy	202	28	42	70
Ferry Hall	150	23	40	44
Totals	5,575	409	352	852

Grand Total 7,188.

Lake Forest has no industries, but among its residents are many industrialists. The heads of many businesses and corporations reside in Lake Forest to enjoy the educational environment, the out-of-doors, and the privacy in a friendly personalized community. They deem the quiet life away from the scenes of the metropolitan marketplace a welcome contrast.

Lake Forest citizens are proud of the many leaders who have lived here, some of whom are in the following list: J. Ogden Armour, President of Armour & Company; Clifford Barnes, founder and President of the Sunday Evening Club; Hobart Chatfield-Taylor, author; E. A. Cudahy, President Cudahy Packing Company; A. B. Dick, President of A. B. Dick & Company; T. E. Donnelley, Chairman of the Board, R. R. Donnelley & Sons Company; Henry C. Durand, President of Durand Brothers; J. V. Farwell, President of J. V. Farwell & Company; C. B. Farwell, U.S. Senator; Charles S. Frost, Architect; Alfred Hoyt Granger, Architect; John J. Halsey, educator and author; Ernest A. Hamill, President of Corn Exchange Bank; D. R. Holt, President of Holt & Balcom; Marvin Hughitt, President of Chicago and Northwestern Railroad; Noble Brandon Judah, Ambassador to Cuba; William V. Kelley, President of American Steel Foundries; Robert Patterson Lamont, Secretary of Commerce; William Mather Lewis, President of Lafayette College; Clayton Mark, President of Clayton Mark & Company; Cyrus H. McCormick, President of International Harvester Company and member of Diplomatic Mission to Russia in 1917; John T. McCutcheon, author, cartoonist, philosopher; D. R. McLennan, President Marsh & McLennan Inc.; Admiral William Adger Moffett, U.S. Navy; Sterling Morton, Chairman of the Board of Morton Salt Company; Walter Neef, European head of the Associated Press; John T. Pirie, Jr., President Carson, Pirie, Scott & Company; Edward A. Ryerson, President of Ryerson Steel Company; Delevan Smith, President United Press; Albert A. Sprague, President, Sprague, Warner & Company; Louis F. Swift, President of Swift & Company; Robert J. Thorne, President Montgomery Ward; Howard Van Doren Shaw, architect; Frederick Wacker, Sr., President Chicago Plan Commission; Ezra J. Warner, President Sprague, Warner & Company; Percy Wilson, President Wilson Mortgage & Finance Corporation.

Among the current residents, who are well known beyond our borders, are: Dorothy Aldis, author; Waldo M. Allen, President Mayflower Society; John D. Ames, President U.S. Golf Association; General William H. Arnold, General of 5th Army; Ralph Bard, Under Secretary of the Navy; Lilace Reid Barnes, President of the World Y.W.C.A.; Otis Carney, author; G. S. "Mickey"

Cochrane, Baseball Hall of Fame, Most Valuable (twice); Mrs. Jane Warner Dick, United Nations; James Douglas, Secretary of the Air Force and deputy Secretary of Defense; Stanley Field, President of Field Museum; Charles Haffner, Chairman of the Board of R. R. Donnelley & Sons Company; Sylvia Shaw Judson, artist and sculptress; Mrs. Buell Mullen, metal fresco artist; James F. Oates, President of Equitable Life Assurance Company; Admiral Francis P. Old, U.S. Navy; John S. Reed, Vice President (Finance) of Atcheson, Topeka & Santa Fe; Hermon D. Smith, President Marsh & McLennan Inc.; Solomon A. Smith, President Northern Trust Company; R. Douglas Stuart, Ambassador to Canada; General Robert E. Wood, President Sears, Roebuck & Company; and others.

THERE ARE several sagas which are peculiar to Lake Forest. A collection of stories would make colorful reading. They tell about Alfred Hamill who played golf for years wearing a stiff collar. It is whispered that Solomon A. Smith has played golf at the Onwentsia Club every year for sixty years, though he won't admit it.

A story involving the high price of medicine dates from the depression period. A customer walked into one of our drug stores and bought a small but unusual item of medication. The clerk walked back of the store and asked the owner what to charge for the purchase. He replied: "Charge her 85¢." The clerk walked to the customer and mumbled the price. She misunderstood the quoted price, left 15¢ on the counter and walked out. The clerk was upset and returning to the owner explained what had happened and added: "I don't even know who she is. What do I do now?" The owner replied: "Never mind, we made 10¢ on the deal anyway!"

Another story involves one of our best known citizens who passed away. A close friend of the family had just received a box of flowers at her house which she hadn't opened. She sent it to the church for the funeral. Later, the widow checked through all the cards to thank all who had sent flowers. She found a card which read: "Happy birthday, and one big smack."

Everybody liked to tell stories about the Samuel Chase family. One of the most unusual involved Mrs. Chase's unorthodox driving habits. One day she made a U-turn on a busy intersection and completely snarled the traffic. An officer soon untangled the mess and in a gruff voice and manner ordered her to the curbing. He then walked to her car with ticket and pen in hand and demanded: "What's yer name?" She answered coyly: "My name is Mary, what's yours?" The officer was so disarmed by her reply, he put away his tickets and said: "All right lady, you can go now!"

Another story involved Mr. Chase and a cat which adopted his family. After a long life the cat died. Then arose the question of the suitable disposal of the family pet. The ground was frozen rock-hard and deep in snow, so a burial underneath the old apple tree in the back yard was not a suitable final resting place. Mrs. Chase had an inspiration. She packaged the cat carefully with newspaper and then parcelled him neatly in brown paper and twine. Mr. Chase took the package with him on the 8 o'clock train to Chicago, expecting to drop the package into the Chicago River, on the way. Mr. Chase was an avid bridge player. When the train pulled into the Northwestern Station, he had forgotten to dispose of his burden, so he took it to his office and placed it on the window ledge. Homeward bound his secretary gave him his winter coat, hat, scarf, boots, *and* package.

On the 5:10 train he sat with Horace Martin, an old friend he hadn't seen for ages, and they had a fine ride home. As they got off at the Lake Forest station, the conductor reminded him of his package in the overhead rack. Mrs. Chase met him at the train and seemed displeased to see what he was carrying. There were some loud exchanges of words as both were quite hard of hearing.

Home again Mr. Chase tossed his parcel on the kitchen table. As the package split open both stood staring at each other and at the leg of lamb which emerged.

PROBLEMS of retaining the natural beauty of Lake Forest along with health and sanitation, have been constantly before the city fathers. During the 1940's the lake was dangerously high. Where people used to ride horseback or to take walks along the entire shore area of Lake Forest it was no longer possible to do so. The high water undermined trees and damaged several homes on the bluff in spite of expensive breakwaters which had been erected during the previous decades. The sand which formerly drifted to the leeward along the waters' edge was now carried into the deep waters. All this was accompanied by a city water pollution problem which forced the expenditures of considerable sums of money in 1947 to lay a 24 inch pipe 3,000 feet out from the shore in 28 feet of water. The new improvement took care of the 80 miles of water pipes and 410 public fire hydrants with sufficient margin for the anticipated increases in the coming years.

A new caucus system, with a broadened electorate was introduced during World War II, to nominate the Mayor and other city officials. Today the caucus has been enlarged further, so that it is open to all who care to come and voice their opinions. This has increased public interest in all phases of city government.

On December 5, 1960, the Zoning Ordinance was greatly altered after revisions in 1955, 1957, and 1959. Residential areas west of Green Bay Road required 60,000 square feet, east of Sheridan Road required 40,000 square feet. Between Washington and Sheridan Roads 20,000 square feet were required. Altogether ten zones were redefined; five residential, one duplex, one office, and one neighborhood shopping, one business and one service.

The face of Lake Forest has changed appreciably since World War II. The new architecture endorses the ranch house, modern colonial and modern American. The trend is toward smaller properties and smaller homes with a view toward independence in maintenance. All dwellings stress light and convenience and recognize, for the first time, the existence of the automobile with ample garage space. Air conditioning, central heating, and efficient kitchens are standard requirements. All have stressed the building of houses "inside out" instead of "outside in," but now in modern American, an outward beauty is also achieved which has enduring quality. The new architecture is often exquisite and chaste indicating good taste and charm.

Among the new generation of architects, Jerome Cerny has devised a transitional style of architecture which embodies the symmetry and balance of the Georgian in outline but which incorporates all the essentials of convenience, efficient operation and low maintenance. He has designed houses not only in Lake Forest, but in many parts of the country, and has just completed one in the Bahamas. In 1960 I. W. "Ike" Colburn was awarded the American Institute of Architect's National Award for the William L. McLennan house on Lake Road. The house was cited as having the classic ideals of order, dignity and controlled sensuousness. In May 1961 the McLennan house was the subject of a *Life* magazine article titled "The Romantic Swing in Architecture." He also designed the Bath and Tennis Club buildings and outlay, on the north end of Green Bay Road. Boyd Hill has achieved a happy inward and outward beauty combined with utility by "striving toward the modern with a traditional feeling." Herman Lackner, too, realizing the varying tastes of our cosmopolitan and heterogeneous community, has been able to please his constituents and meet local needs. Ralph Milman, following the classical French architecture of Gabriel Jacques Ange, has designed a modernized version of Le Hermitage one tenth the size of the original and containing electric heating, a modern small kitchen, no fireplace and no chimney. This house was built for the Edward Cummings at 999 Green Bay Road. Stanley D. Anderson Associates have designed some of our most attractive homes in the Georgian style, also several public buildings.

Many public and private buildings are proud of some work of art, some little gem which adorns it. The annual art exhibits in Market Square stress the high quality of the work of the large colony of artists who are Lake Forest residents. One of these, Sylvia Shaw Judson, a daughter of the man who designed the Market Square, has pleased many with the high quality of her sculpture. On July 9, 1959, her heroic statue of Mary Dyer was dedicated on the grounds of the Massachusetts State House. She was the Quaker martyr who was hanged on the Boston Common in 1660. The statue, remarkable for its depiction of strength and serenity, is a witness to the concept of freedom.

NEW SUBDIVISIONS with diverse architecture have mushroomed over the 15.2 square miles of Lake Forest. We have 96 miles of paved streets. There are 300 acres of public parks, a high ratio of open space to private homes and properties. In 1958 $5,820,259 of new private and institutional construction was started. The 1950 census showed a population of 7,819; in 1955 it increased to 8,963; in 1960 it rose to 10,658. The 1961 census is estimated at 11,300. Births have numbered about 120 each of the last six years; deaths about 50. The assessed evaluation has now passed $75,000,000.

Other miscellaneous vital statistics show that in 1960 22,000 people used the beach, 26,074 rounds of golf were played at the Deerpath Golf Club, 56 fires occurred in buildings, 4,899 passenger cars were licensed, 325 automobile accidents and 20 auto thefts were reported, 1,259 dog licenses were issued, 585,073,000 gallons of water were purified and delivered to 2,653 customers; the Library containing 54,649 volumes circulated 81,169 books; 1,370 pupils attended public schools; eighty teachers taught in 58 class-rooms; 3,463 man hours of work was employed for snow and ice control.

Trees on parkways, roads and parks include 4,594 elms, 2,562 oaks, 1,146 hard maple, 901 ash, 533 locust, 383 hawthorne, 220 hickory, 195 linden, 121 cedar, 118 cottonwood, 100 willow, 95 aspen, 91 spruce, 91 wild cherry, 71 boxelder, 55 white pine, 42 balsam fir, 35 walnut, 27 buckeye, 25 apple, 17 birch, 16 blue beech, and a considerable variety of others, totalling 11,478 trees.

In 1940 the City of Lake Forest received 57 acres in the southeast corner of the City which has become a unique forest preserve. This is probably the only forest preserve of this kind in the country, comprising virgin timber and 600 feet of lake front.

Lake Forest is one large park, its trees being its glory. In the spring, the delicate sprouting of trees and shrubbery cover the city with a cloak of unsurpassed beauty. White and red oaks, red maple, hickory, elm and the hundreds of imported varieties of pines, elms, beeches, and poplars, display their richness in the summer growth. In the fall, nature is most generous with its brilliant shades of red and yellow, when every street competes with every other in natures most colorful display: when the beeches glow, maples burn and oaks smoulder. Some like Lake Forest, in her winter garb, when a sudden cold snap brings varieties of glittering splendor, all beyond description.

A host of citizens have preserved and enhanced this beauty. The unsung heroes are the hundreds of gardeners who have gathered here from all parts of Europe, to share their knowledge and skill, to introduce new varieties, to experiment with others, and to cooperate with nature to make our little world a beautiful spot in which to live.

Another group deserving of praise, especially for the hundreds of lovely gardens in Lake Forest, are members of the Lake Forest

Garden Club, who, by dint of hard work and application, have gathered a great fund of knowledge and applied their findings. They seem to believe that happiness can only be achieved by creating a garden of one's own. It is rumored that many a Lake Forest matron would prefer a load of manure for her garden to the gift of a new pearl necklace.

Lake Forest, being heterogeneous and cosmopolitan, is not for all who come an easy place in which to live. We have here a complicated social structure with endless groups made up from varieties of interests, most of them originating in the great city nearby. To some, party or prominence is the whole of life. Others are absorbed in their own business or profession, finding it difficult to find time for new friends. Through patience and friendliness many have made friends, thus making their residence here a happy experience for all.

In 1957 Lake Forest Academy, Ferry Hall, and Lake Forest College celebrated the centennial of the chartering of Lind University, the first Lake Forest charter. At the centennial dinner, in Durand Commons of Lake Forest College, Harold H. Corbin, Jr., Headmaster of Lake Forest Academy, said:

We meet to bid goodbye to a dying century and ring in the second hundred years of a great educational enterprise. It is no secret that the perilous decisions of our day make clear the need for intellectual and moral discipline on a scale never before contemplated in America's history. The City of Lake Forest, born in an educational dream, should never allow itself to forget that in one vital sense it is a manufacturing town—not merely residential—and its sole demonstrable product is education. In this city of 9,000 persons, some 13 schools are far, far out of proportion in number and excellence to the size of the city; they embrace virtually the whole range of American education—public, independent, sectarian; primary, elementary, secondary, collegiate; coeducational, boys, girls, boarding and day.

By geography and inclination, by tradition and service, by resources and desire, education in Lake Forest must continue to flourish and abound. Let no citizen imperfectly understand this reality and this hope. The example of this community is of incalculable value as an inspiration and a pattern for other cities.

I would hope, and this most deeply, that the College, Ferry Hall, and the Academy, having shared the same nest, and having explored, in their fledgling century, the diverging paths of their special missions, will find in the years ahead a new spiritual if not a corporate bond. We, in our individual services to that process called youth, have much to share together, and even more to offer to the city of our founding.

The Academy spread out its centennial celebrations over the entire year of 1957. A Centennial Ball with several hundred guests was held in Reid Hall. The General Robert E. Wood house, a residence to be built for the Headmaster, was announced. An anniversary booklet was published. Robert Frost, the American Poet Laureate, was a guest of the school for a week, and read his award-winning poems before a large audience. Dr. Harold W. Dodds, President of Princeton University, was entertained by a group of a hundred friends and graduates of Princeton, at the Onwentsia Club, then lectured before a large audience in Glore Gymnasium, praising the Academy for its role as a leading unit of secondary education. He spoke of the leadership, foresight and courage of her faculties. He said it was

founded by Calvinists, who felt learning and piety were the two main achievements of a man's life. One of the heresies of American education is that democracy means equality at the polls and in education. The fear of intellectual snobbery is one of the deterrents of quality education. Schools like Lake Forest Academy must be kept strong to protect American freedom.

THE 1959 centennial celebration of the First Presbyterian Church of Lake Forest included a banquet at the Calvin Durand Commons with Arthur R. McKay, President of McCormick Theological Seminary as the chief speaker. This was especially suitable since the first President of the Seminary, Dr. James G. K. Mc-Clure, was pastor of this Church and one time President of Lake Forest University. Photographs were collected and a small but informative anniversary historical pamphlet was written by Louis E. Laflin, Jr., and Edward Arpee. The great anniversary effort consisted of a campaign to raise $500,000 for an expansion program to improve the facilities for Christian education and other services of the church.

THE city's centennial celebration was also a whole year's affair. It included a Garden Club series of exhibits in the windows of Lake

Forest business houses, June 28–29, a Lake Forest College Ten-panel historical exhibit under the direction of John Anderson of Lake Forest College and Robert Vogel of the Lake County Museum, Wadsworth, Illinois. This exhibit was on display at the College Library for ten days, and then moved to City Hall, where it continued for two more weeks. The Lake Forest Public Library displayed several different exhibits composed of books, maps and pictures related to the one hundred years of Lake Forest history.

One of the most exciting Centennial events was Lake Forest Day, on August 2, which did double duty celebrating the Civil War as well. Thousands lined the parade route—Western, Deer Path, and Green Bay Road to West Park—they were mostly children, wearing headgear reminiscent of the Civil War centennial. Louis Ellsworth Laflin, Jr., was at the "mike" at the head of Market Square, the parade judges were Mr. and Mrs. Harold H. Corbin of Lake Forest Academy, Dr. and Mrs. Robert G. Andrus of Ferry Hall, and Dr. and Mrs. William Graham Cole of Lake Forest College. Two Spanish-American war veterans were introduced.

The 9:30 siren started off the children's parade with a hundred children of a few months to a few years old taking part in two dozen displays. Though slow moving, it has always been one of the most interesting to the audience. The second siren at 10 o'clock announced the adult parade which was led by Mayor and Mrs. George R. Beach, Jr., driven in an antique Packard touring car by Mrs. Charles H. Brown. As usual, the Lake Forest American Legion Rifle Squad came next, followed by the Fifth Army Band and a Company of crack riflemen.

In all there were more than a dozen bands including one from Great Lakes. The long ribbon of music was punctuated by showers of ball-point pens and an assortment of wrapped candies tossed upon the boys and girls along the streets. There were many reminders of the years past: A conestoga wagon reminded us of the pioneers; a Treasure chest bore the inscription "The Treasured Years"—the hundred years. An 1880 model bicycle, owned by Stanley Kiddle, was ridden in style and showmanship over the parade area; several O'Neill carriages were reminiscent of Lake Forest businesses in the 1870's onward. It was unfortunate that the Julian Matthews' original sleigh which had served as a taxi in Lake Forest, not being seasonable, could not be displayed. Two dozen exhibitions advertised medicines, beverages and cars. One of the most impressive was the Hawthorne-Mellody wagon with a team of six huge horses. Hardly had these passed when a North-western streamliner roared by parallel to the parade.

The crowds and the floats gathered at West Park where prizes were announced. This was followed by various races, baseball, rides and all the carnival that continued until midnight.

Perhaps the most significant centennial effort was the dinner in the college Field House on February 18, when a pageant of the first City Council meeting was presented, followed by an address by Senator Barry Goldwater of Arizona before 1,300. The Invocation by William Graham Cole at this dinner seemed to condense the hopes and dreams of all, when he prayed:

O Thou who art the Lord of years, the Potentate of Time; one hundred years in Thy sight are but as yesterday when it is past, but to us it is a long time; a time to remember, a time to celebrate. Bless us as we gather here tonight, looking to our past with pride and to our future with faith. We thank Thee for what we have been, a City of homes, a City of culture, a City that has cared and dared. Grant that as we go forward into our second century, we may continue with the courage, the vision and the faith of our forebears, to build here a community always mindful of Thy favor and glad to do Thy will. Keep us grateful to those who have gone before us, who have given of themselves and their substance to make us what we are. They are with us in spirit in this hour, and we touch hands with them across the barriers of time, in glad remembrance and happy hope. Grant that we may individually and severally leave our town better than we found it, and to Thee be the glory and the honor and praise now and for ever more.   Amen.

William Holt Spalding, great great grandson of pioneer D. R. Holt, was born at Lake Forest Hospital the night of the Centennial dinner.

Miscellany

MISCELLANY

1. Mayors of Lake Forest

Adminis- tration	Mayor		Tenure of Office
1.......	1. Harvey M. Thompson ......First Term		1861–1865
2.......	2. William S. Johnston, Jr.		1865–1866
3.......	3. David J. Lake		1866–1867
4......	Harvey M. Thompson ....Second Term		1867–1868
5.......	4. Sylvester Lind ....First Term		1868–1870
6.......	5. Samuel Ezra Barnum ....First Term		1870–1871
7.......	6. John V. Farwell		1871–1872
8......	Samuel Ezra Barnum .....Second Term		1872–1874
9......	Sylvester Lind ....Second Term		1874–1877
10......	7. Amzi Benedict ....First Term		1877–1878
11......	Sylvester Lind ....Third Term		1878–1879
12......	Samuel Ezra Barnum ......Third Term		1879–1881
13......	Sylvester Lind ....Fourth Term		1881–1884
14......	Amzi Benedict ....Second Term		1884–1885
15......	8. Joseph B. Durand		1886–1888
16......	9. Moses L. Scudder		1888–1889
17.......10.	Walter C. Larned		1889–1891
18.......11.	Calvin Durand		1891–1895
19.......12.	Edward F. Gorton		1895–1902
20.......13.	Mark Morton		1902–1903

269

Miscellany

21.......14. Fredrik Herman Gade ......*First Term* 1903–1906
22.......15. David H. Jackson 1906–1909
23....... Fredrik Herman Gade ....*Second Term* 1909–1910
24.......16. C. Frederick Childs 1910–1911
25.......17. John T. Pirie, Jr. 1911–1914
26.......18. Leverett Thompson 1914–1915
27.......19. William Mather Lewis 1915–1917
28.......20. Keene H. Addington 1917–1919
29.......21. Henry A. Rumsey 1919–1925
30.......22. Farwell Winston 1925–1928
31.......23. Albert B. Dick, Jr. 1928–1931
32.......24. Albert D. Farwell 1931–1934
33.......25. Francis E. Manierre 1934–1937
34.......26. Kent Chandler 1937–1940
35.......27. Richard H. Mabbatt 1940–1943
36.......28. Charles F. Clarke 1943–1946
37.......29. Edward K. Welles 1946–1948
38.......30. John O. Giles 1948–1951
39.......31. W. Paul McBride 1951–1954
40.......32. Elliott Donnelley 1954–1957
41.......33. Morrison Waud 1957–1960
42.......34. George R. Beach, Jr. 1960–1963

2. Lake Forest Population

Year	Population	Ten Year Increase
1860............	300?	
1870............	800............	500
1880............	1,000............	200
1890............	1,750............	750
1900............	2,215............	465
1910............	3,300............	1,085
1920............	3,600............	300
1930............	6,500............	2,900
1940............	7,200............	700
1950............	7,819............	619
1960............	10,658............	2,839

3. LAKE FOREST ANNEXATIONS

Square Miles

Original Plat 3.262

November 11, 1894. .245 Generally the High School area. North of Woodland Road to Lake Bluff. East of the Northwestern tracks to Sheridan Road.

August 22, 1899. . . 1.638 Township line on North to Old Elm in the South. From Lake Michigan to a N.S. line from Onwentsia Stables.

September 2, 1907. .056 Atteridge Road South, including West Park.

April 2, 1912. . . . . . .005 Small triangle between Laurel Avenue and west of the Northwestern tracks.

May 12, 1926. . . . . 9.000 Area generally west of the Skokie Highway.

May 2, 1927. . . . . . .402 Knollwood Club area.

April 1, 1957. . . . . . .611 Part of Vernon Township east of the Toll Road and south of Everett Road.

Total 15.219 Square Miles

4. PRINCIPALS AND HEADMASTERS OF
LAKE FOREST ACADEMY

1. Samuel Fisher Miller, A.M., Principal 1858–1862
2. Prof. Milford C. Butler, Principal 1862–1864
3. Lewis M. Johnson, M.A., Principal 1864–1868
4. Dr. Edmund Adams Jones, Principal 1868–1869
5. Ira W. Allen, Principal 1869–1874
6. Albert R. Sabin, Principal 1874–1879
7. Walter L. Rankin, A.M., Principal 1879–1881
8. Samuel Woods, A.M., Principal 1881–1883
9. Rev. Alexander G. Wilson, D.D., Principal 1883–1887
10. Rev. George R. Cutting, M.A., Principal 1887–1890
11. Charles Alden Smith, M.A., Principal 1890–1897
12. Alfred Gardner Welch, M.A., Headmaster 1897–1900
13. Conrad Hibbeler, Acting Headmaster 1900–1901
14. Joseph Curtis Sloane, Headmaster 1901–1905

15. William Mather Lewis, Headmaster 1905–1913
16. John Wayne Richards, Headmaster 1913–1941
17. Ebenezer Francis Bowditch, Headmaster 1941–1951
18. Harold H. Corbin, Headmaster 1951–

5. PRINCIPALS OF FERRY HALL

1. Edward P. Weston 1869–1876
2. Emily M. Noyes (Lady Principal) 1869–1872
3. Martha Sprague 1876–1878
4. Rev. Alexander G. Wilson 1878–1880
5. Mrs. Esther E. Thompson 1880–1886
6. Sarah M. Van Vleck 1886–1887
7. Levi Seeley 1887–1894
8. Dr. J. M. Coulter............................1894–1895
9. Sabra L. Sargent 1895–1904
10. Frances L. Hughes 1904–1914
11. Miriam S. Converse (Acting Principal) 1914–1915
12. Marion Coats 1915–1918
13. Eloise Ruthven Tremain 1918–1945
14. Frances Wallace 1945–1958
15. Rev. Robert Gardner Andrus 1958–

6. PRESIDENTS OF LAKE FOREST COLLEGE

1. Rev. Robert Wilson Patterson, D.D. 1875–1877
2. John H. Hewitt (Acting President) 1877–1878
3. Rev. Daniel S. Gregory, D.D. 1878–1886
4. Rev. William C. Roberts, D.D., LL.D. 1886–1892
5. Rev. James G. K. McClure, D.D. (Pres. pro tem) 1892–1893
6. John M. Coulter, Ph.D. 1893–1896
7. Prof. John J. Halsey (Acting President) 1896–1897
8. Rev. James G. K. McClure, D.D. 1897–1901
9. Rev. Richard Davenport Harlan 1901–1906
10. Prof. John J. Halsey (Acting President) 1906–1907
11. John Scholte Nollen, Ph.D. 1907–1917
12. Henry Wilkes Wright (Acting President) 1918–1920
13. Herbert McComb Moore, D.D. 1921–1942
14. Ernest Johnson (Acting President) 1942–1944
15. Ernest Johnson 1944–1959
16. William Graham Cole 1960–

7. PASTORS OF ST. PATRICK'S CHURCH

1. Rev. John Guegnin . . . . .c. 1840 *Missionary from Waukegan*
2. Rev. Bernard McGorrish . . . .
3. Rev. James Kean . . . .
4. Rev. John Hampstead   1852
5. Rev. Henry Coyle   1854
6. Rev. John McGee . . . .   1855 *First Resident Pastor*
7. Rev. Edward O'Reilly   1900
8. Rev. Thomas Quinn   1910
9. Rev. William Ryan . . . .
10. Rev. James Fielding . . . .
11. Rev. Lawrence Daly   1937–1951
12. Rev. Raymond T. McCarthy .   1951–

8. CLERGY STATIONED AT ST. MARY'S CHURCH

1. Rev. J. Coyle 1859–1860
2. Rev. William Herbert 1860–1861
3. Rev. William M. Phew 1861–1862
4. Rev. P. O'Dwyre 1862–1866
5. Rev. J. W. Kennedy 1866–1867
6. Rev. M. Lyons 1867–1868
7. Rev. Dominick Egan 1868
8. Rev. M. Donohoe 1868
9. Rev. P. L. Hendricks 1868–1869
10. Rev. P. T. McElherne 1869
11. Rev. James Maloney 1869–1872
12. Rev. R. H. McGuire 1872–1875
13. Rev. James J. McGovern .1875–1880
14. Rev. M. Welby 1880–1881
15. Rev. Thomas Carroll 1881–1883
16. Rev. J. H. Grogan 1883–1890
17. Rev. Edward O'Reilly 1893–1906
18. Rev. Francis J. Barry 1906–1923
19. Rev. John J. O'Hearn 1923–1931
20. Rev. Charles A. Murphy 1931–1941
21. Rt. Rev. Msgr. Thomas Vincent Shannon, LL.D. 1941–1959
22. Rev. Robert J. Madden 1959–

9. PASTORS OF THE FIRST PRESBYTERIAN CHURCH

1. William C. Dickinson 1864–1867
2. James H. Taylor 1868–1875
3. William R. Brown 1877–1881
4. James Gore King McClure 1881–1905
5. W. H. Wray Boyle 1905–1913
6. George Roberts 1915–1935
7. William Oliver Brackett 1936–1945
8. Robert Gardner Andrus 1946–1957
9. Richard H. Hutchison 1958–

10. RECTORS OF THE CHURCH OF THE HOLY SPIRIT
(*Episcopal*)

1. Owen J. Davies 1902–1904
2. Albert Glenn Richards 1904–1912
3. John Herbert Edwards 1912–1922
4. Herbert W. Prince 1923–1946
5. Wood B. Carper, Jr. 1946–1956
6. George F. Tittmann 1956–1962

11. LAKE FOREST ARCHITECTS

1. Adler, David
2. Anderson, Stanley D.
3. Cerny, Jerome
4. Clark, Edwin H.
5. Cobb, Henry Ives
6. Colburn, I. W.
7. Dangler, Henry C.
8. Farwell, Granger
9. Frazier, Walter
10. Frost, Charles Sumner
11. Granger, Alfred
12. Heun, Arthur
13. Hill, Boyd
14. Jobson, C. E.
15. Lackner, Herman
16. Lindeberg, Harris T.
17. Milman, Ralph
18. Morphett, A. S.
19. Olmsted, Frederick Law
20. Perkins, Frederick W.
21. Platt, Charles A.
22. Rogers, James Gamble
23. Shaw, Howard Van Doren
24. Suter, W. Lindsay
25. Warren, William Arthur
26. White, Sanford
27. Whitehouse, Meredith
28. Zimmerman, W. C.

BIBLIOGRAPHY

Anderson, George. A Personal History of Lake Forest's Pioneer Resident.
Andreas, A. T. History of Chicago, The Lakeside Press, 1884.
Anonymous. A Biography of James Gore King McClure.
Articles of the Lake Forest Association. February 28, 1856. The Democratic Job Office, Chicago.
Barnet, James. Martyrs and Heroes of Illinois in the Great Rebellion, 1865.
Beautiful Suburban Towns. The Chicago and North Western Railway. 1909.
Bross, William. History of Chicago. 1880.
Bryant, William Cullen. Picturesque America. D. Appleton & Company. 1874.
Campbell, Neil N. and Vaughn, F. A. Lighting a Residential Suburb. Reprinted from the American City. 1930.
Chamberlin, Everett. Chicago and its Suburbs. T. A. Hungerford & Co. 1874.
Coulter, John M. Lake Forest University. Herald Publishing Company. 1895.
Currey, J. Seymour. Chicago, Its History and Builders. 1912.
Diamond Jubilee of the Archdiocese of Chicago. 1920.
Ehrlicher, James G. A History of Lake Forest Academy. The Caxy. 1933.
Facts for Lake Foresters. The League of Women Voters. 1950–1960.
Ferry, Abby Farwell. Reminiscences of John V. Farwell. Ralph Fletcher Seymour. 1928.
Field, Stanley. History of Old Elm.
Flinn, John J. History of the Chicago Police. 1887.

Bibliography

Forest Gem, The. Newspaper, 1861–1863.
Truxell, F. M. A Physiography of the Region of Chicago. University of Chicago Press. 1927.
Gale, Edwin O. Reminiscences of Early Chicago. 1902.
Gilbert, Paul Thomas. Chicago and Makers. 1929.
Granger, Alfred H. Reminiscences of the Winter Club.
Haines, Elijah M. Historical and Statistical Sketch of Lake County. 1852.
———History of Lake County. William Le Baron & Co. 1877.
Haley, J. E. The XIT Ranch of Texas. Lakeside Press. 1929.
Halsey, John Julius. History of the University. 1892.
———A History of Lake County. R. S. Bates, Philadelphia. 1912.
———Historical Sketch of Lake Forest University. American Communities Company. 1916.
Harrison, Carter. Stormy Years, 1935.
———Growing Up with Chicago, 1944.
Historical Pictorial Review. Udell Printing Company. 1923.
Hughitt, Marvin. The Illinois Central Magazine, September 1925.
Ingraham, Charles A. Elmer Ellsworth. The University of Chicago Press. 1925.
Jackson, Johnathan J. Lake Forest in the 1890's. M. S. 1955.
Kirkland, Caroline. Chicago Yesterdays. Daughaday and Co. 1919.
Kirkland, Joseph. The History of Chicago. 1894.
Know Your Town. League of Women Voters. 1938–1939.
Lake Forest Association. Minutes of the Board of Trustees.
Lake Forest News. 1929–1943.
Lake Forester, The
Le Baron. History of Lake County.
Little Fort Porcupine. Waukegan newspaper. 1845.
Masters, Edgar Lee. The Tale of Chicago. 1933.
McClure, Rev. J. G. K. Lake Forest University, 1893.
———Report of the President, 1897–1901.
———History of the Presbyterian Church, 1905.
———A Pastorate of Twenty-Four Years, 1905.
———The History of Ferry Hall, 1906.
———Historical Address, 1921.
McGann, Mrs. Robert Greaves. Early Lake Forest. Daughaday and Co. 1919.
Manierre, George. Reminiscences of Lake Forest Academy. The Illinois State Historical Society. October 1917.
Minutes of the Session of the First Presbyterian Church of Lake Forest.
Nordyke, Lewis. Cattle Empire. Morrow. 1949.
Onwentsia Club. 50th Anniversary Celebration. 1945.
Our Suburbs. From The Sunday Times, May 4, 1873, Chicago.
Pease, Theodore Calvin. The Story of Illinois.
Quaife, Milo M. Chicago's Highways, Old and New.
Randall. Colonel Elmer Ellsworth. Little Brown & Co., 1960.
Randall, Frank A. History of Chicago Buildings. 1949.

Reichelt, Marie Ward. History of Deerfield, Illinois. Deerfield Post 738, American Legion.

Reminiscences of Chicago During the Great Fire. The Lakeside Press. 1915.

Runnion, James B. Out of Town. From *The Chicago Times.* 1869.

Schick, L. Chicago and its environs. 1891.

Shea, John Gilmony. Discovery and Exploration of the Mississippi Valley. 1903.

Smith, Hermon Dunlap. The Desplaines River. The Cuneo Press. 1940.

Waukegan Daily News. Articles on Lake County, Lake Forest, and Great Lakes Naval Training Station.

White, Marian A. Second Book of the North Shore. 1911.

Wissler, Clark. The American Indian. Oxford University Press. 1938.

Yesterday and Today. A History of the Chicago & North Western Railway System. 1910.

Index

INDEX

Index

Index

Index

Index

Index

McIntosh, Henry, 73
McKinlock, George Alexander, 188, 195
McLaughlin, Frederick, 145
McLoughlin, Mary, 122, 127
McMahon, Kate, 124
McVay, James, 22
Medical School, 66, 69
Medill, 89
Meeker, Arthur, 188
Meeker, Joseph, 37
Melody, Patrick, 18
Mellody Farms, 201, 215
Merriam, W. F., 38
Mettawa, 5
Metzger, William, 97
Military Drill, 70
Milk Strike, 196
Miller, Charlotte H., 58
Miller, Ellery S., 42, 46
Miller, James A., 148
Miller, Samuel Fisher, 27, 42, 44, 50, 57, 64, 65, 78
Miller, Spencer, 42
Mitchel Hall, 54
Mitchell robbery, 217
Moffett, Capt. W. A., 125, 176, 193, 221
Monmouth College, 30
Mott, John R., 140
Moody, Andrew, 64
Moody, Dwight L., 110
Mooney, Michael, 21
Mooney, Peter, 21, 34
Morgan, W. A., 160
Morton, Mayor Mark, 161
Motto, City, 63
Movies, 211, 212

N

Neef, Walter, 50
Neefe, M. A., 37, 62
Nergararian, Hovhannes, 101
New Hotel, 85, 99

New York Tribune, 103
Newcomb, George W., 37
Nichols, Rev. Washington Adams, 141
Night School, 77
Nollen, Pres. John S., 126
Norkat, William, 64
North Shore Line, 140, 153, 214
Northwestern Railroad, 26, 47, 50, 61, 72, 103, 106, 112, 118, 129, 212
Northwestern University, 30, 99
Norton, Rev. A. T., 58
Norton, Nathaniel, 37
Norton, Wilbur T., 70

O

O.C.D., 238
O'Dwyer, Father Patrick, 18
Old, Admiral F. P., 234
Old Elm Club, 179
Old Hotel, 38, 41, 43, 44, 53, 57, 62, 64, 77, 85, 96, 104, 164
O'Leary, John, 142
Olmstead, Frederick Law, 78
Olmstead, Vaux & Co., 35
O'Mara, Father, 17
O'Neill, Joseph, 81, 113, 128
O'Neill, William, 113, 142
Onwentsia Club, 129, 141, 144, 145, 155, 157, 158, 161, 213
Onwentsia Polo, 144, 145
Opera, 214
Opposition Coaches, 133
O'Reilly, Rev. E., 153

P

Page, Peter, 31, 33, 34, 38, 39, 43, 47, 50, 57, 68
Paley, Arthur D., 156
Parks, 65, 76, 81, 85, 94, 173
Passenger Pigeons, 46, 47
Patterson, John C., 42, 43, 46, 69
Patterson, M. H., 96, 129

Index

Personal Reminiscences

Personal Reminiscences

Personal Reminiscences

Personal Reminiscences

Personal Reminiscences